# STRANGE REVELATIONS

# THE MAGIC IN HISTORY SERIES

The Magic in History series explores the role magic and the occult have played in European culture, religion, science, and politics. Titles in the series will bring the resources of cultural, literary, and social history to bear on the history of the magic arts, and will contribute towards an understanding of why the theory and practice of magic have elicited fascination at every level of European society. Volumes will include both editions of important texts and significant new research in the field.

MAGIC IN HISTORY

# STRANGE REVELATIONS

## MAGIC, POISON, AND SACRILEGE IN LOUIS XIV'S FRANCE

LYNN WOOD MOLLENAUER

THE PENNSYLVANIA STATE UNIVERSITY PRESS
UNIVERSITY PARK, PENNSYLVANIA

Library of Congress Cataloging-in-Publication Data

Mollenauer, Lynn Wood, 1966–
    Strange revelations : magic, poison, and sacrilege in
    Louis XIV's France / by Lynn Wood Mollenauer.
        p.      cm. — (The magic in history series)
Includes bibliographical references and index.
ISBN 0-271-02915-3 (cloth : alk. paper)
ISBN 0-271-02916-1 (pbk. : alk. paper)
1. Poisoning—France—History—17th century.
2. France—Court and courtiers—History—17th century.
3. France—History—Louis XIV, 1643–1715.
4. Trials (Murder)—France—History—17th century.
5. Murder—France—History—17th century.
I. Title.
II. Series: Magic in history.

DC126.M5 2007
944'.033—dc22
2006015081

The Pennsylvania State University Press is a member of the Association of
American University Presses.

# Contents

# LIST OF ILLUSTRATIONS

# ACKNOWLEDGMENTS

Not the least pleasurable aspect of finishing a long project is the opportunity it presents to express my gratitude to all those whose support made it possible. I would like first of all to thank my teachers. I cannot pinpoint the day upon which I decided to study history, but I arrived at the resolution during a course on American history taught by Marshall Cohen at Newton South High School. At Amherst College, Margaret Hunt's seminars on the cultural history of early modern Europe introduced me to a new way of considering the past. I still turn to—and now assign to my own students—the works I first read in her classes. At Northwestern University I was fortunate to work under the guidance of three gifted historians whose knowledge, insight, and encouragement shaped the development of this project. Sarah Maza, William Monter, and Edward Muir have each provided a model of scholarship and mentoring that I value increasingly over the years. The support of Henry Binford was just as instrumental; he was ever ready to lend a willing ear (or shoulder), and his good humor always brightened a dark day of writing.

I am indebted to the friends and colleagues who, throughout the years, have read drafts both long and short, commented upon papers, and otherwise offered their advice, expertise, and encouragement: Michael D. Bailey, Sarah Beam, Louisa Burnham, Mita Choudhury, Kate Hamerton, Thomas Kaiser, Henry Kamerling, Cherilyn Lacy, Carol Loar, Heather McHold, Laura Sinclair Odelius, Sharmishtha Roychowdhury, Meredith Rusoff, and Judy Walden. I am especially grateful to Claire Waters, the best of friends and scholars. I must also thank my colleagues at the University of North Carolina, Wilmington, particularly Diana Ashe, Kathleen Berkeley, Mark Boren, Susan McCaffray, and Kate Montwieler. Toward the completion of the project, I received great inspiration from Austin Sarat and the members of the 2004 National Endowment for the Humanities summer seminar, "Punishment, Politics, and Society."

The staffs of the Bibliothèque Nationale, the Bibliothèque de l'Arsenal, and the Archives de la Préfecture de la Police provided invaluable assistance during my research trips to Paris. I owe a particular debt to the interlibrary loan staff of UNCW's Randall Library, whom I suspect I kept working overtime. Research support from an Amherst College Memorial Scholarship, a summer stipend from the University of North Carolina, Wilmington, and the Thomas Moseley Fund allowed me to visit archives and libraries over the course of the project. The invaluable critiques from James R. Farr and an anonymous reader helped to sharpen my arguments and point the work in new directions. I would also like to thank Peter Potter, Cherene Holland, and Laura Reed-Morrisson of Penn State Press for their support and timely editorial advice, and Suzanne Wolk and Doug Krehbiel for their deft copyediting skills. Any mistakes that remain are mine alone.

It is to state the obvious that this book could never have been completed, or even begun, without the encouragement—and forbearance—of family and friends. I am grateful to my parents and brother, who have always offered their unstinting support. My husband has seen this project through from inception to completion, cheerfully read the manuscript many more times than could possibly be expected, and endured with great equanimity the many jokes of those newly acquainted with the book's subject regarding the wisdom of eating any meals I prepared. It is to him and our son that I dedicate this work.

# Introduction

The reign of Louis XIV reached its zenith in 1679. The Sun King was the richest ruler in Europe, his glittering court the envy of his fellow monarchs, and his magnificent palace at Versailles was approaching completion. Almost every endeavor Louis had embarked upon during his thirty-six years on the throne of France had proved a triumph. By virtue of his patronage, France had become the center of high culture in Europe. He had established order within his realm, subduing major rebellions in Bordeaux and Burgundy, bending the regional parlements to his will, and promulgating sweeping legal and administrative ordinances. Louis had been victorious abroad as well, gaining substantial territories and diplomatic concessions in the War of Devolution and the Dutch War. Primi Visconti was not exaggerating unduly when he wrote, "The king was at the height of his power: everything within and without his realm submitted to his will. He had only to desire something to have it; all, until this time, favored him; if it was raining when he wanted to hunt or to go for a walk, it stopped. . . . Moreover, he had money, glory, and above all great health; in sum, he lacked nothing but immortality."[1]

At the apex of his success, however, Louis XIV found the glory of his accomplishments undermined by a scandal of unprecedented proportions. The first macabre details of the Affair of the Poisons came to light in the fall of 1678, when Nicolas de la Reynie, the first lieutenant general of the Paris police, uncovered evidence that suggested the existence of a plot to poison the king. During his three-year investigation, La Reynie encountered a loosely knit community of magicians, sorceresses, and renegade priests who formed the nucleus of the criminal magical underworld of Paris. Their wares included magical remedies, love charms, and poisons known as "inheritance powders." The inheritance powders, usually made from dessicated toads steeped in arsenic, lent the Affair of the Poisons its name, and the purchasers of the powders gave the affair its notoriety, for

Louis XIV, Roi de France, et de Navarre, né le 5 Septembre 1638, Roi en 1643.

**Fig. 1** *Louis XIV.* This 1664 engraving by Robert Nanteuil shows the king in the early years of his personal rule.

the suspects arrested accused the king's official mistress of having tried to poison her royal lover.

While La Reynie's investigation concluded that Mme de Montespan had not attempted to poison the king, it did determine that she had done her utmost to increase her influence over him through magical means. She sprinkled a variety of love potions into his food and bolstered their efficacy with an assortment of aphrodisiacs. Furthermore, she commissioned a variety of magical rituals intended to vanquish her rivals for the king's affections and to solidify her hold over him. The suspects in the affair even maintained that she had participated in a series of demonic conjurations known as amatory masses. Madame de Montespan's sacrilegious activities were not unique; the scandal further revealed that a score of Louis's courtiers had sought to further their political and amatory aspirations by purchasing magical ceremonies and love potions from denizens of the criminal underworld to gain advantage over their rivals.

Determined to eradicate what he termed "this miserable commerce in poisons," Louis XIV appointed a special commission to try all suspects implicated in the affair and compelled duchesses and day laborers alike to present themselves before it. By the time the king dissolved the Chambre de l'Arsenal in 1682, its judges had investigated more than four hundred of his subjects. Louis XIV marked the close of the commission with a royal edict that restricted the sale of poisons and decriminalized witchcraft in France. All those alleging to perform "so-called acts of magic," it declared, were simply frauds "who profane all that religion holds sacred."[2] The Sun King, in effect, forbade his subjects to believe in magic.

Drawing largely upon police and court records, memoirs, and private correspondence, this study explores the underside of Louis's splendid century exposed by the Affair of the Poisons. Many scholars, leery perhaps of the sensationalist accounts that dominate the literature on the affair, have avoided the subject entirely.[3] Most of those who have broached the topic, such as Georges Mongrédien and Jean-Christian Petitfils, have concentrated upon historical detective work, attempting to determine whether a plot to poison Louis XIV actually existed and the extent of Mme de Montespan's participation in it—although as the king himself burned the documents that held the answers to this puzzle, the mystery is ultimately unsolvable.[4] Historians of witchcraft have tended to regard the affair as significant primarily because it prompted the French crown to simultaneously decriminalize and deny the reality of witchcraft in the edict of 1682.[5] This study argues, however, that the Affair of the Poisons opens a unique window into the social, cultural, and religious values of Louis XIV's subjects. Moreover, the affair offers a singular opportunity to analyze the hidden forms of power which men and women of all social classes attempted to access in order to achieve their goals. While the exercise of state power during the ancien régime was quintessentially visible—ritually displayed through public ceremonies such as royal coronations, entrées, and funerals—the Affair of the Poisons exposes the simultaneous presence of otherwise invisible sources of power available to Louis XIV's subjects: poison, magic, and the manipulation of sexual passions.

The public that so avidly followed the latest details of the Affair of the Poisons was an extensive one. While Louis and his ministers would have undoubtedly preferred that the entire affair remain secret, the sheer number of people arrested and the status of the most prominent suspects ensured that a wide audience took an ardent interest in the unfolding scandal. No official channels imparted news; the *Mercure galant,* a court circular, remained scrupulously silent on the subject and no *factums,* or trial briefs, of the secret trials were published. The majority of Parisians therefore relied upon hearsay and innuendo for the latest information. Those with court connections clearly stayed abreast of the latest gossip, as the letters of Mme de Sévigné and her cousin the comte de Bussy attest.[6] Similarly, the correspondence of several ambassadors at Louis's court indicates that they were able to report to their governments a considerable amount of well-informed gossip.[7] Those without links to the court, however, were forced to rely upon the rumors circulating in the city, a form of communication more difficult to substantiate.

Word of mouth was not the only means by which Parisians learned about the magical activities of the "so-called sorceresses." Six months after the first hint of the Affair of the Poisons electrified the city, the playwrights Jean Donneau de Visé and Thomas Corneille premiered *La devineresse, ou les faux enchantements.* Hundreds flocked to the theater to enjoy the spectacle of the quasi-fictional sorceress La Jobin and her partner peddling bogus charms for eternal youth, love magic, and séances with the devil to a collection of naive clients. The satire's allusions to the events of the day were clear, and its "torn-from-the-headlines" approach proved wildly successful; *La devineresse* became the longest-running play in the history of Parisian theater.[8] Those who did not attend the play could follow its plot by leafing through the engravings in the *Almanach de la devineresse,* circulated by the playwrights to advertise their new work.[9]

The theater of ancien régime justice presented the crimes committed by the suspects of the Affair of the Poisons to a broader public still.[10] People of all classes lined the thoroughfares of the city to watch those sentenced to death proceed from prison to the place de Grève. Nobles gathered at friends' *hôtels* that lined the route; the less privileged crowded into the streets. Parisians heard the prisoners admit their guilt in *amendes honorables,* or public apologies made before the main portal of Notre-Dame, and in final confessions offered at the foot of the scaffold. Onlookers were further edified by a recital of the convicts' crimes delivered immediately before they were put to death. At the execution of the notorious La Voisin, nearly the entire population of Paris formed the audience before which the French state performed its ritual of justice.

The judicial records of the Affair of the Poisons unveil the shared culture of magic and poison that permeated all levels of French society, connecting the lower classes to the very center of power, the court. However, the reliability of the testimony of the suspects, who confessed to a litany of crimes both magical and material in their efforts to please their interrogators, remains highly uncertain.[11] Like the murderers' pardon tales analyzed by Natalie Zemon Davis in *Fiction in the Archives,* the statements of the sorceresses, magicians, and renegade clerics of the Affair of the Poisons were carefully constructed to ring true.[12] Rather than attempt to determine the validity of the suspects' claims, this study seeks to establish the reasons their testimony seemed believable to the French public, La Reynie, Louis XIV's judges, and the king himself.

The narrative fictions presented by the suspects indeed corresponded to the expectations of La Reynie and the judges of the Chambre de l'Arsenal, for the magistrates had ample reason to presume that a considerable percentage of the Parisian population, from the top to the bottom of the social scale, believed in the efficacy of magic. Louis's court itself had its own resident fortune-teller, Primi Visconti, who offered predictions based upon his noble clients' handwriting samples.[13] Statements from letters written by court observers such as Mme de Sévigné indicate that the practice of visiting magicians and palm readers in the capital was commonplace. When questioned, artisans and aristocrats alike admitted that they had visited sorceresses to purchase innocuous items such as spells of love magic or charms to bring luck at cards or dice.[14]

Physical evidence corroborates the clients' testimony. The police inventories of the sorceresses' merchandise list ingredients for magic charms and assorted poisons, as well as signed receipts from clients. The police also seized *grimoires* and other magic manuals owned by the sorceresses and renegade priests that contained recipes for various potions and instructions for conducting ceremonies of ritual magic. Although the confessions of the suspects were given under various forms of duress, such indubitable physical evidence convinced the judges that at least some of the suspects in the Affair of the Poisons were indeed practicing sorcery and peddling poisons, and at least some of the accused had been their clients.[15]

But what of the testimony regarding the practice of demonic magic? The suspects clearly recognized that, like Scheherazade, their lives depended upon spinning out their tales, and their statements certainly became increasingly fantastic over the course of their imprisonment. But unlike the statements elicited under torture during the great witch hunts of the early modern period, Louis XIV's sorceresses and magicians did not confess to—and tellingly, neither did their interrogators inquire about—the performance of any manifestly impossible activity. They did not purport to fly through the air on broomsticks, attend sabbats, copulate with devils, or worship Satan. Rather, they claimed to have practiced a traditional form of Christian magic that exploited the rituals and imagery of the Catholic Church.[16] Their alleged magical activities had all the appearance of verisimilitude to the judges of the Chambre de l'Arsenal because the judges, as members of the Parlement of Paris, had long been accustomed to hearing similar confessions.[17]

Moreover, the suspects' belief in the existence of demons was licit, if their attempts to call up Satan's minions were not—and at no time did they contend that any demons had actually manifested themselves as a result.[18] The claims of the suspects that must have most strained the credulity of the judges, in fact, were not about the magical practices in which they professed to engage but about the clients for whom they professed to be working: Louis XIV's courtiers.

The judges investigating the Affair of the Poisons did not inquire about manifestly impossible actions because they had long held that the performance of such magic could not be proved in a court of law. As the court of appeal for more than half the country, the Parisian Parlement (from whose ranks the judges of the Chambre de l'Arsenal were drawn) had not upheld a death sentence for witchcraft in more than fifty years. Scholars such as William Monter and Alfred Soman have demonstrated that the *parlementaires* of Paris became increasingly chary of upholding lower court convictions for witchcraft over the course of the seventeenth century.[19] Magistrates at the appeals courts were reluctant to countenance procedural irregularities or the relaxation of legal standards of proof—the only methods by which someone accused of a manifestly impossible crime could be convicted—and many were progressively more doubtful about the reality of witchcraft as well.[20]

If magistrates were less inclined to believe in magic over the course of the seventeenth century, the majority of ordinary Europeans were not. The Affair of the Poisons provides ample proof that the decriminalization of witchcraft in France in no way marked the end of belief in magic. Nor was belief in magic limited to the uneducated or underprivileged.[21] That members of the popular classes, rural and urban alike, shared a general credulity regarding magic during the ancien régime is well documented; historians have found evidence that sorceresses and magicians continued to market their wares and services to an appreciative audience well into the twentieth century.[22] That much of the criminal magical underworld enjoyed the patronage of a noble clientele may be a more surprising finding among those who would anticipate that the twin forces of Cartesian skepticism and mechanical philosophy would have eviscerated elite belief in magic by the time of the Affair of the Poisons. Certainly scholars have long argued that the early end of the witch trials in France (the last execution for witchcraft within the jurisdiction of the Parlement of Paris took place in 1625) was a result of skepticism on the part of magistrates at the French parlements. But the reluctance of *parlementaires* to try individuals for crimes of magic stemmed more from their growing conviction that such crimes were impossible to prove at law than from a belief that they were simply impossible. Refusal to try witches was in essence a premodern form of judicial activism; the *parlementaires* legislated de facto skepticism from the bench. As Alfred Soman has argued, "Witchcraft trials came to an early end in France not because people stopped believing in witches, but because the central authorities considered the trials scandalous and unbefitting the dignity of the king's justice."[23] While some judges came to the conclusion that witchcraft was "not only unprovable but impossible" by the late seventeenth century, most of Louis XIV's subjects continued to participate in a shared culture of magic.[24]

Despite their professional skepticism, the magistrates of the Chambre de l'Arsenal continued to regard magical activities such as those perpetrated during the Affair of the Poisons as serious breaches of public order. Louis XIV and his judges deemed the members of the criminal magical underworld to be a threat to French society because they cheated the credulous, corrupted the faithful, and profaned religion.[25] The city's sorceresses and magicians were accounted guilty of sacrilege, impiety, and the misuse of holy things—all proscribed by the criminal code—for their spells and charms exploited a Christian magical tradition with deep roots in the Middle Ages. Because their transgressions placed the community at risk of divine retribution, they were condemned to suffer the most extreme forms of punishment inflicted during the old regime. The criminal prosecution of the members of the magical underworld of Paris is therefore best understood within the framework of a larger Catholic Reformation drive to ensure social order and enforce religious orthodoxy.

In addition to illuminating the magical practices and beliefs shared by Louis XIV's subjects, the Affair of the Poisons serves to shed new light on the multiple ways in which power was exercised at Louis's court. The court was the heart of the political system in seventeenth-century France, where Louis had succeeded in gathering the most powerful nobles in the country around his throne.[26] Louis XIV's court society has long been a subject of interest to scholars since the work of Norbert Elias, whose analysis of the sociopolitical significance of the ritual, etiquette, and structure of the court has shaped almost all subsequent studies of the institution.[27] Elias argues that the king carefully distributed privileges and honors in order to keep the various factions in balance with one another. The court thus became, in the words of Roger Mettam, a "ritualized battlefield" where an intense struggle for power and prestige was enacted through etiquette and ceremony, intrigue and innuendo, as courtiers fought fiercely to increase their access to the king.[28]

Most historians, however, have neglected to distinguish between the experiences of male and female aristocrats within the world of the court. Elias fails to consider the considerable role played by noblewomen except to note that "women, considered as social groups, have far greater power at court than any other formation in this society."[29] Jeroen Duindam similarly gives court women short shrift in his analyses of the French court, as does Jean-François Solnon in his latest work on the subject.[30] This gap in the historiography represents a crucial oversight, for while Louis XIV's attempt at domestication instituted a court society that restricted traditionally male forms of power, it proved to be highly responsive to the exercise of female influence. To ignore the central place of women at Louis XIV's court is to fundamentally misapprehend its structure.

The literature on the political significance of the king's body is of great use in conceptualizing the avenues open to women to exercise power at Louis XIV's court. In seventeenth-century France, the concept of kingship was not just represented but was understood through the king's body; the monarch therefore served as the literal embodiment of royal authority. While several historians (Ernst Kantorowicz, Ralph Giesey, Sarah Hanley, and Richard Jackson) have studied the ritual manifestations of this emphasis on the king's sacralized body, few scholars have considered the king's physical body as the locus of power and status at court.[31] The advantage of an emphasis on the king's body "in the flesh" is that it restores Louis's *maîtresses en titre* to the central place they occupied in the world of the court. As a sexual relationship ensured the closest possible physical proximity to the king, a mistress's intimate access to the monarch granted her a position atop the highest reaches of the court's unofficial, or shadow, hierarchy. From her elevated position, she was able to exercise a prodigious amount of influence through the networks of patronage and brokerage at the court. The considerable rewards available to the woman acknowledged as Louis's official mistress help to explain why a dozen of his female courtiers—including his most prominent and successful mistress—might turn to amatory magic in their quest to gain or retain power over the passions of the king.

Each chapter of this study explores an aspect of the exercise of power in seventeenth-century France. Through an analysis of the legal investigation into the Affair of the Poisons, the first chapter examines the dimensions and exercise of royal power within the judicial system of the ancien régime. It also explores the conflict between Louis XIV's need for secrecy and his resolve to impart justice; while France's most absolute monarch proved powerful enough to conceal the illicit activities of his mistress and courtiers, he could do so only at the expense of the courts. This chapter argues that the king's decision to circumvent his own judicial system highlights some of the limits on royal absolutism that existed even at the very peak of his powers.

The following three chapters turn to the shared culture of poison and magic that connected the lower depths of society to the very center of state power, the court, and examine the ways in which Louis XIV's subjects attempted to manipulate occult sources of power in order to achieve their goals. Chapter 2, "Medea and the Marquise: Understanding the Crime of Poison in Seventeenth-Century France," argues that two main cultural scripts informed the way in which a learned seventeenth-century audience read the crime of poison: the myth of Medea and the legend of the marquise de Brinvilliers. While Medea had long served as the archetypal poisoner—a woman who acted out of vengeance toward a romantic rival—the 1676 case of the marquise de Brinvilliers demonstrated to French society that the female affinity for poison was not merely myth. Executed only three years before the Affair of the Poisons erupted, her crimes helped to cement in the minds of the French public the links between poison, adultery, and greed. The dangerous characteristics of both Medea and the marquise were therefore readily at hand to be mapped onto the women implicated in the Affair of the Poisons.

Chapters 3 and 4 examine the clients and magical practitioners of seventeenth-century Europe's most sophisticated underworld. I argue here that the criminal magical underworld functioned as an illegitimate but influential source of power in seventeenth-century French society. The danger its members represented was compounded by their sinister alliances with Mme de Montespan and other aristocrats who had allegedly sought supernatural assistance to further their financial, political, or amatory aspirations. Chapter 3, "The Criminal Magical Underworld of Paris," demonstrates that the practices of Paris's sorceresses and magicians reflected the persistence of a Christian magical tradition dating to the early Middle Ages, and looks at the differences between men's and women's use of magic and poison. Chapter 4, "The Renegade Priests of Paris and the Amatory Mass," turns to the rogue clerics whose illicit activities lay at the heart of the Affair of the Poisons. Situating the transgressions of the city's magical practitioners and their priestly assistants in the highly religious atmosphere of Catholic Reformation France, this chapter explores their introduction of a deeply sacrilegious ritual and the challenges their activities posed to Catholic orthodoxy.

Finally, this study assesses the ways in which male and female nobles were able to exercise power and influence at Louis's court through their access to the physical body of the king. Chapter 5, "The Magic of Mistresses at the Court of Louis XIV," contains an analysis of the two hierarchies that together determined the relative power and place accorded to Louis XIV's courtiers. Furthermore, it seeks to explain why a score of noblewomen at court might commission rituals of love magic directed at the king: for Mme de Montespan, at least, the magic seemed to work.

# INVESTIGATING THE AFFAIR OF THE POISONS, 1676–1682

It will put us into such a poisoning humor that we will all be astonished.
—Madame de Sévigné, *Correspondance,* 2:342–43

The duc de Saint Simon once observed, "It seems that there are, at certain moments, crimes which become the fashion, like clothes. Poisoning was *à la mode* at the time."[1] His judgment about the reign of Louis XIV echoed the opinions of his contemporaries, for French society saw poison lurking behind every mysterious or untimely death. Public opinion speculated that Cardinal Mazarin had been poisoned in 1661, and another persistent rumor attributed the sudden death of Henrietta Maria, Louis XIV's first sister-in-law, to a poisoned glass of barley water provided by her husband's lover. Over the course of the 1670s, Nicolas de la Reynie, lieutenant general of the Paris police, heard a rash of similar accusations. He was not the only one to do so. In 1673, for example, the monks of Notre-Dame apparently grew so concerned about the sins related by their penitents that they warned the authorities that the majority of people seeking absolution at the cathedral had confessed to having poisoned someone.[2]

La Reynie's investigation into the apparent rash of poisonings uncovered what would become the greatest court scandal of seventeenth-century France. The Affair of the Poisons revealed the existence of a criminal magical underworld whose members offered for sale an array of products and services that ranged from abortions to love magic to poisons known as "inheritance powders." Furthermore, La Reynie discovered that some of the king's highest-ranking courtiers—among them his official mistress, Athénaïs de Montespan—had connections to the sorceresses, magicians, and renegade priests of Paris. The course of the police lieutenant's investigations, directed by the king himself, eventually revealed the limits on royal absolutism that existed even at the peak of Louis XIV's powers.

## PROLOGUE: THE CASE OF THE MARQUISE DE BRINVILLIERS

Spectacular proof of the female affinity for poison emerged three years prior to the Affair of the Poisons. The Parlement of Paris ordered Marie-Madeleine d'Aubray, marquise de Brinvilliers, beheaded in 1676 for poisoning the brothers with whom she might otherwise have had to divide the family fortune. The marquise's case seized the attention of the French public, who followed it closely through the *factums* or trial briefs (later known as *mémoires judiciaries*) published by the lawyers on the case.[3] The story was so well known that the celebrated correspondent Madame de Sévigné reported its latest details in her daily letters to her daughter. The story of the marquise's crimes, subsequent flight, and spectacular capture and trial prepared the French public, the Parisian police, and even Louis XIV and his ministers to believe that the extraordinary revelations of the subsequent Affair of the Poisons were possible. Her case became the thin end of a wedge that would widen to expose the existence of Paris's criminal magical underworld; it eventually led the police not just to one notorious poisoner but to an entire network of criminals. Furthermore, her example brought a heightened awareness of a propensity to poison that apparently lurked within the most unlikely of hearts.

The case of the marquise de Brinvilliers not only captured the public imagination far beyond Paris, but also recast the popular conception of a poisoner. The marquise did not conform outwardly to the stereotype of a duplicitous criminal. She was young, beautiful, and of an ancient and distinguished family.[4] She and her husband, Antoine Gobelin, were extremely wealthy. In a society that saw nobility of character conferred by noble status, the marquise's rank rendered criminal behavior nearly unthinkable.[5] "The advantages of quality, birth and fortune of the Dame de Brinvilliers," contended her lawyer, "must strongly argue that she would not be capable of the cowardly and horrible crimes of which she is accused."[6] As for Marie's signed confession, elucidating each detail of those "cowardly and horrible crimes," her lawyer argued that it must be disregarded because it was "a sacred and secret religious confession" that was "addressed only to God and to her confessor."[7] It is from her confession, the *factums* published regarding her case, and secondary sources that the following account is drawn.

While Marie's face, family, and fortune argued for her innocence, her behavior and character belied her angelic countenance and irreproachable connections. According to the *factums* for the prosecution, the marquise was a woman whose passions ran unchecked. To the French public who followed her case, this rendered her far more likely to poison than her social position would initially admit. Marie was by all accounts dissolute, greedy, and promiscuous—attributes she shared with her husband. The marquis, it seems, did not subscribe to the prevalent sexual double standard that zealously regulated female behavior while ignoring male dalliances. Thus for several years the Brinvilliers marriage was a contented one, with both partners free to pursue independently their common interests: love affairs, gambling, and overspending. However, Marie's family was less complacent about her conduct and repeatedly admonished her to amend her behavior.

Despite their reproaches, the marquise continued to run up enormous debts, take lovers, and otherwise scandalize her relatives.[8]

Matters did not come to a head between Marie and her family until her husband introduced her to Jean-Baptiste Gaudin de Sainte-Croix. The Gascon cavalry captain was handsome, arrogant, and infinitely charming, and Marie fell passionately in love with him. Their affair drew further remonstrations from the d'Aubray family, but Marie blithely continued to lavish both her fortune and her favors on the adventurer. After two years, Sainte-Croix grew concerned that Marie's husband was selfishly squandering the lion's share of the couple's estate, thus endangering Sainte-Croix's comfortable lifestyle. He convinced Marie to institute legal proceedings to separate her fortune from her husband's. Apparently unaware that the court would probably award all joint assets to her husband because of her adultery, she followed Sainte-Croix's advice.[9] Appalled, Marie's family finally took decisive action. On March 19, 1663, her father obtained a *lettre de cachet*[10] and had Sainte-Croix thrown in the Bastille for six weeks.[11]

Sainte-Croix's brief imprisonment did not bring about the result that Marie's father and brothers intended. Rather than inspiring Marie to amend her behavior, they unwittingly instituted a chain of events that would lead to their deaths. In the Bastille, the vengeful Sainte-Croix made the acquaintance of an Italian prisoner named Egidio Exili, who was rumored to be an "artist of poison." The French authorities took Exili's reputation seriously; released from prison shortly after Sainte-Croix, he was escorted to Calais by the police and put on a boat bound for England. Despite such efforts, Exili reappeared in Paris and was promptly installed by Sainte-Croix in a workshop on place Maubert.[12] Aside from the opportunity to take his revenge on Marie's father, Sainte-Croix seems to have speculated that there was a profit to be made manufacturing poisons. Before Exili vanished six months later, he apparently passed on to Sainte-Croix a great deal of what he knew about the art of poisoning.[13]

Sainte-Croix next recruited the noted Swiss chemist Christophe Glaser to help him continue his research. Why Glaser, a royal apothecary and author of several notable scientific tracts, agreed to help Sainte-Croix remains a mystery. Glaser and Sainte-Croix began two sets of experiments, believing that the success of either would earn a fortune. The first, a search for the Philosopher's Stone to turn base metals into gold, proved fruitless. The second was more successful. Over a period of three years they were able to manufacture a tasteless, odorless poison that left no trace upon its victims. Marie helped to develop the recipe, which contained a solution of arsenic.[14] She paid daily visits to the Hôtel-Dieu, the poor hospital, where she piously distributed pastries and other delicacies laced with Sainte-Croix's current formula to the indigent patients. She was thus able to observe closely the effects of the poison and to make suggestions on how to refine the necessary dosages.[15]

For Marie and Sainte-Croix, the recipe was perfected just in time. Both Marie and her husband had continued to incur tremendous debts, and their creditors had begun proceedings to repossess some of their properties; the Brinvilliers (and hence Sainte-Croix) found themselves in desperate need of money. Marie and Sainte-Croix cast covetous eyes on her father's fortune, a considerable portion of which was to be inherited by Marie. To that end, the pair recommended a servant to Marie's father, who upon his entry into the household began to poison Antoine d'Aubray's food and drink, causing his health to deteriorate gradually. After eight months, Marie's father was near death. Marie (with whom he thought he had been reconciled since Sainte-Croix's prison term) stayed devotedly by his side, so that she could administer the fatal dose. Antoine died on September 10, 1666, of what the doctors termed a "crisis of gout." Neither doctors nor family members suspected that his death had other than natural causes. Antoine's estate was divided among his daughters Marie and Thérèse and his sons Antoine and François.[16]

Perhaps buoyed by her success, Marie decided that her family tree was in need of some additional pruning. She made several attempts to become a widow so that she might marry Sainte-Croix, with whom she remained passionately in love. Sainte-Croix had recently married an heiress, though, and evidently preferred his current domestic arrangements. Whenever Marie slipped a dose of poison into her husband's food, Sainte-Croix promptly administered an antidote. As Mme de Sévigné later wrote her daughter, the unfortunate marquis de Brinvilliers "was thrown back and forth five or six times in such fashion; sometimes poisoned, sometimes unpoisoned, he stayed alive."[17] Marie also proved unable to rid herself of her female family members. Her attempts to poison her sister Thérèse, a Carmelite nun, were to no avail, and while she was tempted on several occasions to poison her own daughter (who was apparently "too stupid" to live), she always relented and gave the unfortunate girl a counterpoison.[18] "Medea did not do so much," remarked Mme de Sévigné.[19]

In 1668 Marie found herself once again pressed by her creditors. She turned her attention to her brothers, with whom she had divided their father's estate. Antoine d'Aubray d'Offémont, intendant of Orléans and civil lieutenant of Paris (offices inherited from his father) and François d'Aubray, a *conseiller au Parlement,* lived together in Paris, and if they died without issue, Marie believed that she stood to inherit a large part of their estates. She began to plan. She did not have access to her brothers' kitchen, however, and Antoine had recently married a woman who was scandalized by Marie's lifestyle and apparently none too eager to entertain her sister-in-law with any frequency. An opportunity presented itself when Marie learned that her younger brother, François, was in need of a new valet, and she seized the chance to make a recommendation for the post. La Chaussée, Sainte-Croix's loyal servant, made a suitable candidate for her needs—he was sorely in need of money and quite without scruple. In exchange for promissory notes for thirty thousand and twenty-five thousand *livres,* Sainte-Croix agreed to furnish La Chaussée and the necessary poison. No longer romantically involved with Marie, Sainte-Croix refused to rely solely on her future generosity for payment.

La Chaussée ingratiated himself with both brothers and soon became indispensable to their household. He began to supervise the kitchen staff and make recommendations about how the Messieurs d'Aubray wished their food prepared. Apparently he believed that they preferred it seasoned with arsenic, for by the middle of June of 1670 Antoine was dead of what was determined to be a natural, albeit puzzling, ailment. The autopsy report noted that "the stomach and duodenum of the victim were black . . . the liver gangrenous and burnt."[20] Within a few short months François too was dead of mysterious symptoms, but despite the suspicions that prompted the doctors and remaining family members to order an autopsy, his death too was declared to be from natural causes. François's fortune went to Marie and her sister, Thérèse.

Marie's crimes might have gone undetected if not for the untimely death of Sainte-Croix on July 31, 1672. Rumor later attributed his demise to divine justice; it was said that the mask he wore while working in the laboratory on place Maubert slipped and the poisonous vapors from his experiment killed him instantly.[21] Upon learning that Sainte-Croix was dead, Marie dispatched La Chaussée to recover some incriminating letters and promissory notes of hers that Sainte-Croix had stored in a red leather trunk in his laboratory, but to no avail. Instead, La Chaussée's attempts to obtain the trunk aroused the curiosity of the Paris police.[22] They seized the casket and discovered not only Marie's letters but dozens of vials filled with poisonous substances and instructions from Sainte-Croix requesting that, in the event of his death, the contents of the case be handed over only to the marquise herself. The matter began to look as though it bore further investigation. The police immediately issued an arrest warrant for La Chaussée but hesitated to seize the marquise, as arresting someone of her rank was a matter of some delicacy. Marie took advantage of their reluctance and caught a boat bound for England, abandoning La Chaussée to his fate. Two weeks later, the police caught up with him. The packet of *vitriol de Chypre* hidden in his clothes at the time of his arrest confirmed their gravest suspicions.[23]

On February 23, 1673, the Tournelle, the criminal chamber of the Paris Parlement, convicted La Chaussée and Marie (in absentia) of murder.[24] Tortured after his sentence had been passed,[25] La Chaussée confessed to his crimes and admitted those of his employer before he was broken on the wheel at the place de Grève.[26] The marquise, sentenced in absentia to death by beheading, continued to thumb her nose at French justice from across the channel. She was forced to flee to the Low Countries, however, when Louis XIV's ambassador requested her extradition from the English government. Safely ensconced in a convent in Liège for three years, she was not captured until she was lured out of her sanctuary by an enterprising captain of the Paris police named Desgrez on the day before the French-controlled town fell back into the hands of the Spanish. Desgrez posed as an abbé smitten with Marie, and the vain marquise agreed to a tryst. When she left the safety of the convent to meet her admirer, he promptly placed her under arrest, bundled her into a carriage, and whisked her off to the Conciergerie, the prison of the Paris Parlement.[27]

Marie's fate was sealed by evidence from her own hands. Among her possessions found in the convent in Liège was a signed confession that she had written when she was apparently considering suicide. Sixteen pages long, it detailed her crimes: among other peccadilloes, she admitted to poisoning her father and two brothers, attempting to poison her sister and daughter, and even setting fire to one of her residences lest it be seized by her creditors. After reviewing the evidence from Sainte-Croix's casket, La Chaussée's conviction and confession, and testimony provided by Jean Briancourt (her children's tutor and one of her lovers), the *Grand-Chambre* of the Paris Parlement and the Tournelle ordered that Marie-Madeleine d'Aubray, marquise de Brinvilliers, "make a public apology before the main portal of Notre-Dame . . . be taken and conducted in the said tumbril to the place de Grève of this city, to be beheaded on the scaffold that will be erected for this purpose; her body burned and her ashes thrown into the wind; having been previously subjected to the questions ordinary and extraordinary that she may reveal her accomplices."[28]

Between her trial and her day of execution, Marie apparently made a sincere spiritual transformation. Testifying before the Parlement, she vehemently denied all responsibility for her crimes, displaying a strength of will that astonished her judges.[29] After her conviction, her sister Thérèse asked that a confessor be appointed for Marie. According to his own later account, the abbé Pirot proved to be a powerful spiritual advisor whose counsel at last inspired Marie to make a full confession of her crimes. Having received absolution, she proceeded through her public ordeal with such humility and serenity that the vast crowd gathered to watch her death in the place de Grève considered that she had been redeemed and sanctified. After her body was burned, people gathered bits of bone and ash as grisly souvenirs of her edifying death.[30]

While the marquise de Brinvilliers made a full confession of her own sins, she did not implicate any accomplices, either during or after torture. Some of her testimony, however, seemed to indicate that she knew more than she had admitted. After her arrest in Liège, she insisted repeatedly, "Half the well-born people have also, and I would ruin them if I wanted to speak about them."[31] The police understood her to mean that she was not the only notable in Paris to have used poison. The marquise made other troubling statements as well. Perhaps because she had been responsible for so many poisonings herself, she was questioned about the mysterious deaths of several prominent people, including Cardinal Mazarin. In response, she said only, "many people were involved in the miserable commerce of poisons, people of rank,"[32] and refused to elaborate further. The case of the infamous marquise, which initially appeared to have been a single cause célèbre, was to prove instead the thread that unraveled the whole cloth of Paris's criminal magical underworld.

## THE UNFOLDING OF THE AFFAIR OF THE POISONS, 1676–1679

La Reynie and the Paris police made little immediate headway in uncovering any of the poisoners to whom the marquise had so ominously alluded. Over the next two years, however, connections emerged between a series of seemingly unrelated cases that lent credence to the marquise de Brinvilliers's final warning. As her notorious case helped to persuade the Parisian public that poisonings by aristocrats were believable, so the unpublicized cases of Mlle de la Grange and the Vanens cabal helped to convince La Reynie and the Paris police that a veritable conspiracy of poisoners and other miscreants threatened the Sun King and his subjects.

In February 1677 the police arrested Magdelaine Guénisseau (known as Mlle de la Grange) and her lover, the abbé Nail, on suspicion of murder. The two stood accused of poisoning her elderly patron, a lawyer at the Parlement, and then forging a marriage certificate so that Mlle de la Grange might inherit his considerable estate. She was, according to her police dossier, "an artist in poisons. . . . She is the first who taught their use and who put the weapon into the hands of people who would not have indulged in such crimes but for the ease with which they found they could commit them."[33] The police believed that Mlle de la Grange had obtained her poisons from a Parisian sorceress named Marie Bosse (of whom much will be said later).

Nine months later the police arrested a band of criminals led by Louis Vanens.[34] Under the guise of searching for the Philosopher's Stone, Vanens and his cronies were producing both counterfeit coins and genuine poisons for what appeared to be a widespread clientele.[35] La Reynie seemed to have uncovered a broad, if loose, conspiracy of alchemists, counterfeiters, and poisoners. He and the minister of war, the marquis de Louvois,[36] strongly suspected that the group had been responsible for the death of the duke of Savoy in June 1675, although they were unable to prove it despite interrogating their suspects over the course of a year.[37]

The success of La Reynie's investigation into this ring of poisoners took a dramatic turn in the fall of 1678 when the police lieutenant encountered evidence of a plot against the king. In a church on rue Saint-Antoine, a mysterious woman slipped a letter to the Jesuit to whom she was making her confession, murmured that she had found it at the Galerie du Palais, and disappeared from the church. The letter hinted ominously of a conspiracy to poison a man so powerful his name could not be mentioned: "This white powder you want to put on the handkerchief

MESSIRE GABRIEL NICOLAS DE LA REYNIE,
Conseiller du Roy en ces Con.ᵉⁱˢ    Maistre des Requestes Ordinaire
de Son Hostel, et Lieutenant    General de La Police de la Ville
Preuoste et Vicomte de Paris,    &c.⁴

**Fig. 2** *Gabriel-Nicolas de la Reynie,* 1709. An engraving by Larmessin presenting the
police lieutenant as he appeared soon after his appointment to the office.

of you-know-who, could it not be recognized by the very effect for which you intend it? I leave you to judge what may happen! If you do not abandon forever such a criminal design, you will lose me forever."[38] Lest there be any doubt that the king was the intended target, the writer alluded to the crime of *lèse-majesté*: "I ardently believe that our letters are seen and that I will be believed guilty, although I am entirely innocent. Because while for all other crimes one must be an accomplice to be punished, for this one it is necessary only to have known of it."[39] Merely possessing knowledge of *lèse-majesté*, or a threat to the king's life—whether real or imaginary—warranted the death penalty.[40] The troubled priest handed the letter to his superior, who promptly dispatched it to the king's confessor, Père de La Chaise. The minister Jean-Baptiste Colbert was next shown the note, and it was he who brought it to La Reynie.[41] The missive seemed to confirm La Reynie's worst suspicions but brought him no closer to discovering the conspirators.

Finally, in the winter of 1679, La Reynie received the information for which he had been waiting. A lawyer of the Parlement had apparently been keeping rather unusual company for a man of his station. Monsieur Perrin reported to the police that he had attended a dinner with several people interested in the occult arts, hosted by a palm reader named Marie Vigoureux. After a glass or so too many, a guest named Marie Bosse boasted that with three more poisonings she would be able to retire with her fortune made. When the other members of the party laughed knowingly, Perrin decided that perhaps these were not his sort of people after all and denounced them to the police. To check the lawyer's story, the police captain (Desgrez, the same officer who had entrapped the marquise de Brinvilliers at Liège) sent a subordinate's wife off to consult the indiscreet poisoner. After spinning a tale about her abusive husband, the policeman's wife returned home with a remedy that promised a sure means for restoring domestic harmony: arsenic. Both Marie Bosse and Marie Vigoureux were promptly thrown in the Bastille, where they lost little time implicating both their colleagues and their clientele.[42]

With the two arrests, La Reynie finally penetrated the heart of the criminal magical underworld of Paris, whose members offered palm readings as well as poisons. The police lieutenant's discovery that the sorceress had dispensed inheritance powders, distilled from a mixture of arsenic and dried toad, to customers of every social class launched the Affair of the Poisons. The scandal would eventually extend into the highest reaches of the Louis XIV's court, when the investigation implicated the king's *maîtresse en titre*.

### THE SORCERESSES OF PARIS

Under police interrogation, Marie Bosse and Marie Vigoureux protested that they were merely fortune-tellers who occasionally dabbled in a little harmless love magic. The culprits who offered a genuine threat to the city's well-being, they insisted, were at that very moment conducting business in the back alleys of Paris. "The king could not perform a greater good for Paris and his kingdom than to exterminate this evil breed of people who are mixed up with divinations and such business. It will be the ruin of everyone, and I believe that there are more than four hundred people so occupied in Paris," contended La Bosse.[43]

The contents of her apartment, however, belied her protestations of harmlessness. When the police and their panel of experts searched La Bosse's living quarters, they discovered an assortment of herbs, powders, and distillations. La Reynie relied upon the expertise of two doctors, a member of the faculty of medicine at the University of Montpellier and an apothecary, to identify the substances. La Reynie's panel followed standard police procedure (as would a similar team of medical experts later assigned to the official investigation into the Affair of the Poisons). Its members, accompanied by a judge, traveled to La Bosse's sealed-off apartment to inventory its contents. Her medicine cabinet contained, they ascertained, a considerable quantity of arsenic in addition to a number of ingredients commonly used in love potions: Spanish fly, powdered menstrual blood (the experts could tell it was not ordinary blood because of its "blackish color"), and packets of nail clippings.[44]

If they encountered anything unfamiliar, the members of a medical team obtained permission from the judge who accompanied them to remove it for further testing. Police procedure dictated that the experts, in the presence of the same judge, administer a dose of the material to an animal (often a dog of "middling size") and record its symptoms: "the said dog vomited the said matter a moment after and continued to vomit several times until evening, and threw up again in the morning without eating either bread or meat, and only drank a little water the night before, and seemed to be battered and sick, having remained lying down and dejected [fort triste] until the present time, such that they can estimate that the said drug contained orpiment, lime, and powdered mustard."[45] If the dog survived but the experts still harbored some suspicion of poison, they would next administer an equivalent amount of the substance to a smaller animal, such as a rooster. If the rooster too survived, they would dose an even smaller bird.[46]

When La Bosse was confronted with the testimony of the apothecaries and doctors who tested the powders found in her home, she admitted that she had "amused herself" by dabbling in chemistry.[47] She and La Vigoureux then started to name their accomplices, and the prisons of Paris rapidly began filling up with the members of the criminal magical underworld, whose names would soon become synonymous with the Affair of the Poisons. Among dozens of others, the midwives/abortionists La Lepère and her daughter; the sorceresses La Filastre, La Trianon, and La Voisin; the toad vendor La Chéron; the herbalist Maître Pierre; the renegade priests Cotton, Mariette, and Guibourg; the magician Lesage; the mysterious chevalier de la Brosse; and the shepherd Galet all were arrested over the course of the following two years.[48]

Marie Bosse claimed that one of her principal customers was Marguerite de Jehan, dame de Poulaillon. Daughter of a noble Bordeaux family and considered one of the most beautiful women in Parisian society, she was arrested in February 1679.[49] The elements of Mme de Poulaillon's case, as of those of other women later accused in the scandal, bore an unmistakable resemblance to that of the marquise de Brinvilliers: an unhappy marriage, an adulterous affair, and an attempted poisoning. Madame de Poulaillon had been married at a young age to an elderly *parlementaire* from Champagne. Soon after her wedding she made the acquaintance of the self-styled marquis de la Rivière, an enterprising man who supported himself by seducing women with rich husbands. His favors proved so expensive that Mme de Poulaillon sold nearly everything she owned—her furniture, her silver, even her clothing—in order to retain his attentions. With her own resources exhausted, the besotted woman turned to her husband's considerable property. Marie Bosse (to whom Mme de Poulaillon had pawned her belongings) suggested that Mme de Poulaillon break into her husband's strongbox. When M. de Poulaillon foiled the plan by adding another lock to his safe, his wife apparently decided to make use of another of the services provided by Marie Bosse and rid herself of her inconvenient husband entirely.[50] She purchased *savon noir,* or black soap, an arsenic-based product that when rubbed into a victim's shirts irritated the skin, causing lesions and blisters similar to those generated by syphilis. While nursing her seemingly promiscuous spouse, a wife earned sympathy for her husband's infidelities as well as the opportunity to daub more of the arsenic-based compound on his sores. Mme de Poulaillon, too impatient to poison her husband in such a painstaking fashion, decided to hasten his end and bribed a servant to add arsenic to his wine. M. de Poulaillon, however, managed to avoid both poisoned beverage and a subsequent assassination attempt. He fled to a monastery and swore out a complaint against his wife.[51]

La Reynie's investigation into the Affair of the Poisons accelerated dramatically with the arrest of Catherine Montvoisin, known as La Voisin, on March 12, 1679. Denounced by her sometime rival Marie Bosse, La Voisin was arrested as she left her parish church after Sunday mass.[52] Paris's most celebrated sorceress, the forty-two-year-old La Voisin found so lucrative her many trades—selling cosmetics and perfumes, fortune-telling, palm reading, poisoning—that she was said to fling handfuls of coins from her carriage as she drove around the city. Often wearing her magnificent "sibyl's" robe, La Voisin received clients in a small consulting room located at the back of her garden.[53] Her house on rue Beauregard was situated in Ville-Neuve, an isolated area of northern Paris just outside the city walls. She lived with her husband, Antoine, and her daughter, Marie-Marguerite, both of whom she kept in a state of abject terror. Marie-Marguerite served as her assistant, but Antoine apparently had little to do with La Voisin's business ventures or clients.[54] She boasted that she had earned more than a hundred thousand *écus* during her career, an amount surely exaggerated, although she did charge her often exceedingly wealthy clients according to their means and demanded payment in advance for her inheritance powders.[55] Business was cyclical, however. During lean times, La Voisin claimed that she was forced to pawn her clothes.

During her first interrogations, La Voisin dismissed the notion that she was involved in anything sinister or illegal. She advised her judges to concentrate on real criminals like Marie Bosse. Her own knowledge of chiromancy and physiognomy, La Voisin claimed, had been given to her at age nine and had been found licit by "several doctors at the Sorbonne."[56] She had begun her practice after her husband lost his shops, requiring her "to cultivate the knowledge that God" had given her so that she might support her family.[57] She denied that she had been involved in any sort of love magic other than to advise her clients that they might rectify their husbands' abusive behavior by praying to Saints Nicolas de Tolentin, Anthony of Padua, or Ursula. In fact, she stated, she had often counseled her clients to visit the chapel of Saint Ursula at the Abbey of Montmartre and ask the saint to help their marriages.[58]

La Voisin did concede that if one of her clients lacked the time or the inclination to make the requisite prayers, she was willing to go to Montmartre herself and say the novena, or cycle of prayers, on the client's behalf. If Saint Ursula failed to reform the errant husband, La Voisin did offer some other remedies. A client might attempt to increase her husband's ardor (thus rendering him more amenable) by wearing La Voisin's cosmetics or perfumes, guaranteed to be irresistible to the opposite sex, or by applying a cream that increased breast size in order to bring about the same result. A client could also try charms of Christian magic: being sprinkled with holy water, saying *quarantaines* of prayers while surrounded by incense and burning candles, or writing her wishes on a slip of paper that was then waved over the chalice at a mass during the consecration of the host. Such practices were believed to be efficacious because they co-opted the rituals, imagery, and sacramentals of the Catholic Church. In later interrogations La Voisin declared that the same techniques could also be used to solicit supernatural help to other relatively benign ends: to make marriages come about, find treasure, or win at cards or dice. Furthermore, she confessed, she also performed magical ceremonies at her clients' behest, the potency of which was derived not from saintly intercession but from demonic assistance. She transfixed wax figures with needles, burned the disinterred skulls of criminals, and buried eggshells and urine in the intended victim's garden.[59]

The testimony of La Voisin and her associates revealed a tangle of related crimes that to La Reynie had all the appearance of a wide-ranging conspiracy. Even before the sorceress's revelations, La Reynie and Louvois had recommended to the king that he create a special commission to investigate and try those implicated rather than have the cases heard by the judges of the criminal chamber of the Paris Parlement.[60] Over the objections of Colbert, the superintendent of finances, who worried not only that such a commission would prove tremendously expensive but that its discoveries would also discredit the crown if made public, Louis XIV agreed to the proposal.[61] The establishment of order within his capital seemed worth the risk to the glorious reputation the king so carefully cultivated both at home and abroad.[62] The king could not have gambled lightly with his own reputation or that of his court, for he believed that his personal *gloire* served France's political ends. As he loftily declared to his son, "The glowing image of [the monarch's] greatness travels everywhere on the wings of his renown. Just as he is the admiration of his subjects, he soon becomes the wonder of neighboring nations, and if he only knows how to use this advantage, there is nothing, either within or without his dominions, that he cannot eventually accomplish."[63] Louis XIV evidently regarded his reputation as a critical instrument of state.

Establishing a special commission, or *tribunal d'exception,* was an unusual but not unprecedented step. French monarchs had appointed such tribunals throughout the Middle Ages and as recently as the 1660s with the special court that judged Colbert's predecessor as superintendent of finances, Nicolas Fouquet.[64] Louis XIV seems to have based his decision to create the Chambre de l'Arsenal (named after the building in which its cases were to be heard) on two considerations. First, the sheer number of people who seemed to require investigation promised to tie up the regular Parisian criminal courts for years. A panel that could move quickly and decisively to bring the perpetrators of such crimes to justice would help to assuage the public's fears of poison and to stem the flood of rumors that was already sweeping the city.[65] Second, if one member of a robe family (such as Mme de Poulaillon) could be implicated, more might follow.[66] A judicial panel whose members had been handpicked by the king and that met in secret would ensure that the Parisian public remained ignorant of the unsavory or possibly even treasonous activities of any more high-ranking suspects.[67] While some historians have seen the appointment of a special tribunal as evidence that Louis and his ministers wished to cover up the illicit activities of his courtiers, the most prominent people implicated in the affair by March 1679 were the widow of a royal musician, the marquis de Feuquières, and the aforementioned Madame de Poulaillon.[68] Apparently neither Louis nor his closest advisors suspected that their investigation would eventually implicate members of the king's inner circle, including the mother of five of his children.

## THE INVESTIGATIONS DIVERGE, MARCH 1679–OCTOBER 1680

Over the objections of the Paris Parlement, whose members argued that the cases should be tried according to regular procedure (and therefore by themselves),

Louis XIV created the Chambre de l'Arsenal.[69] The king selected thirteen magistrates from the Parlement of Paris, which functioned as the supreme court for approximately half the kingdom, to serve on the new commission.[70] The judges were charged to investigate and try those "accused of involvement in evil spells and composing, distributing, and administering poison."[71] *Magie,* because it was understood to comprise idolatry and necromancy, was a capital offense, as was poison.[72] Louis designated Jean Sagot as clerk, responsible for the sensitive task of recording each meeting of the judges as well as their interrogations of the prisoners. The king also appointed two doctors and two apothecaries to examine any physical evidence and furnish medical and toxicological reports.[73] The *procureur général* M. Robert was responsible for bringing charges against the accused, making recommendations for pursuing prosecution, and recommending sentence if a suspect was found guilty. As *rapporteurs,* La Reynie and Claude Bazin de Bezons directed the investigation and submitted detailed reports to the judges of the Chambre.[74] These reports and the recommendations they included served as the basis of the judges' rulings. As the affair ran its course, Louis closely monitored each detail of the proceedings, receiving precise updates each morning on the suspects' interrogations and the judges' deliberations.

Officially convened at the beginning of April, the Chambre de l'Arsenal began to hear cases in May. The Chambre was a deluxe production in the genre of the seventeenth-century theater of justice. Its proceedings a state secret, its members sat in judgment in the basement of the Arsenal, the windows draped in black cloth, the only light provided by flaming torches. These torches lent the tribunal its unofficial name, the Chambre ardente, or Burning Chamber.[75]

The Chambre de l'Arsenal followed standard French judicial procedure as recently revised by the Edict of Saint-Germain-en-Laye in 1670.[76] La Reynie and Bezons identified the suspect to be arrested and submitted a request for a *lettre de cachet.* After the king signed this warrant it was dispatched to La Reynie, who then ordered the arrest of the suspect named. Once caught, the suspect was imprisoned in the Bastille, the Châtelet, or the fortress of Vincennes. In light of La Reynie's initial interrogations of the suspect, the *procureur général,* Robert, determined whether a *réquisition,* or indictment, would be issued and a preliminary investigation launched. This preliminary investigation, conducted by La Reynie and Bezons as *commissaires instructeurs,* included the interrogations of the suspect and the witnesses, the *récolements* or verifications of the testimony of the witnesses, and the confrontations between accusers and the accused.[77] The court clerk, or *greffier,* recorded each encounter in a bound volume, the relevant pages of which were countersigned by all participants at the conclusion of the session. However, the clerk did not transcribe dialogue verbatim, as direct discourse, but documented statements indirectly, in the third person. After their initial investigation had been completed, La Reynie and Bezons submitted their findings on the case to the Chambre. Based on the *rapporteurs'* report, the judges then met in session to decide whether the accused should be remanded into custody (*recommandé*) or set free. If the suspect was imprisoned, an *instruction,* or further investigation into the case, followed. La Reynie and Bezons conducted this second investigation as well. Upon its completion, the prosecutor, M. Robert, drew up the resulting indictment. After the judges as a body formally questioned the suspect one last time (formal questioning took place *sur la sellette,* or while the suspect sat before them on a three-legged stool), they issued a ruling on the case. Their sentence was without appeal, although the king reserved the right to modify the sentence if he so chose.[78]

The judges of the Chambre ardente had a considerable range of rulings at their disposal. They could dismiss the charges and set the suspect free. All prisoners who were released were not necessarily declared innocent, however; the judges could order the accused *mise hors de cour,* or released from prison, but not acquitted of the charges. When the judges were suspicious of the accused but did not have enough evidence to convict, they could issue a ruling of *plus amplement informé,* setting the prisoner at liberty but leaving the case open should new evidence be uncovered. Other rulings left a defendant physically alive but legally dead; *mort civile* (a status shared by those condemned to death, to the galleys, or to perpetual banishment) rendered a person unable to hold office, testify in court, or write a will.[79] Defendants found guilty received sentences that ranged from fines and periods of banishment to death.

If the judges found the suspect guilty of a capital crime, they could impose the *question préalable,* or torture before execution, to force the suspect to reveal the names of any accomplices.[80] According to royal law, torture could also be administered in capital cases before a guilty verdict had been reached (the *question préparatoire*). A sentence to the *question préparatoire* required grave suspicion, or proximate proof, of guilt. According to legal precedent, proximate or half-proofs included some forms of written evidence (such as written spells of diabolic magic), the testimony of two disinterested witnesses that the accused had confessed outside the courtroom, and the testimony of one eyewitness to the crime. The confession of the accused under torture, in combination with an extant half-proof, added up to a complete proof of guilt.[81] Unlike the modern practices of state torture analyzed by Elaine Scarry, which are hidden, illegal, and intended to extinguish the very voice and humanity of their victims,[82] the employment of torture in ancien régime France was openly acknowledged, enshrined in law, and intended, as sentences to torture read, "to know the truth from [the prisoner's] mouth."[83] Torture was not conceived of as a punishment but as a means of eliciting truthful statements that otherwise would be left unspoken. Only pain, Louis XIV's judges believed, allowed the truth to be freed from the body.[84]

The criminal ordinance of 1670 carefully circumscribed the practice of torture.

A prisoner could be tortured only once unless additional evidence came to light; torture could last no more than eighty-five minutes; no leading questions could be asked; and any confession made under torture had to be reaffirmed without torture within twenty-four hours. Prisoners could be sentenced to "ordinary" torture (*la question ordinaire*) or the more severe "extraordinary" torture (*la question extraordinare*). Within the jurisdiction of the Parlement of Paris, authorities employed two methods: the boot or *brodequins* and the water torture or *question d'eau*. In the first, the prisoner's feet and legs were placed in a wooden mold and "coins" or wedges (four for the ordinary, four more for the extraordinary) were driven into the sides of the boot, causing the mold to tighten and crush the prisoner's bones. In the second, the prisoner was stretched naked over a short stool placed in the small of the back, hands and feet tied and pulled in opposite directions. He or she was then forced to swallow four *coquemards* (a *coquemard* was roughly three pints) of water, which distended the stomach almost to bursting and nearly drowned the prisoner. For the extraordinary, the prisoner was bent backward over an even higher stool, causing greater distention of the stomach, and forced to drink four more jugs of water.[85] Despite the acute agony that they endured, very few people tortured during the seventeenth century confessed. In the jurisdiction of the Parlement of Paris, for example, confession rates for the *question préparatoire* hovered at 2.3 percent.[86] Nonetheless, French judges continued to impose sentences of torture throughout the ancien régime and continued to regard it as a viable means of extracting truth.[87]

By the time Louis XIV dissolved the Chambre de l'Arsenal on July 31, 1682, the tribunal had held 210 formal sessions; it had indicted 442 people and issued 319 arrest warrants or *décrets de prise de corps*. The fate of more than half remains unknown. Of those people whom the Paris police succeeded in placing under arrest, the judges of the Arsenal sent thirty-six to their death, condemned five to the galleys for life, banished twenty-three, fined and sentenced ten to public apologies, and set forty-three free.[88] Two died in prison. Approximately sixty prisoners were never tried at all; Louis and Louvois judged their potential testimony and confessions too dangerous to the crown to be heard even by their handpicked judges. The possessors of such incendiary knowledge were instead placed in solitary confinement for the rest of their lives, chained to the wall of one of France's fortresses and forbidden to speak even to their jailors.[89] The king imposed perpetual silence upon these last inconvenient reminders of the Affair of the Poisons.

La Reynie wasted no time while awaiting the official installation of the Chambre de l'Arsenal during the months of March and April 1679. He expanded his investigation into the allegations made by La Voisin and La Bosse concerning their clients among the robe nobility. His findings only reiterated the need for a special commission, for several additional witnesses confirmed that two widows of *parlementaires,* Mmes de Dreux and Leféron, were indeed involved with the sorceresses. La Reynie and the judges, unsurprisingly, were less interested in the activities of clients who indulged themselves with magical cosmetics and love charms than they were in capital offenses. Fortune-telling and palm reading were minor infractions; murder, trafficking in poison, abortion, and sacrilege were crimes the judges were determined to punish.

During the confrontation that followed La Voisin's first interrogation, she and La Bosse began to charge each other with crimes of increasing gravity.[90] La Voisin, asserted La Bosse, had tried to murder her own husband so that she might marry the magician Lesage, and furthermore La Voisin had sold inheritance powders to two women from prominent robe families.[91] Mmes de Dreux and Leféron, La Bosse claimed, had sought not to manipulate their husbands' behavior through prayers, perfumes, or love charms but to rid themselves of their husbands for good—with poisons supplied by La Voisin.[92]

Determined to punish the crime of poison regardless of a suspect's rank or social status, Louis ordered the arrests of Mmes de Dreux and Leféron at the beginning of April. As with Mme de Poulaillon and the marquise de Brinvilliers, adultery and unchecked passion had led to the crime of poison. Madame de Dreux, wife of a *maître des requêtes* in the Parlement of Paris, had purchased poison from Marie Bosse to administer to her inconvenient husband. She had also made attempts on the lives of four others: two lovers, the fiancée of one, and the wife of the other.[93] Madame Leféron stood accused of poisoning her first husband in 1669 so that she could marry her lover.

The robe nobility in Paris was particularly horrified to learn of the arrests of two of its own. No one knew who might be next. In a letter to her brother-in-law, Bussy-Rabutin, Mme de Scudéry described the waves of anxiety sweeping the city: "One only talks of the people arrested for poisoning . . . all this has made everyone afraid; thank God I have never bought any cosmetics or had my fortune told."[94] The tumult within Parisian society only intensified when the first fruits of the Chambre ardente's labors were exhibited on the scaffolds of the place de Grève. Scarcely a month after their first meeting, the judges condemned both Marie Bosse and Marie Vigoureux to death for "having distributed poison to several women to poison their husbands."[95]

Like all punishments ordered by the Chambre, the executions of the two sorceresses reflected a hierarchical conception of punishment in which the level of the criminal's suffering was to correspond to the gravity of the offence.[96] Sentences were carefully calibrated to communicate the state's disapprobation to the crowds who gathered to watch the spectacles enacted in the place de Grève.[97] Petty thieves were branded and whipped, incorrigible blasphemers had their tongues pierced by hot irons, and parricides' right hands were severed before execution. The trial papers of criminals whose offenses were deemed particularly reprehensible (such as sodomy, blasphemy, or *lèse majesté*) might also be ritually burned on the scaffold, symbolically expunging even the memory of their existence.[98] Formal shaming ceremonies exacerbated physical suffering; the public and abject apology, or *amende honorable*, was meant to dishonor the prisoner as he begged remission for his sins.[99] The punishments of those convicted can thus be read as evidence of the weight accorded their transgressions.

Both La Bosse and La Vigoureux, as the marquise de Brinvilliers had been, were sentenced to make a public apology "before the main portal of the cathedral of Notre-Dame, naked but for a shirt, the hangman's noose around the neck, holding a burning candle of two pounds, then conducted to the place de Grève to there be burned alive"—an extremely rare form of execution, reserved for the perpetrators of the most atrocious crimes. La Bosse was put to death on May 10, 1679.[100] To the priest who stood at the foot of the scaffold to offer the sorceress a final opportunity to confess the sins weighing on her soul, she said only, "Pray to God for me."[101] The stake prepared for Marie Vigoureux stood empty, for she had died of an "abscess in the head" as she was tortured the day before.[102] Marie Bosse did not go to her death alone, however. Her son, convicted as her accomplice, was hanged at the same time, as was Marie Ferry, convicted of poisoning her husband.[103]

The judges of the Chambre could not bring themselves, however, to pass such severe judgment on women of their own class. Despite the weight of evidence against them, the judges exercised considerable clemency toward Mmes de Poulaillon, Leféron, and de Dreux. Madame de Poulaillon was banished for life and all of her goods were confiscated,[104] while Madame Leféron received a sentence of nine years of banishment and fifteen hundred *livres* in fines. Madame de Dreux, with two cousins (d'Ormesson and Fortia) sitting in the Chambre, escaped with only a warning, or *admonestation*.[105] Apparently her ordeal did not teach her much of a lesson. She found herself before the tribunal again a year later, accused of returning to the *empoisonneuses* to try to get rid of another rival for her lover, M. de Richelieu. She did not escape so lightly the second time; banished, she spent the remainder of her life repenting of her deeds in a convent in the Low Countries.[106] The leniency shown toward the three noblewomen, rather than creating public support for La Reynie's investigation, contributed to *le monde*'s displeasure over the entire process. Madame de Sévigné complained to her daughter, "Such a scandal for nothing."[107]

La Reynie's investigation continued to expand throughout the spring and summer of 1679. Following the allegations made by La Voisin and La Bosse, the judges of the Chambre issued arrest warrants for dozens of members of Paris's criminal magical underworld. Several abortionists were among the first imprisoned.[108] Unsurprisingly, there were close connections between sorceresses who supplied women with love charms and abortionists who disposed of the evidence of adulterous liaisons. La Voisin regularly referred clients to abortionists like the sinister Catherine Belleau (known as La Lepère) and her daughter.[109] *Faiseuses d'anges,* or angel makers, offered women of all classes a means of escaping the relentless cycle of pregnancy and childbirth. According to their statements, these abortionists had extensive practices. Usually midwives as well, they provided herbal abortifacients, performed surgical procedures with an "iron syringe,"[110] or simply took away an unwanted infant after delivery. Apparently, many of Paris's abortionists hid the evidence of their work by bringing it to La Voisin to destroy.[111] Several witnesses attested that La Voisin, an inveterate self-promoter, had bragged that she had burned the bodies of twenty-five hundred infants in the little stove in her garden consulting-room.[112]

The Chambre continued to issue warrants for a number of other sorceresses and practitioners of related trades. La Trianon and La Dodée were two of the more colorful sorceresses then operating in Paris. After poisoning La Dodée's husband, they "lived together as man and wife" and conducted a lively trade in charms and spells. La Trianon was considered to have ghoulish tastes even by her fellows; she kept a skeleton in her apartment and saved the fingers of condemned criminals whose bodies had been left exposed to make her magical charms.[113] La Trianon and La Dodée also sold poisons, often imported from shepherds or monks in nearby provinces, a number of whom were also arrested that spring.[114] Anne Petit and François Belot, suspected of brewing and distributing poisons, found themselves in the fortress of Vincennes as well. They were joined by a collection of underemployed curés, vicars, and abbés who had supplemented their meager livings by performing magical rites and demonic invocations.[115] In the space of a few short months, La Reynie had filled the prisons of Paris to overflowing.

The man who was to become La Reynie's most valuable (and voluble) prisoner, the magician Lesage, was arrested on March 22, 1679. Also known as Adam Dubuisson, his actual name was Adam Cœuret. He first arrived in Paris in 1667 at the age of thirty-eight, sporting a red wig and claiming to be a wool merchant. Rather than sell wool, Lesage and his partner, the abbé Mariette, supported themselves by performing demonic ceremonies for those hoping to find buried treasure or requited love. By 1668 Lesage had been sentenced to a life term in the galleys for his "impieties and sacrileges."[116] His reappearance in Paris five years later was due not to the influence of his sometime lover La Voisin, as some historians have speculated, but to an extraordinary stroke of luck. In 1673 Lesage's galley distinguished itself during a battle and the king rewarded the bravery of the crew by granting a pardon to fifteen Frenchmen serving on board.[117] Lesage found himself among the fortunate few granted their freedom and lost no time returning to the capital to resume his trade and renew his friendships.

Like La Bosse, La Vigoureux, and La Voisin before him, Lesage initially denied any involvement in serious crimes. He protested that his only offenses had been to swindle the credulous—including, he boasted, the duc de Luxembourg and the

marquis de Feuquières—with fraudulent *pistoles volants* and bogus demonic invocations.[118] But the poisons found in his apartment, his relationships with unsavory
characters such as La Voisin and La Bosse, and the discovery of his prior conviction
for sacrilege told La Reynie that Lesage was more than just a talented charlatan.[119]

Lesage no doubt realized that his only hope of saving his skin was to begin to
talk, and talk he did. Throughout the summer and fall of 1679 the garrulous Lesage
accused not only his accomplices but many prominent aristocrats who he claimed
had been his clients. He lodged his most serious charges against his former lover.
La Voisin, Lesage maintained, provided dissatisfied wives with poison to rid themselves of their husbands. She worked with a "véritable empoisonneur" named
Maître Pierre who furnished her (as well as La Bosse and La Trianon) with venomous herbs with which she brewed various concoctions (*décoctions*) and teas
used for "evil spells." She also performed strange rites of love magic for clients.
Lesage also claimed that La Voisin told an acquaintance that twenty-five hundred
aborted infants were buried in her garden.[120]

When confronted with Lesage's statements, La Voisin immediately struck back.
Her disclosures regarding their mutual endeavors were sensational; revenge was
apparently worth self-incrimination. On September 12 the clerk Sagot recorded
La Voisin's change of heart. She prefaced her statement by saying that she wanted
"to reveal to us the truth of all she knew . . . declaring to us moreover that she
had not told until now all that she knew about all the things about which she had
been interrogated."[121] La Voisin declared that she had furnished some of La Leroux's poisons to Mmes Leféron and de Dreux and that she and Lesage worked
together for Mme de Vivonne, sister-in-law of the king's mistress Athénaïs de Montespan, and Mme de la Mothe, another prominent courtier.[122] La Voisin claimed
that both women had come to her seeking a way to escape their marriages.[123]

Interrogated on September 17, Lesage retaliated with an even more startling
accusation that moved the Affair of the Poisons into ever-higher circles at court.
La Voisin, La Bosse, and La Vigoureux, he said, had tried to place a woman named
Marie Vertemart as a servant in Mme de Montespan's household.[124] His accusation was grave indeed, as it revealed that even the king's *maîtresse en titre,* mother
of five of his children, had been targeted by Paris's network of sorceresses and
poisoners. Furthermore, Lesage divulged, La Voisin traveled frequently to the court
at Saint-Germain during 1676 to deliver powders of Spanish fly to members of
Mme de Montespan's entourage, a Mlle des Œillets and a maid named Cato.[125]
La Voisin, however, stoutly denied any participation in the business whatsoever.
Cato had asked for her help to win a post with Mme de Montespan, she admitted,
but her assistance had been limited to saying three novenas, for which, by the way,
she received only an *écu* and a cheap ring. She had not laid eyes on Cato since.[126]
Not so, responded Lesage. La Voisin had not only participated in the plot to
place La Vertemart but the sorceress had met frequently with Mlle des Œillets in

**Fig. 3** *The marquise de Montespan with four of her legitimized children*, c. 1677. The painting is attributed to Charles de Lafosse.

connection with "an affair" concerning Mme de Montespan. If La Reynie arrested a woman named Françoise Filastre, "he would learn of strange things."[127]

Louvois reported Lesage's latest revelations to the king immediately. The magician's statements only served to justify the precautions that the minister and the king had taken just five days earlier to prevent any whisper of the accusations made against those close to Mme de Montespan from reaching the ears of the public. In response to Lesage's statement of the 17th, the king had instructed the clerk of the Chambre de l'Arsenal to record La Voisin's interrogations on separate sheets of paper rather than in the customary bound volume, so that any charges against or mention of Mme de Montespan, her children, Mlle des Œillets, or even her maids could be removed before copies of the interrogations were made for the Chambre.[128] The judges were never to see the unexpurgated statements.[129]

From this point on, La Reynie, Louvois, and the small circle of royal advisors who knew of these accusations referred to them only as the *faits particuliers*. These facts would eventually inspire the king to order a separate, clandestine inquiry into the magical activities of his *maîtresse en titre*. The king would effectively create a two-pronged investigation; one branch semipublic and conducted with the full knowledge of the judges of the Arsenal, the other secret and investigated only by his faithful police lieutenant. La Reynie's covert inquiry would grow in scope over the next two years as an increasing number of suspects began to make allegations about Mme de Montespan and her entourage. When the official investigation threatened to expose the revelations of the unofficial one, the king suspended the Chambre de l'Arsenal altogether. The king's interference ensured that neither the judges of the Chambre nor the French public learned of the many accusations leveled against Mme de Montespan. Most important, no major aristocratic observer—neither Mme de Sévigné, Primi Visconti, nor Saint Simon—would ever make any mention of the suspects' most explosive charge: that Mme de Montespan had attempted to poison the king.[130]

Lesage, scrambling to save his neck (as a recidivist on the charge of sacrilege, he faced capital punishment), found a way to make himself indispensable to La Reynie's investigations: he raised the social bar of suspects ever higher. As he broadened the scope of his accusations, Lesage amplified the seriousness of his charges against his alleged clients. The marquis de Feuquières, he said, wanted to do more than "speak with the spirits." The marquis had sought out Lesage because he sought to contrive the death of the uncle of a girl he wanted to marry— the uncle opposed the match.[131] Furthermore, Lesage claimed, the duc de Luxembourg, captain of the king's guard, had employed him to further a variety of nefarious objectives. The duke wanted the magician to bring about the death of his wife and of the maréchal de Créqui, to ensure the marriage of his son with Louvois's daughter, to win the love of the sister-in-law of the princesse de Tingry, and, finally, to be assured of victory in the field. Lesage explained that the duke had written all his wishes on a scrap of paper that Lesage had pretended to insert into a ball of wax and throw into a fire. (By palming the note instead of burning it, Lesage secured a useful item with which to blackmail his client at a later date.) The gunpowder-laced ball immediately exploded, supposedly sending the duke's requests straight to the devil, who was to reply within three days.[132]

Lesage's accusations against the much-decorated duc de Luxembourg fell delightfully on Louvois's ears. He felt an intense rivalry toward the captain of the king's guard and took care to draw the king's attention to the duke's alleged diabolical dealings. "All that your Majesty has seen against M. de Luxembourg and M. de Feuquières is nothing compared to the declarations contained in this interrogation," he wrote to the king. The gratified minister promised even more startling revelations to come, after he paid a visit to the magician himself. "M. de la Reynie assures me that he is persuaded that if I speak to Lesage he will decide to reveal all that he knows."[133] Thus Louvois and La Reynie, rather than Luxembourg, became Lesage's ultimate clients.

Lesage's statements seemed to demonstrate such an intimate knowledge of the activities, clients, and membership of the criminal magical underworld that La Reynie and Louvois came to believe that the magician's information was essential to their investigations, both official and unofficial. La Reynie and Louvois decided to offer Lesage what he so desperately sought—"the king's grace"—in return for his complete cooperation. Louvois implied in his report to the king that the offer had been La Reynie's idea. La Reynie, he wrote, believed that Lesage, "who as of now has not been convicted of having poisoned anyone himself, has a perfect knowledge of all that has been done in Paris for the past seven or eight years."[134] Extraordinarily, Louvois did in fact travel to Vincennes to urge Lesage to continue to talk, "making him hope that Your Majesty would grant him grace provided that he made the necessary declarations to provide information about all that he knows in regard to poison."[135]

Lesage did his utmost to satisfy his new clients. His next allegations, made after his visit from Louvois, seemed to justify the confidence that the minister and La Reynie had in his "perfect knowledge of all that has been done in Paris." The magician had in fact kept some of his best material in reserve, revealing not only poisonings but also startling acts of sacrilege and other religious impieties that must have shaken the devout La Reynie to the core. Lesage's most spectacular allegations concerned amatory masses held at the home of La Voisin. The magician contended that two renegade priests celebrated the masses over the prone body of a woman (whom Lesage did not identify at this time). One of the priests kissed the woman's "shameful parts" during the mass and had "carnal knowledge" of the woman at the ceremony's conclusion. Furthermore, similar rites had been conducted by several other priests in Paris.[136]

Lesage also began to accuse notable members of the court of participating in other, albeit less fantastic, sacrilegious rituals. Aiming his charges ever higher up the social hierarchy, he alleged that the duchesses of Angoulême, Vitry, and Vivonne (sister-in-law of Mme de Montespan), and the princesse of Tingry had sought his help in arranging a pact with the devil that "had something to do with the king." Furthermore, the magician purported, Mesdames de Polignac, Gramont, and du Roure had employed magical means in their plot to supplant Louise de la Val-lière during her reign as *maîtresse en titre*. They had gone so far as to commission spells involving the burial of pigeon hearts that symbolized those of the king and his mistress. The comte de Cessac, he added, was in love with his sister-in-law and had sought to do away with his own brother, and the duchesse de Bouillon wanted to murder her husband so that she might marry her lover.[137] La Voisin seconded Lesage's allegations against his aristocratic clients. He had confided, she told La Reynie, that "all these women are crazy and only want to get rid of their husbands, and she [Mme de Bouillon] really wanted to be a widow."[138]

While his investigation lurched into an increasingly prominent group of sus-pects, La Reynie had no intention of ignoring the numerous magical practices uncovered in his investigations that were accounted "superstitious" rather than criminal. It was clear that the thousands of Parisians who kept the city's fortune-tellers, palm readers, and the like in business were in need of a lesson illustrating the true nature of such magical chicanery.[139] To that end, he encouraged Jean Don-neau de Visé and Thomas Corneille to write a play that would induce the Parisian public to view the so-called sorceresses with the proper skepticism as well as to help purge the fear of poisonings running rampant in the city. A tremendous spec-tacle, *La devineresse, ou les faux enchantements* opened in Paris's Théâtre Guéné-gaud on November 19, 1679 (see Fig. 4).[140] The play ridiculed the credulous clients of two con artists posing as a sorceress and a magician. Although the Affair of the Poisons was never alluded to explicitly, it was clear to all that the play depicted people like La Voisin and Lesage and their foolish clients. Like those of La Voisin, the clients of the fictional sorceress sought spells that would protect them in battle, charms for larger breasts and younger-looking skin, and the oppor-tunity to converse with the devil.[141] La Reynie must have been heartened by the results of his attempt to encourage Paris to laugh at "so-called sorceresses"; the play sold out for an unprecedented five months, the longest run ever recorded to that point.[142]

As the play's successful run continued, so too did La Reynie's investigations. Despite, or perhaps because of, the alarming revelations of the *faits particuliers* concerning his mistress, Louis remained adamant that the official investigation into the Affair of the Poisons continue. The interests of justice and order still out-weighed the Sun King's need for secrecy. In his personal notes on the case, La Reynie recorded the orders that he and the judges of the Chambre received from

**Fig. 4** *La comédie de la devineresse.* Originally engraved to promote Corneille and Visé's 1679 play *La devineresse, ou les faux enchantements.* Each vignette depicts a magical fraud perpetuated by the sorceress of the title.

Louis on December 27: "His Majesty desires that for the public good we penetrate as deeply as is possible for us into the unhappy commerce of poisons in order to root it out, if that were possible; he commanded us to exercise scrupulous justice, without any regard to person, condition, or sex, and His Majesty told us this in such clear and vivid terms, and at the same time with such good will, that it is impossible to doubt his intentions in this regard."[143] La Reynie and the judges took Louis's commands to heart.

With the January arrests of several courtiers named by Lesage and La Voisin, the French public learned that the Affair of the Poisons reached high into the ranks of the ancient families of the sword as well as those of the robe. The Chambre issued warrants for the comtesse de Soissons, the marquise d'Alluye, the vicomtesse de Polignac, and the duc de Luxembourg. The marquis de Feuquières, the princesse de Tingry, the duchesse de Bouillon, and the comtesse du Roure were subpoenaed to appear before the judges.[144] Paris, despite having been inundated with rumors about the affair and its participants for months, was in an uproar. Madame de Sévigné described the furor: "One is in a state, one sends for the news, one goes out visiting to learn of the latest, one is curious. . . . The tone of today is of the innocence of the accused and the horror of the scandal; maybe tomorrow it will be the opposite. . . . One doesn't talk of anything else in company; in effect, there has scarcely been an example of such a scandal in a Christian court."[145] Reports circulated wildly about the charges facing the unfortunate courtiers. Bussy kept himself well informed:

> The comtesse de Soissons is accused of having poisoned her husband; the marquise d'Alluye, her brother-in-law Sourdis; the princesse de Tingry, babies she had given birth to; Mme de Bouillon, a valet de chambre who had got to know of her love affairs. The King has sent back to the duchesse de Foix a note which she had written to La Voisin, and which included the phrase: "The more I rub, the less they project." His Majesty demanded an explanation of this phrase, and she replied that she had asked La Voisin for a prescription to make her breasts grow larger.[146]

Parisian society initially discounted such seemingly preposterous accusations against members of the aristocracy as the desperate attempts of hardened criminals to avoid the scaffold. The marquis de Feuquières offered his father the explanation that his fellow courtiers found most appealing: "Some male and female poisoners by trade have succeeded in prolonging their lives by making successive denunciations against men of quality, who have consequently to be arrested and interrogated, and thus the prisoners gain a respite."[147] However, the lofty rank of those accused did indicate to some observers that the courtiers could not be entirely innocent. The English ambassador informed his government that Parisian society was inclined to believe that the suspects would never have been arrested without substantial evidence against them.[148]

Before it had time to digest the news of the arrest warrants that had been issued, Paris and the court were further scandalized to learn that some of the aristocrats under suspicion had fled the country rather than face the Chambre de l'Arsenal. The comte de Cessac headed for England, while Olympe Mancini (niece of Cardinal Mazarin), comtesse de Soissons, scampered over the border to Flanders, accompanied by her loyal friend and fellow suspect, the marquise d'Alluye. The comtesse's flight was no surprise to the king. Despite evidence that she had poisoned her husband and plotted to poison Louise de la Vallière, Louis gave his former lover the choice of exile or a trial and she had chosen the former.[149] Madame de Sévigné described how the comtesse had justified her flight: "Mme de Soissons . . . disappeared at night, saying that she could not face the prospect of prison and the shame of being confronted with hags and villains." Madame de Sévigné believed wholeheartedly that the comtesse had behaved honorably. "I consider her action to be perfectly natural and noble, and entirely approve of it," she wrote.[150]

The uproar over the proceedings of the Chambre arose not only over the insult to the estate of its defendants, but also from the apparent triviality of many of the crimes under investigation. Primi Visconti recalled: "The Chambre ardente set up at the Arsenal caused a great stir at the time, for, besides the poisonings, it investigated all sorts of superstitions and vices; it seemed like a state inquisition of conscience. All France trembled, especially at the sight of even princesses and marshals in flight, or in prison, on mere suspicion."[151] Madame de Sévigné shared his sentiments. Apparently unaware that the comtesse de Soissons was alleged to have poisoned anyone, she puzzled, "it is said that the things of which she is accused consist of mere stupidities, things she herself has mentioned time and time again, as one does after visiting one of these so-called sorceresses."[152] Such "bagatelles" simply did not merit much scrutiny in the eyes of the Louis's courtiers.[153] Furthermore, she sniffed, the accusations of myriad sacrileges and abortions "are filling all Europe with horror."[154] Soon enough, she wrote, "a Frenchman will be synonymous with a poisoner in foreign lands."[155]

For Louis XIV and the judges of the Chambre de l'Arsenal, however, trying the suspects of the Affair of the Poisons was well worth scandalizing *le monde*. The trials provided an opportunity to cleanse the capital not only of poisoners but also of those whose truck with magic, based as it was on the power of holy things, so clearly corrupted the teachings of the Catholic Church. The transgressions of members of the magical underworld were not only accounted criminal, they were held to be deeply sinful as well. As historians such as Stuart Clark and Robert Muchembled have demonstrated, the Tridentine ideals that infused seventeenth-century French society contributed to a "sacralization of justice" in which members of the judiciary came to envision themselves as "custodians of religion as well as law."[156] Indeed, the concepts of sin and crime were so closely entwined during the seventeenth century that neither religious nor political authorities distinguished particularly between them.[157]

The criminalization of sin had its roots in late medieval Catholic reform. The decrees of the sixteenth-century Council of Trent, intended to discipline lay piety, continued the trend; the council explicitly defined as criminal any sin that compelled a baptized Catholic to require the sacrament of confession.[158] In France, the Tridentine association between sin and crime was advanced by the efforts of lay religious organizations such as the Company of the Holy Sacrament, whose noble members dedicated themselves to stamping out "public sins" (pornography, prostitution, and begging, among others) in order to create a morally pure society.[159] Popular devotional tracts reiterated the link between sin and crime, as did the priests who confirmed the connection between the moral and social order and urged their parishioners to follow the dictates of both church and state. "Religion is nothing other than a bond that . . . subjects us to God. . . . [This bond] . . . subsumes . . . all the duties and all the obligations which hold men together [in a civil society]," preached the Jesuit Louis Bourdaloue.[160]

The Gallican church's conflation of sin and crime was enshrined in the jurisprudence of the French state. Offenses against religion that might conceivably have come under the purview of ecclesiastical courts were instead tried under royal law. Louis XIV's lifelong concern to ensure that his subjects adhered to the teachings of the Roman Catholic Church manifested itself in a series of ordinances that disciplined his subjects' religious lives and enjoined a strict Catholic Reformation morality. His prolonged campaign to outlaw Protestantism would culminate in the revocation of the Edict of Nantes only a few years hence. The king's crusade to eradicate irreligion encompassed far more than the persecution of Protestants, however. In the name of public order, his courts vigorously enforced existing ordinances against heresy, sacrilege, and blasphemy.[161] Heresy, the most serious of violations, threatened to divide the kingdom; blasphemy (subject of a series of sporadically severe edicts, the last issued in 1681) promised to bring divine anger down upon the entire community; and sacrilege insulted God, for "to insult the things of God is to insult God himself."[162] The king also issued decrees that required that Sunday be kept as a holy day, that Lenten fasts be observed, that clerical misconduct be condemned, and that prostitutes be incarcerated.[163] In effect, Louis XIV's criminal code punished those who broke the Ten Commandments.

Therefore, when Louis XIV expanded the scope of the Chambre de l'Arsenal to include "sacrilege, impieties, profanities, production and introduction of counterfeit money,"[164] his actions were entirely in keeping with his contemporaneous attack on sin.[165] Likeminded magistrates and theologians agreed that rooting out the members of the criminal magical underworld was of paramount importance.

Spiritual offences, perhaps even more than secular ones, threatened the "right order" of the city. This logic did little to mitigate the unpopularity of the Chambre, however. Public indignation was such that its judges had to be reassured by Louvois that the king would place them under his protection.[166]

With the king's support, the judges continued their inquiry despite the public outcry. The subpoenas issued against members of the aristocracy were enforced and Louis's courtiers were compelled to appear or flee the country. The duchesse de Bouillon, furious that a woman of her rank and ancient lineage was to be questioned by mere members of the robe, arrived for her hearing on January 29, 1680.[167] Alleged to have poisoned a valet who had uncovered her plan to poison her husband so that she might marry the duc de Vendôme, the duchess entered the courtroom with her lover on one arm and her husband on the other. Stating that she had appeared before the commission only because it was the pleasure of the king, she arrogantly denied all charges against her and swept out of the room.[168] Perhaps overly pleased with her performance, she later regaled her friends with her version of what had transpired. When asked by La Reynie whether or not she had seen the devil during her visits to Parisian sorceresses, the duchess now recalled that she had answered, "Yes, I saw him, and he looked just like you!"[169]

After the excitement created by the appearance of the duchesse de Bouillon and other courtiers, it seemed to the Parisian public that the Affair of the Poisons might have finally run its course. Madame de Sévigné, ever attentive to the latest gossip, let her daughter know on February 9 that "the Affair of the Poisons is all over, one doesn't hear any more that is new. The rumor is that there will not be any more blood spilled." She was mistaken. Only five days later, she sent word, "The Chambre de l'Arsenal has recommenced."[170]

Even before Louis XIV's courtiers testified before the Chambre, La Reynie's investigations had begun to focus on the statements made by Françoise Filastre, the woman from whom, Lesage had promised, the judges would "learn of strange things."[171] La Filastre first came to La Reynie's attention during his inquiry into the international cabal of Louis Vanens in the fall of 1677. Vanens and his cronies maintained a discreet laboratory in the home of Madeleine Chapelain in the faubourg Saint-Antoine, where they concocted alchemical formulas and assorted poisons.[172] There, La Chapelain and La Filastre practiced various forms of demonic magic in the company of several renegade priests, all of whom also worked with Lesage and La Voisin.[173] La Reynie's police did not locate La Filastre until December 1679; she had been searching for buried treasure in the Auvergne, or so she maintained. Her statements would soon threaten to expose the secrets of La Reynie's clandestine investigation to the judges of the Arsenal and the public.

La Reynie was finally able to interrogate La Filastre on December 22. Until her execution the following October, she confessed to an increasingly macabre litany of crimes: pledging her own baby to the devil, arranging pacts with the devil for clients such as the duchesse de Vivonne, and assisting at amatory masses. An accomplice also accused her of attempting to poison several people, including her lover's wife.[174] Furthermore, La Reynie discovered that La Filastre's lover was a counterfeiter and poisoner who had not only collaborated with members of Louis Vanens's cabal but had served as La Voisin's agent in the provinces.

Most worrisome of all were the letters of recommendation found in La Filastre's possession addressed to the king's latest favorite. La Filastre protested that she had merely hoped to gain a post in the service of Mlle de Fontanges and thus "advance her family."[175] Mademoiselle de Fontanges, though, was not just another lady-in-waiting at the court. Daughter of the comte de Roussille, "beautiful as an angel and stupid as a basket," she was Louis's last great passion and the last great threat to Mme de Montespan's reign as *maîtresse en titre*.[176] The discovery that an associate of the notorious poisoners Vanens and La Voisin had plotted to install herself close to the king's newest mistress was an ominous discovery indeed.[177] Moreover, La Filastre's statements were soon to be corroborated by a member of La Voisin's own household: her daughter Marie-Marguerite.

As La Reynie pursued his inquiry into the activities of La Filastre, the public was preoccupied with the spectacle of La Voisin's public apology and execution. On February 19, 20, and 21, La Voisin was interrogated on the *sellette* for a final time by the judges of the Chambre de l'Arsenal. Her death sentence was a foregone conclusion. When subjected to the questions ordinary and extraordinary, La Voisin added little to her previous statements. She maintained that La Lepère and her daughter were abortionists ("more than ten thousand abortions") and that La Lepère had attempted to poison her husband. She persisted in her accusations against her former lover Lesage and against La Trianon and La Dodée, and denounced a score of other devineresses and poisoners as well: La Petit, La Duval, La Chapelain, La Belhomme, La Delaporte,[178] La Pelletier, and Vautier. Even as the bones in her feet and legs were crushed in the *brodequins,* however, La Voisin continued to deny any participation in the plot to place La Vertemart in Mme de Montespan's retinue and maintained that the petition she planned to hand to the king at Saint-Germain was merely a request for the release of François Blessis from prison. While she admitted that she had helped Cato enter the service of Mme de Montespan several years before (albeit through ardent prayer only), she claimed she had not seen her erstwhile friend since.[179] La Voisin also continued to deny Lesage's charges that she had had dealings with, or ever knew, Mlle des Œillets, as well as any participation in amatory masses or the delivery of powders to Mme de Montespan.[180]

La Voisin was burned alive on February 22, 1680.[181] Even before her execution, Paris was rife with rumors over the way in which she had passed her final days. Madame de Sévigné described the scenes to her daughter: "In the evening she said to her guards: 'What! No *medianoche?*'[182] She ate with them at midnight, out of whim for it was not a fast-day, drank a great deal of wine, and sang a number of drinking songs. On Tuesday she received the questions ordinary and extraordinary, after having dined, and slept for eight hours. She was confronted, while under torture, with Mesdames de Dreux and Leféron and several others. Her answers have not yet transpired, but everyone expects strange revelations."[183] The streets of Paris filled with people wishing to catch a glimpse of the notorious sorceress in her tumbrel as she was taken to the scaffold. The curious gathered in friends' homes that lined the route to the scaffold to watch the procession: "[La Voisin] appeared in the tumbrel dressed in white, a kind of garb worn by those condemned to be burnt. She was very red in the face, and was seen to push away the confessor and the crucifix with great violence. M. de Chaulnes, M. de Sully, the countess, myself, and several others, saw her pass by the Hôtel de Sully."[184]

For anyone unfortunate enough to have missed her final journey, booksellers offered broadsheets that commemorated the event, featuring a portrait of the sorceress by Antoine Coypel. The engraving depicts an unremarkable middle-aged woman gazing wearily at Death, the three Fates, and a multitude of snakes and demons encircling her. A verse beneath the portrait floridly intones, "Spring of so much evil, cursed creature / Who by a thousand poisons destroyed nature, / Even though the Fates have made death reign by spinning out your detestable days and prolonging their length, / A terrible torture, full of ignominy / Has been able to cut short the thread of your horrific life" (see Fig. 5).

La Voisin's daughter, Marie-Marguerite, arrested one month before her mother's execution, had little to say during her initial interrogations.[185] Once her mother's body had been reduced to ashes, however, Marie-Marguerite began to make statements that no doubt stood La Reynie's hair on end. The twenty-one-year-old declared that she had served as her mother's assistant, sure that if she objected to anything that she witnessed—the strange invocations and ceremonies, the preparation of mysterious liquids and powders—her mother would poison her without turning a hair. She had often seen her mother and Lesage performing ceremonies of love magic. Some involved baptizing wax figurines, some called for charms assembled from ingredients such as the heart and blood of a white pigeon, while others were conducted with elements of traditional Christian magic: holy water, incense, salt, and sulfur. These ceremonies often called for a consecrated host, which was furnished by the abbé Mariette or another priest from La Voisin's stable of renegade clerics.[186] Marie-Marguerite had also seen La Voisin and a fellow sorceress performing a rite of love magic directed at the king. While holding a piece of wood over an open flame, the sorceress read an incantation written on a slip of paper: "*Fagot*, I set fire to you, but it is not you that I burn, it is the body, the soul, the will, the heart and the understanding of Louis de Bourbon; that he shall not come or go, rest or sleep until he fulfills the wishes of [this client] and

LE PORTRAIT DE LA VOISIN.

Source de ⟨⟩ tant de maux maudite creature
Qui par mille poisons destruisoir la Nature,
Si la parque en sillant tes detestable jours
A fait regner la Mort, en prolongeant leur cours,
Vn suplice effroyable et plein d'Ignominie
A sceu trancher le fil de ton énorme Vie.

Ant. Coypel Sculpsit                                      Chasteau, ex.

**Fig. 5** *Le portrait de la Voisin.* Antoine Coypel's engraving celebrated the sorceress's execution in 1680.

this will hold true forever."[187] The client who sought to so compel the king, Marie-Marguerite alleged, was none other than his official mistress, Mme de Montespan.

Marie-Marguerite's statements promised to be the key that would unlock the two related mysteries at the heart of La Reynie's covert investigation. First, was there any connection between Mme de Montespan's lady-in-waiting Mlle des Œillets—and hence Mme de Montespan—and La Voisin and other members of the criminal magical underworld? If Mme de Montespan had had dealings with La Voisin, to what end? To purchase love potions or poisons? Second, did a conspiracy exist to poison the duchesse de Fontanges[188] and the king? If so, at whose behest had the conspiracy been organized? La Reynie weighed Marie-Marguerite's statements carefully against those of corroborating witnesses: the abbés Guibourg, Cotton, and Mariette, La Filastre, La Trianon, and his preferred informant, Lesage. Interrogated by La Reynie over the summer and fall of 1680, their claims grew more fantastic and their denunciations penetrated further and further into the court hierarchy.

Marie-Marguerite first hazarded mention of a conspiracy to poison Mlle de la Fontanges during her interrogation of March 28. She claimed that she had overheard her mother and a man named Romani (whose brother, Lapierre, was the confessor of Mlle des Œillets) discussing the details of their plot. With the aid of a crony, Romani planned to pose as a cloth merchant with wares to show Mlle de Fontanges. The lengths of fabric and a pair of gloves were to be treated with a poison that would cause La Fontanges to "fall into a languor and die."[189] Romani was confident of the plot's success, assuring La Voisin that Mlle de Fontanges would not be able to resist trying on the gloves because he "would import them from Grenoble and they would be exquisitely made."[190] "They said," Marie-Marguerite added, "that it would be rumored that she had died of despair over the death of the king."[191]

As La Reynie had feared, the conspirators evidently planned a simultaneous attempt on the life of the king. Louis was to be poisoned through the petition that Romani and La Voisin had sought to hand him only days before her arrest.[192] On July 20 Marie-Marguerite hinted at the plot's instigator. According to the notes taken by La Reynie, she stated that she had overheard a conversation between her mother and La Trianon during which they discussed the petition intended for the king and the money they would receive for delivering it. La Reynie recorded, "La Voisin *mère* named Mme de Montespan several times, and said that she had been well assured on her part and that the woman would not deceive her." La Trianon had then exclaimed, "A scorned woman is a wonderful thing!" Marie-Marguerite further testified that her mother had told her that "the resolution against the king had been taken only because the lady had not succeeded with the other designs she had, which hadn't gone anywhere, and for which several conjurations had been said that hadn't had any effect."[193]

The "other designs" were the aphrodisiacs, charms, and ceremonies of love magic that La Voisin and her associates had supplied to Mme de Montespan for several years via her lady-in-waiting, Mlle des Œillets. Marie-Marguerite asserted that she had always known that the woman who bought love potions from her mother for more than two years was none other than Claude de Vin des Œillets. Mademoiselle des Œillets had collected the powders from La Voisin herself or La Voisin had delivered them to her at designated meeting places, including Clagny,[194] outside Saint-Cloud, and the Church of the Petits-Pères in Paris.[195] In fact, Marie-Marguerite claimed, Mme de Montespan dispatched Mlle des Œillets to La Voisin whenever the king's wandering eye focused elsewhere. When Mlle des Œillets arrived, La Voisin would prepare a love potion out of ingredients such as bat and human blood, semen, and Spanish fly, and send for the abbé Guibourg, who would slide the mixture under the chalice while celebrating mass.[196]

The king and Louvois, who continued to monitor carefully each step of La Reynie's investigations, received news of the direction the prisoners' accusations had taken with grave concern. Louvois wrote to the police lieutenant, "Monsieur, I have given an account to the king of the letters that you took the trouble to write to me. . . . His Majesty heard with indignation the calumnies that were made by the last prisoners [Marie-Marguerite Montvoisin, Lesage, and La Filastre] that you interrogated."[197] Their accusations against Mme de Montespan could not be permitted to reach the ears of the public. But while Louis was able to have any hint of Mme de Montespan's involvement in the scandal expunged from the transcripts sent to the magistrates of the Arsenal, he had no command over what those prisoners might say when they were formally questioned by his judges. With the Affair of the Poisons threatening to spiral out of his control, the king decided to suspend the proceedings of the Chambre while he toured recently completed fortifications along the frontier.[198] La Reynie evidently sent off a protest, to which Louvois responded, "His Majesty persists in his decision that the Chambre not judge the prisoners of Vincennes in his absence, but he permits you to enter into all the procedures that you believe necessary to find evidence. He deems that you, in order to calm the spirits of the prisoners who know that their crimes have been discovered . . . may tell them that the king will be absent for several months, and that the Chambre will not judge anyone in his absence."[199]

While Louis XIV inspected his forts, the dutiful La Reynie continued to follow the trail of the *faits particuliers*. Other prisoners began to corroborate Marie-Marguerite's allegations about the sacrilegious activities of the king's mistress. The abbé Guibourg and his two assistants described taking part in magical ceremonies said for Mme de Montespan. The abbé, arrested in June, admitted that he had performed a series of demonic ceremonies at the behest of La Voisin.[200] He told his interrogators: "It is true that his weakness had been preyed upon, and that in a chateau near Montlhéry, M. Leroy, former governor of pages at the Petit

Écurie, had him celebrate a mass, in the chapel of the chateau, over the womb of a woman whom he did not know, who was lying on her back on the altar with a piece of linen covering her stomach."[201] Guibourg assured his interrogators that he did not know for what dark purpose the mass was intended, nor did he know the identity of the woman over whom he had performed the ceremony.[202] La Filastre, however, contended that Guibourg had boasted that he was in the employ of Mme de Montespan. "Guibourg showed several people the pact or treaty that he claimed to have made in his name with the devil that gave him the power to negotiate with the devil and the power to negotiate on the behalf of others, and he named Mme de Montespan."[203]

Marie-Marguerite, for her part, eventually decided to accuse Mme de Montespan of more than signing a diabolic pact. Shedding any vestige of her former reticence, she alleged that she had been present at two amatory masses celebrated for Mme de Montespan by the abbé Guibourg. Madame de Montespan's ceremony had taken place at La Voisin's house and had begun at six in the evening and ended at midnight. La Voisin had subsequently promised to have two more masses said over her own body on Mme de Montespan's behalf, as Mme de Montespan had declared that she simply hadn't the time to attend them herself. Moreover, Marie-Marguerite added, Mlle des Œillets had not been the only conduit for the aphrodisiacs and love potions intended for the king; she herself had often delivered her mother's powders to Mme de Montespan. And, five weeks or so before her mother was arrested, her mother told her that "she was sending her to Clagny with Blessis, with a note asking for two thousand écus, because Romani said they didn't have enough money to buy the fabric to show Mlle de Fontanges."[204] Marie-Marguerite, at long last, had accused Mme de Montespan directly.

Such allegations against the most prominent woman at Louis XIV's court, the mother of five of the king's legitimized children, put La Reynie in an exceedingly uncomfortable position when it came to reporting upon the progress of his unofficial investigation. Faithful as ever, though, he forwarded copies of the interrogations that mentioned Mme de Montespan to Louvois and the king, still on his inspection tour. The king did not blame his messenger, but he did decide that Marie-Marguerite's statements were to be concealed from the judges of the Arsenal. He instructed La Reynie:

> Having seen the declaration that Marguerite Montvoisin, prisoner in my chateau of Vincennes, made on the 12th of the last month, and the interrogation of her that you conducted on the 26th of the same month, I am writing you this letter to tell you that my intention is that you exercise all care to clarify the statements contained in these declarations and interrogations, and that you be sure to observe that the *récolements,* confrontations, and all that could concern the future investigation which might

be instituted on the basis of these declarations and interrogations are recorded separately. Meanwhile, suspend your reports regarding the interrogations of Romani and Bertrand to my royal chamber sitting in the Arsenal in my good city of Paris until you receive orders from me.[205]

By further circumventing his judicial system, the king continued the trend he had begun almost a year earlier, when he first ordered La Voisin's statements recorded on loose sheets rather than in the customary bound volumes. Yet, despite his fears that the French public or foreign courts might learn of Mme de Montespan's illicit activities, Louis evidently intended that the sessions of the Chambre de l'Arsenal would resume upon his return from the frontier. Thus far he believed that exterminating "this evil breed of people," as Marie Bosse had once urged him to do, was an undertaking still worth the risks.

### PARALLEL INVESTIGATIONS, OCTOBER 1680–JULY 1682

While the Chambre remained in hiatus, La Reynie pursued his covert inquiry into Mme de Montespan's alleged activities. The notes he kept indicate that he weighed each piece of testimony against the king's mistress carefully. On the whole, he seems to have doubted the extent of Mme de Montespan's criminal activity, if not her gullibility. While Marie-Marguerite claimed in her interrogation of August 13 that she had never exchanged a word with Mme de Montespan herself, he wrote, she contradicted herself in her next interrogation (August 20). The discrepancies in her statements cast doubt on her other testimony. La Reynie reflected, "That which she [la fille Voisin] says in the rest of her declaration seems to have a certain air of ingenuousness where, if the things are false, everyone could be fooled. However, I cannot be sure and it seems to me, I couldn't say why, preferable to presume the horrible things are false than that they are true."[206]

La Reynie could not be certain of Mme de Montespan's innocence in the conspiracy to poison the king, either, as her accusers frequently made statements that contradicted one another's testimony as well as their own. La Filastre seemed to support Marie-Marguerite's claims when she revealed that she had traveled several times to Caen to pick up "powders for the king" from a shepherd named Galet.[207] Questioned in turn, Galet admitted that he had twice prepared powders for La Filastre to deliver to Mme de Montespan for the king, but he emphatically assured La Reynie that they were only love potions made from bread and Spanish fly.[208] As for the poisons he had boasted of to La Filastre, he had only wanted to make her believe that he knew how to prepare such things. His "poisons" would not actually hurt anybody—they were made out of prunes, iron filings, and Spanish fly.[209]

Upon his return from the frontier in October 1680, the king allowed the Chambre de l'Arsenal to resume its sessions. He made this decision reluctantly, however, for the suspects due to be tried next by the Chambre (Galet, the abbé Cotton, and La Filastre) had each implicated Mme de Montespan and her sister-in-law, the duchesse de Vivonne, in the affair. Louvois instructed the *procureur général* of the Chambre to intimate strongly to the judges that they need not inquire too closely into La Filastre's statements.[210] The judges obligingly followed the king's unofficial directive, finding ample reason to send La Filastre to the stake without questioning her closely. Her death sentence, however, posed an even greater threat to the reputations of Mmes de Montespan and Vivonne; *torture préalable* could be imposed upon anyone facing capital punishment, and judicial procedure required that the transcript of the torture session be read aloud to the Chambre. When La Filastre was subjected to the boot, she confessed that her trips to the Auvergne on behalf of Mme de Montespan were to retrieve love potions intended for the king and poison intended for La Fontanges.[211] Ever anxious to protect "the glowing image of his greatness,"[212] the reputations of the mother of his children and that of his court, and unable to find legal means by which to prevent La Filastre's final (and in the reasoning of the time, most truthful) account from being read, Louis simply decided to suspend the Chambre altogether. It would not resume its meetings for nearly eight months.[213]

La Reynie, eager to conclude his investigations, carefully weighed both sides of the case against Mme de Montespan. That she, like Medea, might seek to poison a rival out of jealousy and a desire for revenge seemed quite possible, as it confirmed the contemporary correlations that linked poison, jealousy, and female adultery. But a charge that she had made an attempt to poison the king defied the most elementary common sense, as her lofty position at court was completely dependent upon him. On the other hand, the case of the marquise de Brinvilliers had recently demonstrated that such unimaginable crimes might indeed be committed, even by the most unlikely of criminals. But if the king were to die, Mme de Montespan would certainly forfeit the financial benefits that the king had bestowed upon her (she and her sister-in-law owned monopolies on several goods sold in Paris, for example), lose the considerable influence that she wielded at court, and jeopardize the futures of her legitimized children. Given that the prevalent cultural script explaining the crime of poison was that of Medea, who poisoned her husband's new wife but not her unfaithful husband,[214] La Reynie was inclined to believe that La Filastre had bought powders not for Mme de Montespan but for Mme de Vivonne.[215] La Reynie considered it more likely that Mme de Vivonne, upon whose actions the story of Medea could be mapped much more readily, had purchased the love potions to entice the king away from her sister-in-law, and the poison to ensure that Mme de Montespan would not be there to make any protest.[216]

Although he tended to discount Mme de Montespan's role in any plot to poison the king, the lieutenant did not doubt her involvement with members of the criminal magical underworld. Marie-Marguerite, Lesage, and Guibourg continued to spin their tales about the elaborate rituals of love magic that they had performed at the behest of the king's mistress so that she might win and retain the king's affections. Lesage described in detail the love potions he had prepared for Mme de Montespan, the abbé Mariette recounted how he had read *évangiles* over her head, and Guibourg claimed that he had performed three amatory masses over her naked body, in 1667, 1676, and 1679.[217] The first date coincided with the start of Mme de Montespan's campaign for the king's affections and the second two marked major crises in their relationship—his affairs with the princesse de Soubise and Mlle de Fontanges. La Reynie concluded, "Since 1667, Mme de Montespan was in the hands of La Voisin. She [Mme de Montespan] had already worked with Mariette to say several conjurations for her to gain the good graces of the king, and several others against Mme de la Vallière, and had several love powders passed under the chalice by Mariette and other priests."[218]

La Reynie found his most convincing proof of Mme de Montespan's long-standing ties to the criminal magical underworld in the records of the criminal chamber of the Châtelet. He discovered that Lesage had been sent to the galleys in 1668 because he and the abbé Mariette had been convicted of conducting magical ceremonies for Mme de Montespan, among other clients. The two magicians had nothing to gain from bandying her name about at the time, as Mme de Montespan, not yet the official mistress of the king, held a position of only minor importance at court as one of several maids of honor to the queen. Her name was kept out of the criminal proceedings in 1668, La Reynie deduced, because the *premier juge* was related to both Mme de Vivonne (Mme de Montespan's sister-in-law) and to the abbé Mariette by marriage, and so deliberately did not question the prisoners on the *sellette* about their clientele.[219]

The accusations against Mme de Montespan, despite the fact that they had been almost hermetically sealed off from the judges of the Chambre and from the public, were nonetheless serious enough to alter the delicate balance of power at court, for they threatened the king's relationship with his *maîtresse en titre*. As official mistress, Mme de Montespan still wielded a great deal of power and influence despite her recent eclipse by the teenage duchesse de Fontanges. Courtiers may have recalled that Mme de Montespan's position at the top of the court hierarchy had been challenged on two previous occasions and that those who had concluded her reign was over had been seriously mistaken.[220] Moreover, the king had recently appointed Mme de Montespan to the highest (and most lucrative) office at court that could be held by a woman, superintendent of the queen's household.[221] On the other hand, courtiers recognized that Louis XIV was often wont to end a love affair with a golden handshake; he named Louise de la Vallière a duchess only after he had been smitten by Athénaïs de Montespan.[222]

That Mme de Montespan continued to enjoy the king's good graces was of particular interest to Colbert, who had recently married his daughter to her nephew.[223] To that end, Colbert commissioned Claude Duplessis, a prominent lawyer and legal scholar, to prepare a brief "against the calumnies imputed to Mme de Montespan" in December of 1680. The *mémoire* noted that most clients of Paris's sorceresses and fortune-tellers were not guilty of any serious crime, that Mme de Montespan's accusers were far from reliable sources, that their statements contradicted one another and were in any case untenable, and that if Mme de Montespan had wanted to poison the king, she had no need to devise a convoluted plot to hand him a poisoned petition when she could far more easily administer the poison to him herself.[224] The best evidence of the king's response to Colbert's attempt at exoneration is that he permitted Mme de Montespan to live at court until 1692, more than a decade after their love affair had ended. It seems unlikely that he would have tolerated her presence had he believed she had made an attempt on his life.[225]

There is no evidence, direct or indirect, that Mme de Montespan ever learned of the charge that she had tried to poison her lover. Long after the Affair of the Poisons had come to an end, she remained ensconced in the splendid apartments in Versailles that were so close to those of the king, and Louis continued to pay her daily visits, albeit in the company of others.[226] The king's concomitant attentions to the duchesse de Fontanges and then to Madame de Maintenon no doubt provided Athénaïs ample explanation for the gradual loss of his affections.

Madame de Montespan's attendant, Mlle des Œillets, was probably the real culprit behind the conspiracy to poison Louis XIV. Mademoiselle des Œillets apparently sought revenge for Louis's refusal to recognize the daughter she had borne him. Mlle Œillets orchestrated a plot to substitute arsenic for the love potions that she regularly delivered to Mme de Montespan from La Voisin; Madame de Montespan was to unwittingly poison the king.[227] La Reynie described his theory of the plot to Louvois: "Guibourg said a charm to cause the king's death; claimed that La des Œillets and 'L'Anglais' participated in the plot . . . which would be executed by having Madame de Montespan be given poisoned powders that she would give as a love potion; they claimed, by fooling her, to use her hand to commit the crime."[228]

Whether or not Louis XIV believed that Athénaïs de Montespan had participated in rituals of love magic remains a mystery—but she certainly never regained her place in his heart. La Reynie, in contrast, retained the king's full confidence. Ironically, while the *faits particuliers* that accused Mme de Montespan of having attempted to poison the king and his young mistress were successfully suppressed, the death of the duchesse de Fontanges from complications of childbirth in June 1681 immediately gave rise to speculation that she had been poisoned by her rival. If Athénaïs ever learned of the rumors, they did not dissuade her from suggesting that the duchess "had been wounded in the service of the king."[229] Witticism aside,

Mme de Montespan was branded a Medea for the next forty years, despite all the efforts of the king and La Reynie.

Meanwhile, the king, Colbert, and Louvois found themselves in a quandary regarding the 147 prisoners "vehemently suspected of poison" who still languished in the Bastille and Vincennes. The king and his ministers were at a loss as to how to proceed with their cases without exposing the *faits particuliers* concerning Mme de Montespan. The prisoners simply knew too much that the king did not wish his judges or subjects to learn. No extant records reveal precisely why the king eventually resolved to order the judges to resume their deliberations on May 19, 1681, but the decision was a hotly contested one. According to Jean Sagot, many of Louis's advisors pressed the king to dissolve the Chambre permanently.[230] La Reynie, for his part, urged the king to reinstate the Chambre: "If the course of justice is halted, the majority of these villains will go unpunished."[231] The king may have resolved to continue the process because La Reynie solved the problem of La Filastre's *procès-verbal question.* Following the police lieutenant's suggestion, the royal council issued an act declaring that certain facts contained in the *procès-verbal* touched upon crucial affairs of state that lay beyond the judges' purview. The judges were ordered to content themselves with hearing a summary, rather than the verbatim transcript, read to them.[232]

When the Chambre reconvened, the judges found the scope of their inquiry into the Affair of the Poisons considerably circumscribed. La Reynie continued his now quasi-official investigation into the *faits particuliers,* uncovering other members of the criminal underworld, further evidence of magical practices in the city, and additional connections between Louis's courtiers and Paris's sorceresses. The king deemed much of this new evidence to be too explosive to be heard even by his handpicked judges. The judges, sidelined from La Reynie's inquiry, therefore conducted a parallel but separate investigation that diverged almost completely from that of the police lieutenant. Instructed not to concern themselves with any *faits particuliers,* they were instead set the task of hunting down those suspected of sacrilege, impiety, and *lèse majesté.* The judges turned most of their attention to a case of old-fashioned treason, unraveling an elaborate plot hatched by the chevalier de la Brosse to restore the disgraced minister of finance, Nicolas Fouquet, to power by poisoning Colbert and the king. The chevalier de la Brosse and his fellow conspirators were discovered to have had dealings with Louis Vanens (arrested at the outset of the affair), La Filastre, Guibourg, and even the marquise de Brinvilliers and her lover, Sainte-Croix. France's network of poisoners, it seemed, was frighteningly extensive. The judges handed down sentences as quickly as possible, perhaps aware that the king had little desire to prolong his special commission's sessions indefinitely. The judges of the Chambre could only hope that they had managed to eradicate the most treacherous villains from the kingdom.[233]

Louis XIV dissolved the Chambre permanently on July 21, 1682. The king concluded that to let justice run its course any further would inevitably expose the illicit activities of the mother of his children, as well as those of some of his highest-ranking courtiers, to public derision that might well have material consequences. Approximately sixty suspects, including the abbé Guibourg, Lesage, and Marie-Marguerite Montvoisin, remained in the fortress of Vincennes, but the king decided that he could not permit them to be brought to trial at all. Their cases, therefore, could never be settled. They could not be acquitted or convicted and they certainly could not be simply released from prison, given the extent and depravity of the crimes to which they had confessed. As Louis needed to ensure the prisoners' silence, they could not be banished or sent to the galleys. Finally, the king decided to solve the dilemma through an exercise of supreme absolute power. The richest monarch in Europe, Louis possessed the resources to lock away the remainder of his embarrassing prisoners forever. He dispatched the remaining suspects to his most remote fortresses where, he decreed, they were to remain for the duration of their lives.[234] It was, according to La Reynie, a punishment "a hundred times more terrible than death."[235] The king's unprecedented "Siberian solution" was never to be repeated by another French ruler or court of law.

By the end of the year, all of the *prisonniers retenues* had been transferred to various fortresses around the kingdom. Closely guarded, they were placed in solitary confinement and chained to the walls of their cells. Louvois sent strict instructions as to how the prisoners were to be maintained: "Above all . . . take measures to prevent anyone hearing the stupidities that they [the prisoners] may try to cry aloud, for previously they have often shouted remarks about Mme de Montespan which are wholly without foundation. Threaten them with such rigorous punishment, at the first sound they make, that not one will dare raise a murmur."[236] When the last of the *prisonniers retenues* died in 1717, she had been confined in the fortress of Villefranche for thirty-seven years, outliving La Reynie, Louvois, and even the king himself.

The investigations into the Affair of the Poisons thus expose the fissures in the edifice of royal absolutism that Louis and his ministers sought to construct.[237] To eradicate the "miserable commerce in poisons," the king initially resolved to subject anyone involved, no matter how highly placed, to a regular trial.[238] Duchesses and seamstresses alike were compelled to appear before the judges of the Chambre de l'Arsenal. After he set the wheels of justice in motion, however, Louis discovered that the mother of five of his children was deeply implicated in the affair. The king could not tolerate even the slightest risk that Mme de Montespan's sacrilegious activities might become public knowledge; to do so would certainly damage her reputation but, even more important, would blacken "the glowing image of his greatness."[239] Louis XIV's *gloire* was intended to inspire awe at home, ensuring order within his court and kingdom, and to inspire awe beyond France's borders, advancing his ambitions abroad. The king ultimately found that his ability to manipulate the outcome of events was hampered by the legal procedures required in his own recently revised criminal code.[240] Unable to exercise complete control over the actions of the individuals involved in the affair—both judges and suspects—Louis XIV's only recourse was to bring the entire process to a halt. The Affair of the Poisons reveals that while France's most absolute monarch proved powerful enough to condemn several dozen subjects to rot in oblivion, he could do so only at the expense of his own judicial system. The Sun King was finally caught by the rules of his own devising; only by eradicating the Chambre de l'Arsenal could he impose his will upon it.

The revelations of the Affair of the Poisons furthermore demonstrate that Louis, while capable of entombing dozens of his subjects without legal trials, was nonetheless unable to control the illicit activities of his aristocrats in general and those of his female courtiers in particular. Many of the highest-ranking women at court, seeking to gain advantage over political and amatory rivals, had evidently purchased not only poisons but also magical ceremonies and love potions from the denizens of the criminal magical underworld.

# 2

# MEDEA AND THE MARQUISE:
# UNDERSTANDING THE CRIME OF POISON IN
# SEVENTEENTH-CENTURY FRANCE

Readily available and almost impossible for seventeenth-century science to
detect, poison aroused tremendous anxiety in French society. During
the reign of Louis XIV, two cultural "scripts" in particular interpreted the
crime for an audience eager to make sense of the barrage of cases that culminated
in the Affair of the Poisons. Both drew together powerful, long-standing assumptions about poison and those who used it, assumptions that had been in circulation since classical times. The myth of Medea offered the image of a woman,
scorned in love, who poisoned her young rival through the magical arts. The contemporary legend of the marquise de Brinvilliers, described in the previous chapter,
provided an alternative vision. The marquise, brought to trial in Paris in 1676,
was an adulteress who murdered her own relatives out of greed with a poison
created not by magic but through scientific experiment. Both myth and legend
are critical to understanding how the Parisian public and police read the Affair
of the Poisons, for the motives and methods of Medea and the marquise would
be mapped onto the women accused in the scandal. After the Affair of the Poisons had drawn to a close, the historical archetype of the marquise gradually
eclipsed the mythological Medea in the old regime understanding of the crime.
While assumptions about the incentives of poisoners evolved over time, the sex
of the archetypal poisoner would always remain female.

## THE MYTH OF MEDEA

In seventeenth-century France, the myth of Medea was probably the most prevalent cultural script by which a learned audience understood the crime of poison.
Other cultural scripts certainly circulated; the crime was associated with duplicitous servants as well as insinuating foreigners.[1] By providing an explanatory
narrative that linked the practice of poison to women, to magic, and to rivalry,

however, the story of Medea corresponded far more neatly to the events of the Affair of the Poisons. According to Greek mythology, Jason married Medea after she helped him capture the Golden Fleece. When Jason cast her aside for a young princess, Medea avenged herself by poisoning her rival. Like Medea, seventeenth-century poisoners were imagined to be women who acted out of jealousy or vengeance toward romantic rivals. Popular plays and operas depicting the myth had helped to disseminate the stereotype of the spurned wife who exacted terrible revenge upon the rival who had stolen her husband's affections.[2] Medea was no ordinary woman, however. She was also a powerful sorceress whose occult powers could create kings and destroy kingdoms.

Medea was a familiar figure in Louis XIV's France. The educated classes, steeped in classical learning, were well acquainted with the gods and heroes of Ovid's *Metamorphoses*. Those not familiar with Greek or Latin could read Noël le Comte's *Mythologie* or easily find the *Metamorphoses* in French, as the poet Isaac de Bensarade had translated Ovid's work into verse in 1676.[3] Louis XIV's subjects were also accustomed to projecting the exploits of contemporary figures onto Greek and Roman heroes, both historical and mythological; understanding seventeenth-century events in terms of classical examples was a routine practice.[4] The king, for example, was frequently represented as Hercules in both portraiture and statuary, as his grandfather, Henri IV, had been. Comparable representations of French monarchs over the course of the century may also have given a large percentage of the general population at least a passing familiarity with mythology.[5]

The myth of Medea was told and retold on the ancien régime stage. Between 1553 and 1797 nineteen different plays, operas, and court ballets featured the character of Medea, twelve of those productions debuting during the reign of Louis XIV.[6] The most widely admired, Pierre Corneille's *Médée*, captured the Parisian public's imagination at its first performance in 1635. The tragedy was revived several times over the next fifty years, most notably in 1677 by Molière's company, six months after the execution of the marquise de Brinvilliers.[7] The play was published in 1639 and proved popular enough to warrant twelve more editions before 1682.[8] The myth was also the subject of Corneille's machine play, *La toison d'or* (The Golden Fleece), commissioned for the wedding of Louis XIV and Maria Theresa in 1660 and performed both in Normandy and in Paris the following year.[9] Medea was repeatedly represented in opera as well; Jean-Baptiste Lully's *Thésée,* which debuted at court in 1675 to tremendous acclaim, told of Medea's attempt to poison her fiancé, Theseus, after he had fallen in love with another princess.[10] It too was reprised after the execution of the marquise de Brinvilliers and again at the outset of the Affair of the Poisons.[11] Even Racine's *Phèdre,* written in 1677, contains an unusual reference to the myth of Medea. In his play, the poison with which Phèdre commits suicide is Medea's: "I have taken, I have poured into my burning veins, a poison that Medea brought from Athens."[12]

In the seventeenth century, myths of the sorceress Circe were also used to elucidate the motives of poisoners.[13] The sorceress was a popular subject of theatrical productions, featured in eight plays and operas written during Louis XIV's long reign.[14] Like Medea, Circe poisoned her romantic rival. According to Bensarade's translation of the *Metamorphoses,* Circe was motivated by envy: "Circe, jealous of Scylla whom Glaucus loved, poisoned the stream where this beauty was accustomed to bathe, and turned her into a form so monstrous from head to toe, that out of horror at herself, she threw herself into the sea, and was changed into a rock."[15] The myths of Circe and Medea were closely intertwined; according to Greek mythology, Circe was not only Medea's aunt but also the teacher from whom she acquired her knowledge of the magical arts. In *La toison d'or,* Corneille emphasized the ties between the two sorceresses when Medea's brother revealed the genealogy of Medea's powers: "Circe, sister of my father, and daughter of the Sun, Circe, from whom my sister inherited her unequaled arts."[16]

Circe's qualifications for the position aside, her niece nonetheless dominated the seventeenth-century image of the archetypal poisoner. The *Médée* of Pierre Corneille, which drew its inspiration from the plays of Euripides and Seneca as well as the tales of Le Comte's *Mythologie,* disseminated the version of the myth perhaps most influential to the contemporary understanding of the crime.[17] Most important, Corneille's retelling expressed the connection between women and poison that has long been commonplace in Western culture.[18] Second, the myth underscored the link between poison and magic, and third, it highlighted that between poison and rivalry.[19] These three elements, articulated in Corneille's myth of Medea, played a critical role in determining how contemporaries interpreted the actions and motives of those accused in the Affair of the Poisons.

The events depicted in Corneille's play transpire several years after the sorceress Medea has stolen the Golden Fleece from her father and eloped with Jason.[20] Exiled from Jason's homeland because Medea murdered the uncle who usurped Jason's throne, the pair is now in Corinth, where King Créon has granted them refuge. As the action begins, the audience learns that Créon has amended his offer of sanctuary. After hearing from his daughter Créuse that she and Jason have fallen in love, the king has decided to make Jason his son-in-law and heir. Créon, Créuse, and Jason rather inexplicably imagine that it will be a simple task to rid themselves of Jason's wife, and they blithely arrange to banish the inconvenient Medea and her children from Corinth before the wedding.

Medea, however, envisions a different future for her unfaithful husband and his young bride to be. She marvels that Jason can fear her powers so little, exclaiming, "Jason repudiates me! And who would have believed it? / If he has lost his love, has he lost his memory? / . . . Knowing what I can do, having seen what I dare, / Does he believe that to offend me would mean so little?"[21] "If he has ceased to love me," she resolves, "then he will begin to fear me."[22] Medea's fury is heightened when Jason informs her that his new bride has graciously permitted him to keep the children of his union with Medea. Créuse regards her acceptance of the children as an extraordinary favor to their mother, and demands Medea's jeweled robe "as the price of the children whom I have saved."[23] Créuse's greed presents the sorceress with the opportunity for revenge, and Medea retreats to her magic grotto to prepare a deadly poison. She infuses her magnificent robe with the poison and sends the fatal offering to her rival. Créuse eagerly dons her new finery, only to be incinerated by the poison. Her father, trying to tear the venomous robe from her body, is similarly consumed. Jason, aghast, seeks out the sorceress to avenge his bride, only to find that Medea has prepared him a special revenge. Deciding that "he must suffer as a father as well as a lover,"[24] she has murdered their two sons. Jason catches up with his wife only in time to hear her mocking laughter as she makes her escape in a chariot drawn by winged dragons. Jason kills himself in despair, and the curtain falls.

Corneille's *Médée* articulates the cornerstone of seventeenth-century belief regarding poison: the crime is feminine. According to the innovative work of David Nirenberg, associations between women and poison can be found across cultures and times, from ancient Greece to medieval Europe to twentieth-century Africa. In the Judeo-Christian tradition, perhaps the most famous example is Eve and the apple. Hebrew commentaries equated the apple Eve gave Adam with poison; Eve poisoned her husband and all mankind through him, so that she might indulge her passion with the serpent.[25] According to Hildegard of Bingen, Eve's sin was responsible for the appearance of poison on earth.[26] Similar models remained so prevalent in the Western imagination that by the seventeenth century French commentators could pose the question, "Why has the crime of poison always been more common among women than men?" and point to the Bible, Roman history, and contemporary events in support of the claim.[27]

The connection between women and poison antedates the Old Testament, however. Nirenberg speculates that the association may have its roots in prehistoric systems of communication and exchange, a linkage revealed by language itself. He argues that women have been linked to poison through one of the most ancient rituals of communication, that of gift and countergift. The anthropologist Marcel Mauss, Nirenberg notes, observed that the word for gift and the word for poison are one and the same in a number of European languages, including Danish, Norwegian, and Swedish.[28] Mauss theorized that these linguistic connections arose from primeval anxieties surrounding the gift, that is, its potential for deceit and the reciprocal obligations it necessitated.[29] Nirenberg finds the connection between women and Mauss's analysis of the poisonous implications inherent in the gift in the work of Claude Lévi-Strauss. Lévi-Strauss, Nirenberg writes, finds that "the exchange of women stands at the apex of a system of gift exchange out of which kinship structures, group identity, and economies of circulation all emerge."[30] Because women served as objects of exchange within this system, he posits, the ambivalence about the poison in the gift gradually evolved into ambivalence about the poisonous nature of women.

In the Roman era, women were not only linguistically linked to poison but were seen as producing poison themselves.[31] Menstrual blood was represented as a hazardous substance, simultaneously poisonous and magical. In the second century, for example, Pliny contended that if a menstruating woman walked by, wine would sour, vines would wither, bees would die, dogs would run mad, mirrors would discolor, and knives would become dull. He concluded his litany, "But to come again to women, hardly can there be found a thing more monstrous than is that flux & course of theirs."[32] Pliny's views proved not only influential but also long lived; his works were still in print fourteen hundred years later.[33] Even well into the early modern period, popular belief in Europe held that menstrual blood possessed powerful occult properties. Laurent Joubert's 1578 *Erreurs populaires*, a work intended to debunk popular superstitions, attests to the fact that similar beliefs about the properties of menstrual blood were still prevalent in France in the late sixteenth century. Joubert listed a series of current beliefs, such as that the hair of a menstruating woman, buried in dung, would turn into a venomous snake.[34] Menstrual blood would remove birthmarks and avert natural disasters such as tempests and lightning. The blood was also thought to be a cure, suggested for the bites of mad dogs, the falling sickness, and agues.[35] Thus, in popular culture, not only did women's bodies produce a potentially poisonous substance, but that same material possessed curative properties. Menstrual blood was a *pharmakon*; it could be both poison and antidote.

The powerful properties attributed to menstrual blood made it a favorite ingredient in early modern love magic. Its use persisted despite the efforts of proselytizing doctors who sought to convince the popular classes of the errors of their ways.[36] In the *Erreurs populaires* Joubert admonished, "As regards giving a man some menstrual blood to take by mouth (as does a foolish woman in order to throw a spell on a man and make him fall in love with her, putting menstrual blood on the level of philters), this is a villainous practice, and no less foolish than indecent."[37] His scolding apparently failed to work its desired effect, for a century later the pharmacies of Paris's sorceresses, inventoried during the Affair of the Poisons, were commonly stocked with powdered menstrual blood, ready for use in love charms.[38]

Early modern Europeans and ancient Greeks alike assumed that practitioners of love magic were female.[39] In Western literature, the love charms women prepared often had fatal effects, as Jean de Rotrou's 1634–35 play *Hercule mourant* demonstrates. Taking for its text Ovid's tale of the poisonous shirt given Hercules by his wife, the play examines the revenge taken by Hercules' spurned lover. Hercules' former lover tells his worried new wife that if Hercules dons a shirt suffused in venomous Hydra's blood it will stimulate his passion for her. Instead, the blood-drenched garment eats away his flesh.[40] The myth of Medea, staged by Corneille the following year, similarly served to explore the ambiguities inherent in women's use of love charms, as well as to explicitly equate female magic with poison.

References to Medea as a sorceress versed in the arts of love magic as well as poison can be found in a variety of learned seventeenth-century sources. Among them is Jacques Ferrand's *Treatise on Lovesickness, or Erotic Melancholy,* a lengthy medical treatise published in 1610 and 1623, which proposed to solve the mystery of whether love is a sickness, and whether it can be cured. The author reviewed the opinions of theologians, philosophers, and physicians, from Aristotle to Arnaud of Villanova to Du Laurens. Ferrand often drew on the *Metamorphoses* for his examples, frequently turning to episodes from the myths of Medea and Circe to explore the ability of the magical arts to influence love. Stories of Circe demonstrated the ineffectiveness of magic in swaying the passions. Although Circe was an enchantress so powerful she could turn men into pigs, Ferrand writes, her many spells, "inveiglements, baits, and enticements" could not force Ulysses to fall in love with her, although she tried for ten years to achieve this end.[41] By contrast, Medea's spells always proved successful, perhaps because she did not use love potions per se but found more effective magical means to influence the emotions, such as when she, "using her magic powers, made the women of Lemnos hateful to their husbands by giving them stinking breaths."[42]

The ambivalent nature of love charms, articulated in myth as the Hydra's blood that killed Hercules, found physical expression during the Affair of the Poisons. The charms peddled by Parisian sorceresses that supposedly inspired love if administered in small doses could also act as poisons if given in greater quantities. Sorceresses must have frequently prescribed *cantharides,* or Spanish fly, judging from the quantities of the powder found among their wares.[43] The aphrodisiac is apparently efficacious if given sparingly, but if too great a dose is swallowed it causes burning pain, vomiting, headache, vertigo, and delirium.[44]

The practice of harmful magic and the crime of poison were also intimately associated in the myth of Medea. Although they were not necessarily connected— either activity could be performed without the other—the two were nonetheless frequently perceived as related. After all, both promised to cause harm "at a distance and without visible intermediary."[45] As both sorceress and poisoner, Medea embodied this conflation. Her knowledge of the magical arts allowed her to prepare the most deadly of poisons. Her spells compelled venomous snakes to contribute to the mixture destined for her rival: "See how many serpents at my command / Delayed but a moment / And constrained to obey my baleful spell / Have vomited all their pestilence on this fatal gift."[46] Her brew derived its strength not merely from the venom it contained but from the efficacy of her spells. She proudly assured her servant and accomplice, "These herbs do not have an ordinary quality / I dimmed the moon while gathering them myself. . . . See a thousand other venoms here: this thick liquor / Mixed with the blood of the hydra with that of Nesse; / Python had this tongue; and this black feather / is that which a harpy let fall."[47]

The connection between witchcraft and poison can be found in Greek philosophy as well as myth. In the *Laws*, Plato suggested that the reality of poison lent credence to belief in the existence of witchcraft:

> Mankind practices poisoning in two different ways. The form we have just expressly named is that in which the body is hurt by the actions of some other body in normal ways. There is another form which works by art, magic, incantations, and spells, as they are called, and breeds in the minds of the projectors the belief that they possess such powers of doing harm, in those of the victims the conviction that the authors of their suffering can verily bewitch them.[48]

Plato's observations were echoed by the sixteenth-century skeptic Reginald Scot, who also located the reality of witchcraft in the crime of poison. Arguing against the existence of witchcraft, he maintained that the women accused of practicing magic were far more likely to have been practicing the art of poison instead.[49] Scot asserted that biblical references to the practice, such as "Thou shalt not suffer a witch to live" (Exodus 22:18) in fact referred to poisoners.[50]

The belief that witchcraft and poison were intimately related continued to inform the European imagination. The writers of early modern witch-hunting manuals stressed the connection between witches and poisoners; Jacob Sprenger and Heinrich Krämer, Nicolas Rémy, and Henri Boguet dedicated much of their purple prose to the correlation. As Boguet wrote in his *Discours des sorciers* of 1602, "As for witches, although they cannot do such marvels as Satan, yet with his help they do terrible and shocking things. For they learn from him to compound a poison which they secretly pour into the broth of their enemy, who after tasting this poison sickens and languishes, or suddenly dies, according to the might and virtue of the poison he has received."[51] Popular broadsheets recounting particularly transgressive crimes also reinforced the connections between witchcraft, poison, and the disorderly women who indulged in both.[52] Unsurprisingly, then, accusations of witchcraft and of poison were often one and the same.[53] David Sabean has found that in sixteenth-century Germany, for example, the crime of poison was understood to encompass both the material, or poisoning through actual toxic substances, and the occult, or poisoning through supernatural means. Both methods could kill. He writes, "It was not uncommon in rural Württemberg for a husband or wife to suspect the other of poisoning him or her through magic. In fact the charge of sorcery was often a charge of poison."[54]

In late seventeenth-century France, poison and witchcraft were seen as related if not identical practices. Although they might bring about the same results, they were nonetheless understood as separate endeavors. During the Affair of the Poisons, the clients of Paris's sorceresses seem to have weighed their options carefully, making deliberate choices about which method would serve best to rid themselves of unwanted spouses.[55] Interestingly, medical practitioners characterized the mysterious effects of poison on the body in the same language used to describe the consequences of sorcery in an earlier century. Indeed, the symptoms of natural diseases such as the plague and those of poison were acknowledged to be indistinguishable—both attacked the body under the cover of secrecy, their effects invisible to observers. Jean Baptiste du Hamel, writing in 1670, explained, "We call poisons what in some occult way are wont to attack us or suddenly take away our life."[56]

The final association between women and poison exemplified by the myth of Medea helped to explain the motives of poisoners. Like Medea, poisoners acted out of jealousy or the desire for vengeance. In Corneille's tragedy, Medea's wrath is directed primarily toward the young princess who lured Jason from her. Although repudiated by her husband, the sorceress nonetheless still harbors some love for him: "Jason has cost me too much to want to destroy him; / My wrath grants him mercy, and my first ardor / Bears his interests in my heart. / I believe that he loves me yet, and that he nourishes in his soul / Some secret vestiges of such a beautiful passion." Medea decides that "it will suffice that Créuse dies."[57]

The ancient associations between women, rivalry, and poison articulated in the myth of Medea are of pivotal importance in understanding why the allegations that surfaced during the Affair of the Poisons seemed believable to contemporaries. The investigation revealed that many women in Paris had, like Medea, availed themselves of poison in order to rid themselves of their romantic rivals. The case of Anne de Carada, widow of a *procureur du roi,* is typical. Madame de Carada turned to the denizens of the criminal magical underworld after deciding to take revenge on the woman who had stolen her lover. According to the abbé Guibourg, Mme de Carada resolved to poison her rival because "she was confident that if the woman died, the man would marry her."[58]

Further confirming this explanatory framework, several suspects arrested by La Reynie alleged that aristocratic women at court had also become the clients of Paris's criminal magical underworld. Because the court was the locus of both romantic and political rivalries, it seemed a most likely place to inspire the crime of poisoning—and it was already well known that conspiracies against Louis's *maîtresse en titre* had been hatched by her rivals almost since the beginning of the king's personal reign. As the duc d'Enghien observed in 1667, "There are a thousand intrigues at Versailles among the ladies . . . what agitates their hearts is envy of Mademoiselle de la Vallière."[59] Madame de Lafayette seconded his remark in

*The Princess of Clèves,* writing of the court: "All these different cliques vied with one another. The ladies of one were jealous of those who made up the cliques of the other; all competed for favors or lovers."[60]

At Louis XIV's court, romantic rivalry had deeply political implications. While excluded from all forms of public political participation, women were able to wield unprecedented influence within court circles through extramarital romantic intrigue. The political influence of a mistress, however, was largely defined by the limits of her lover's political power. The king's body was the locus of power at court; access to his person, whether at the ritual *lever* or through sexual encounters, imparted considerable political privilege. His mistress, therefore, could become the most powerful woman at court, particularly as Louis's queen, the highest-ranking woman there, remained largely removed from court intrigues.

The Affair of the Poisons raised the possibility that Louis's would-be mistresses had turned to the magical as well as the pharmaceutical realms in their attempts to reach the summit of the intricate hierarchy of power and place at court. Madame de Montespan allegedly targeted Louise de la Vallière (Louis's mistress between 1661 and 1667) and, ten years later, the duchesse de Fontanges, holding an occasional magical ritual in the interim to head off other contenders.[61] The duchesse de Vivonne, on the other hand, reportedly used diabolic pacts to get rid of her sister-in-law, Mme de Montespan.[62] The magician Lesage alleged that the comtesses de Gramont and du Roure and the vicomtesse de Polignac had all hired him to perform complex magical rites intended to oust Louise de la Vallière from the king's affections. According to the sorceress La Voisin, Mmes du Roure, de Soissons, and de Polignac had not confined themselves to magical attempts on the life of Louis's first official mistress but plotted to poison her as well.[63] Neither did the duchesse de Vivonne rely solely on supernatural aid; Lesage claimed that she purchased poison that she intended to use on Mme de Montespan.[64] The association between women, rivalry, and poison was so prevalent by the late 1670s that insistent rumors about magic and poison swirled around nearly every woman who appeared to have a real opportunity to become Louis's official mistress.

Courtiers and public alike were well aware that the position of *maîtresse en titre* was a short-term appointment that the king could revoke as easily as he could the countless other court offices at his disposal. It was thus easy to imagine that contenders for the post might see attracting the king's attentions as only half the battle; clearing the field of other contestants may have been understood to offer these women a tempting means of winning the war.[65] Hence, when the duchesse de Fontanges died in 1681 after a protracted illness, rumors immediately surfaced that the vengeful Mme de Montespan, like Medea, had poisoned the beautiful young rival who had supplanted her in the king's affections.[66] According to Mme de Sévigné, the duchess herself believed that she had been poisoned, and her illness was protracted enough to allow her to repeat her allegations.[67] Whether or not they believed the reports, Mme de Montespan's enemies vigorously promoted the rumor that she had poisoned her romantic rival. Bussy, for example, included it in his account of the duchess's death in later editions of his *Histoire amoureuse des Gaules:* "Having opened up the body, it was found that the heart and lungs were covered with black blotches, which, it is claimed, is a sure proof of poisoning. The king's grief was so great that it was apparent in his face . . . he was fully convinced that Mme de Fontages had been sacrificed to the jealousy and despair of this ambitious woman [Mme de Montespan] who had cherished the illusion that she would always reign supreme."[68]

Contemporaries understood the alleged use of magic and poison by Louis XIV's would-be mistresses as a function of political as well as amatory competition, for winning the king's affections translated immediately into power and influence at court. Such expressions of rivalry were not unique to the seventeenth century but fit into a tradition of political sorcery whose roots stretch back to the Roman Empire.[69] Analogous charges stemming from political rivalries surfaced during the thirteenth and fourteenth centuries in France, when an assortment of courtiers and counselors were accused of employing the tools of ritual magic to increase or maintain their standing at both the royal and the Burgundian courts.[70] Accusations of political sorcery had been employed in the early seventeenth century as well; Cardinal Richelieu is known to have spread rumors (which he apparently believed) that his rival, the duc de Luynes, used sorcery to maintain the favor of Louis XIII.[71]

The myth of Medea thus helped to shape the seventeenth-century understanding of the events brought to light in the Affair of the Poisons. Like Medea, the women of the Affair of the Poisons were seen as having sought revenge on romantic rivals. These women had apparently turned to sorceresses who possessed knowledge of both magic and poison. Three years before the Affair of the Poisons erupted, however, another cultural script was written that would offer an alternative vision to the myth of Medea.

## The Legend of the Marquise

The 1676 case of Marie-Madeleine d'Aubray, marquise de Brinvilliers, demonstrated to French society that the female affinity for poison was not merely a myth. It seemed that sorcery was unnecessary for the practical marquise, who relied on pharmacology alone to poison her father and two brothers.[72] The activities of the marquise electrified her fellow Parisians with a spectacular contemporary example of the crime of poison; as Mme de Sévigné informed her daughter, "Here, we talk only of the speeches, the deeds, and the exploits of la Brinvilliers."[73] The story of her transgressions quickly achieved the status of legend. Not only was it recounted in the *factums* published throughout her 1673 trial in absentia and again at her capture three years later, but her deeds were also retold over the next century in multiple editions of the perennially popular *Histoires tragiques*.[74] While her actions were initially read against the script of Medea, they were later perceived to transcend it, thus offering another cultural script by which to read the crime of poison. The marquise was not a scorned wife but an adulterous woman; she was motivated by greed rather than rivalry; and she had no truck with magic but perfected the poison she used on her family members through scientific experiment. The marquise de Brinvilliers carved out her own place in the infamous pantheon of poisoners.[75] She herself became an archetype and her trial a preamble to the Affair of the Poisons.

The case of the marquise de Brinvilliers offered the vision of an aristocrat whose wanton character encouraged her to murder for material gain. The crimes of the marquise, who had "poisoned her father by her own hand, her brothers, her sister, her husband and her own children . . . [who] under the pretext of piety, visited the hospitals to poison the sick, and then returned to observe the effects of the different poisons which she had given to them," surpassed the deeds attributed to the sorceress abandoned by Jason.[76] Madame de Sévigné agreed: "Medea did not do so much," she observed to her daughter.[77]

Despite the evidence against her, the marquise de Brinvilliers seemed initially to defy the conventions of a stereotypical criminal, for she was beautiful, wealthy, and of noble descent. "Who could have predicted that a woman raised in an honorable family . . . with a seemingly gentle nature, was capable of such premeditation and such a litany of crimes?" wondered La Reynie, reflecting upon her deeds during his investigation into the Affair of the Poisons.[78] Such actions could only have been committed by an unnatural woman. As one commentator wrote: "How can . . . those who are so sensitive to the misfortunes of others and who shed such charitable tears, how can they take up such terrible resolutions, and decide to commit such a great crime? Beauty, modesty, and reserve are the natural attributes of their sex, and without doubt protect them from suspicion, and if some have been found so unhappy as to have fallen into such excesses, they are monsters. One must not suppose them like others, and they are sooner compared to the most evil men."[79]

After the Parisian public learned of the dissolute conduct of the marquise, however, her monstrous actions could be mapped more satisfactorily onto contemporary beliefs about the crime of poison. Her dissipated behavior had apparently been a scandal to her family ever since her marriage. She had made no secret of her passionate affair with Jean-Baptiste Gaudin de Sainte-Croix. Indeed, it was initially thought that, besotted with love, she had acted at the behest of Sainte-Croix. When the marquise's deeds first came to light, Bussy informed a correspondent, "The affair of Mme de Brinvilliers is frightful, and it has been a long time since one heard talk of a woman as evil as she. The source of all her crimes was love."[80] Her sexual improprieties, to the minds of her contemporaries, explained her propensity for poison. Madame de Sévigné, for example, pointed to Marie's early introduction to debauchery. She wrote to her daughter that the marquise had admitted "that at the age of seven, she had ceased to be a maiden."[81] Salacious rumors that the marquise had tried to commit suicide in prison by thrusting a sharp stake into her vagina proved the extent of her sexual dissipation.[82] Illicit sexuality and adultery became evidence of the marquise's criminal nature.[83]

The enormities perpetuated by the marquise de Brinvilliers seemed to confirm the dire warnings of Catholic theologians who regarded the unregulated passions with deep disapproval. The passions not only wreaked havoc within the individual soul, they threatened the stability of the state as well. Contemporary prescriptive literature described uncontrolled passion as a malady of the soul; even marrying for love invited violence and disorder.[84] Preachers insisted that the passions were deeply destructive: "our passions are the cause of all our disorder because it is from them that comes our unfortunate penchant toward evil."[85] As James Farr has argued, Reformation moralists, deeply influenced by the writings of the early church fathers, gendered the passions feminine and thus considered the sin of lust the most harmful of the passions.[86] *The True Catholic*, a popular devotional book from the early seventeenth century, explained that lust was the province of women; while "people went to hell by all sorts of sins, women were damned by the sins of the flesh."[87] Women, as Saint Augustine had held, were occasions of sin. Thirty years later, Antoine Arnauld warned his female readers that their passions had to be firmly disciplined lest their souls be imperiled. A woman who abandoned her God-given modesty, he wrote, "becomes buffeted by waves of concupiscence as in a stormy sea . . . there is nothing to prevent her from complete and total abandonment in vice and sin."[88] Lust, as Jean-Jacques Olier wrote at the turn of the century, poisoned the soul.[89]

A soul poisoned by lust was a soul that could turn to poison. The seventeenth-century conviction that unregulated passion exacerbated the female propensity to poison was widespread.[90] As the author of *Questions sur les empoisonneurs* explained, "debauchery causes even more trouble and disorder in the wits of women than of men and excites a greater fire in their hearts . . . because modesty is natural to them and the sins that they commit throw them into dangerous extremities. It is for this reason that adultery and poison formerly occurred as joint crimes."[91] Women whose passions ran unchecked might therefore poison their husbands out of desire for another. Such sentiments were not new; the author of the *Questions sur les empoisonneurs* noted that Cato the Elder had expressed the same belief when he wrote, *adultera, ergo venifica*, or "There is no adulteress who is not also a poisoner."[92]

During the Affair of the Poisons, the enduring associations between adultery and poison informed the public's response to the report that a number of high-ranking women had been accused of poisoning their spouses. The legendary marquise had provided fresh evidence for the conviction that women who indulged in adulterous affairs often tried to replace an unsatisfactory spouse with a more congenial lover. Thus, when suspects in the Affair of the Poisons accused the duchesse de Vivonne, the comtesse de Soissons, and the duchesse de Bouillon, among others, of using poison to accomplish just such an exchange, Parisians considered such allegations plausible.[93] For, as Mme de Lafayette explained in *The Princess of Clèves*, the Sun King's court was not only the heart of political and romantic rivalry but the center of adulterous exploits as well: "Ambition and gallantry were the soul of the court and consumed alike the energies of both men and women."[94] The king himself found the accusations serious enough to issue an arrest warrant for the comtesse de Soissons and subpoenas for the other two. As for Parisian society, the English ambassador reported, "*le monde* is inclined to think that there is something considerable against them all, because they are of such a quality that they would not be treated so severely without reliable witnesses against them."[95]

The marquise de Brinvilliers committed most of her crimes against family members, confirming the early modern belief that poison was a domestic crime. Poison presupposed proximity, for it was a murder weapon that usually necessitated intimate and sustained contact with the victim.[96] Unlike the conviction that poison was solely a woman's weapon, the perception that female murderers struck within the household usually proved true in practice as well as theory.[97] Men most often killed outside the home; women murdered within it.[98] Furthermore, the marquise's case substantiated the idea that the female murderer's weapon of choice was poison. Poison could be most easily administered in food, the preparation of which was traditionally women's responsibility. The fear that women might poison the meals they served their families was pervasive in early modern Europe, where relationships of the greatest intimacy were understood to pose the gravest threats.[99] The sharing of food with family members seemed particularly fraught with danger because it encompassed a potential threat to the patriarchal order of the family; food provided by the wife could readily mask the poison intended for the husband.[100]

The marquise found it a relatively simple task to poison the meals served to her husband and daughter.[101] It proved more difficult to do away with her father. Although unable to gain access to his kitchens herself, she managed to place a servant among his staff to act in her place. Over the course of several months, the servant added the undetectable poison developed by Marie and her lover to the food and drink presented to the unfortunate man.[102] Antoine d'Aubray's resulting decline apparently aroused no suspicions, and he gratefully accepted his daughter's offer to move into his house so that she might help nurse him—and ensure that he received his fatal dose. It took only two years for the marquise to squander the inheritance she received, whereupon she infiltrated her brothers' household. Both died at the hand of their valet, a man recommended for the post by Marie.

Similarly, many of those later accused in the Affair of the Poisons, courtiers and commoners alike, were alleged to have served inheritance powders to their own family members. Such cases lent credence to the seventeenth-century belief that women, who "love material goods better than do men, and are naturally more avaricious," sometimes turned to poison to gain their inheritances. "It is the unhappy hope for the death of others . . . it is the terrible avidity to possess and this criminal impatience that is so strongly condemned by Seneca," wrote the anonymous author of *Questions sur les empoisonneurs.*[103] According to the sorceress La Voisin, Mme de Brissart sought to increase her share of an inheritance by poisoning the sister with whom she would have had to share it.[104] La Voisin's friend La Richon went even further, poisoning her father-in-law and three sisters-in-law to ensure that her husband inherited all of his family's assets.[105] Common wisdom to the contrary, cupidity was not the exclusive province of women during the Affair of the Poisons. M. de Lottinet, for example, allegedly poisoned his son-in-law so that his daughter might enjoy her widow's portion early, and then poisoned his daughter, so that he might enjoy it instead.[106]

The domestic crimes of the marquise were made easier by her gift for deceit. In seventeenth-century France, deceit and hypocrisy were traits commonly attributed to the female sex.[107] Deceit enabled women to hide their anger, which could simmer for long periods of time because "their temperament, being more phlegmatic than that of men, makes it more difficult for them to become aroused, but they retain their anger far longer."[108] Duplicity was also widely acknowledged to be the hallmark of the poisoner.[109] The details of Marie's case seemed to confirm that she was both an exceptional actress and remarkably cold-blooded. She and her lover had apparently planned her father's murder for two years but delayed acting until they had manufactured a poison that he would not be able to detect in his food. While the poison was being perfected, Marie contrived a reconciliation with him so that she would be able to gain access to his household once her plan was in place. Moreover, she was deceitful in public as well as in private; she affected a sudden piety so that her regular distribution of poisonous pastries at the poor hospital might pass unremarked.[110]

Louis XIV's subjects recognized that deceit and hypocrisy were traits necessary to the success of courtiers as well as poisoners. Courtiers hid their true emotions behind masks of *politesse* and followed the rules of *bienséance* as they vied with each other to gain the material and social rewards distributed by the king. La Bruyère described the perfect courtier as "a man who knows the court is master of his gestures, of his eyes and of his face; he is profound, impenetrable; he dissimulates bad offices, smiles at his enemies, controls his irritation, disguises his passions, belies his heart, speaks and acts against his feelings."[111] In *The Princess of Clèves,* the soundest advice offered by Mme de Chartres to her daughter was a warning: "If you judge by appearances at court . . . you will always be deceived."[112] Thus the script of the marquise pointed the crime of poison at the court. Not only were courtiers versed in the arts of deception, but they were also members of the same (albeit vast) domestic household—a household that fostered both romantic and political rivalries. Accusations of poison lodged against courtiers could therefore fall on receptive ears.

Like the myth of Medea, the contemporary legend of the marquise encouraged prosecutors and public alike to give credence to the revelations of the Affair of the Poisons. Nicolas de la Reynie reflected that his own response to the scandal had been shaped by the case of the marquise, writing of his investigation, "Perhaps [these crimes] were necessary to leave at least some inclination to listen to what has cropped up since; perhaps by the same order of Providence, the famous example of Mme de Brinvilliers preceded the discovery of the inconceivable number of poisonings and of the abominable commerce in poison."[113] The dangerous characteristics of the marquise—greed, deceitfulness, and illicit female sexuality—as well as those of Medea—rivalry and an affinity for magic—were therefore readily on hand to be attributed to the women implicated in the Affair of the Poisons.

The archetype of Medea, refurbished in seventeenth-century French theater, emphasized the intimate connection between sorcery, rivalry, and poison. During the late 1660s and 1670s, life seemed to be imitating art as a series of Parisian trials reassembled the elements of the myth. The 1668 trial of the abbé Mariette and his partner the magician Lesage hinted that magical practices were thriving in the heart of the city;[114] the 1676 trial of the marquise de Brinvilliers revealed that a pattern of poison (without benefit of religion) might be flourishing as well. By the late 1670s the elements of magic, poison, and rivalry converged in the Affair of the Poisons, to make Medea seem incarnate at the Sun King's court.

Once the myth of Medea had been reanimated, it proved as enduring as ever. Mapped onto Mme de Montespan in 1680, the myth clung to her memory long after she had retired from the court. Elizabeth-Charlotte, Louis XIV's sister-in-law, continued to invoke allegations of poison against her for almost forty years, even after Mme de Montespan's death. "It is certain that La Fontanges died from poison," Liselotte wrote as late as 1715. "She herself accused La Montespan of her death. A lackey suborned by La Montespan contrived her death with poisoned milk, and did away with some of her followers; two have died, and it is said publicly that they were poisoned."[115] Casting Mme de Montespan as a seventeenth-century Medea served political ends. No doubt Liselotte believed that it was in the interest of her son, the regent Philippe d'Orléans, to remind people that his political rival, Louis's legitimized son the duc du Maine, was the son of a poisoner.

The legend of the marquise gradually came to rival the myth of Medea in the ritual repertoire of the old regime. The marquise became the archetypal poisoner most commonly evoked to signify the most depraved refinements of feminine behavior. Her repute spread beyond France's borders; Louis XIV's foreign critics seized upon the trope to cast aspersions on the Sun King's rule. During the War of the League of Augsburg, for example, Dutch pamphleteers churned out a profusion of tracts critical of Louis XIV, depicting the king as a man whose immoderate passions had enslaved him to his mistresses. In the 1695 *L'esprit familier du Trianon,* Louis's mistresses were debauched women who had poisoned their rivals to maintain their positions. The pamphlet described a scene that was to have taken place in Louis's bedroom. The ghost of La Fontanges appeared before the king and his morganatic wife, Mme de Maintenon (who was sharing his bed), to denounce the rival who had given her a "mortal drink," crying, "Villainous Montespan! It is you who poisoned me to satisfy your envious rage; the same valet who brought me the soup . . . waits for you, tigress. . . . You will be placed in the same rank as Brinvilliers and the others who made attempts on the lives of innocent creatures."[116]

Enlightenment authors likewise employed the case of the marquise de Brinvilliers. In Voltaire's *Le dîner du comte de Boulainvilliers,* she served as an example of the most egregious kind of criminal.[117] As the ancien régime drew to a close, opponents of the Bourbons would seize upon both the legend of the marquise and the Affair of the Poisons to criticize the French monarchy as a despotic institution corrupted by poisonous—and poisoning—female influence. During the Revolution, for example, Jean-Paul Marat denounced the pernicious influence exerted by Mme Roland over her husband, the minister of the interior. Madame Roland, he wrote in the pages of *L'ami du peuple,* was a criminal of the same rank as the marquise de Brinvilliers and La Voisin.[118] More than a century after the executions of these notorious poisoners, their names and crimes still resonated with the Parisian public.

Moreover, after the case of the marquise and the Affair of the Poisons, the crime of poison came to be seen as a particularly aristocratic endeavor. Marat's accusations therefore served as a means of linking Girondin ideology to the old regime court and to signal the dangerously reactionary nature of Girondin politics. His readers would have understood that the crime of poison stood metonymically for the entire system of feminized, aristocratic politics that they repudiated. Olympe de Gouges sought to demonstrate the corrupt nature of aristocratic power during the old regime in similar fashion. In the *Declaration of the Rights of Woman and the Female Citizen,* she employed the association between aristocratic women and poison to play upon contemporary suspicions regarding the destabilizing influence of clandestine female political power, writing: "Women have done more harm than good. Constraint and dissimulation have been their lot. What force had robbed them of, ruse returned to them; they had recourse to all the resources of their charms, and the most irreproachable person did not resist them. *Poison and the sword were both subject to them; they commanded in crime as in fortune*" (emphasis added).[119] It is surely no coincidence that the virulent pornographic pamphlets excoriating Marie-Antoinette before and during the Revolution painted her as a depraved voluptuary who "set to work and herself distilled the juice brought to Colchis by the famous Medea" and then attempted to poison her husband with "a lethal dose of crushed diamonds."[120] By the time of the French Revolution, aristocratic women who had once conspired to manipulate the body of the king now allegedly conspired against the body of the French nation itself.

# The Criminal Magical Underworld of Paris

D uring their three-year investigation into the Affair of the Poisons, Nicolas de la Reynie and his police uncovered a criminal magical underworld thriving in the very heart of the Paris. The members of this loosely knit community included treasure-hunters, fortune-tellers, and alchemists. Their personal and professional ties helped fuel La Reynie's conviction that a vast and pernicious conspiracy of criminals threatened the stability and order of Paris, the good of the state, and the life of the king himself. Occupying the innermost reaches of this underworld were magicians, sorceresses, and renegade priests who offered for sale an array of products and services that ranged from relatively benign rituals of love magic to poisons known as "inheritance powders." Their extensive customer base stretched from the poorest suburbs of the capital to the highest reaches of the French court, for Louis XIV's official mistress was apparently a regular client of the notorious sorceress La Voisin.

The practices of the renegade priests, sorceresses, and magicians exposed by La Reynie indicate that the Christian magical tradition of medieval Europe continued to flourish during the ancien régime. Invoking heavenly aid to fulfill their clients' desires, the members of Paris's underworld exploited the practices, imagery, and sacramentals of the Roman Catholic Church to increase the efficacy of their magic. Like their medieval predecessors, they provided their clients with charms and rituals that promised to bestow good health, beauty, wealth, and love. Others offered their clients occult means of causing death, and some provided poisons as well. After mapping out the criminal magical underworld of seventeenth-century Paris, this chapter assesses its sacrilegious activities in the context of the Catholic Reformation, examines the wares offered by the city's sorceresses, and compares the diverse ends to which their male and female clients employed such magic.

## THE COMMUNITY OF THE CRIMINAL MAGICAL UNDERWORLD

The members of the criminal magical underworld of seventeenth-century Paris operated in loose association with one another. Like the residents of a small village, they kept an eye on one another's doings, both legal and otherwise. Consequently, secrets were difficult to keep; gossip and rumor kept members of this community well informed of one another's activities. Although the magician Lesage, for example, declared he had never met Abbé Dulaurens, he told his interrogators, "there was a priest named Dulaurens at Saint-Leu, who was the good friend of the priest Olivier, who told him [Lesage] that Dulaurens and he [Olivier] had searched for treasures and other things."[1] Lesage insisted that he did not know Abbé Deshayes, either, but that he had heard Deshayes was "one of La Filastre's greatest friends, and the comte de Gassilly said he was mixed up with counterfeiting."[2] Lesage claimed familiarity with the activities of the abbé Guibourg as well. He had heard tell, he said, of demonic ceremonies for locating treasures and of several amatory masses from several of the renegade priest's associates, including one of his parishioners, a sorceress, and the duchesse de Vivonne, a client of Guibourg's.[3] While Lesage was undoubtedly attempting to draw the attention of his interrogators away from himself, many of his allegations were later corroborated by other witnesses.[4]

In fact, gossip circulating among the members of the underworld did not have far to travel, for many of those involved in the Affair of the Poisons lived in the same neighborhoods and were members of the same parishes. The sorceresses and magicians tended to congregate in three areas of northern Paris, their addresses stretching along the main avenues that led toward the faubourgs Saint-Martin, Saint-Denis, and Montmartre. The first group settled in the environs of the former cour des Miracles, razed in 1667.[5] Anchored by La Trianon on rue Charlot, the second group lived to the east, near the Temple on rues Pastourelle and Gravilliers. The final group, including La Voisin, La Joly, and La Bosse, conducted business on rues Cléry, Paradis, Beauregard, and Bourbon in the neighborhood of Ville-Neuve on the outskirts of Paris, just beyond the porte Saint-Denis.[6] This area held a particular attraction for those who practiced dubious professions, for it was located far from the center of Paris's corporate government and the watchful eyes of La Reynie's police. The community of Ville-Neuve consisted of villas surrounded by walled gardens that ensured that the activities of their occupants could not be seen from the street. But its residents' poisonous proclivities were an open secret in the city. It was apparently common for women who complained of their husbands' boorish behavior to be advised to solve their marital difficulties with "a soup from the rue Saint-Denis."[7]

The example of Father Gilles Davot, chaplain of Notre-Dame de Bonne-Nouvelle, clearly illustrates the connections that linked members of the criminal magical underworld together. Davot served as the Montvoisin family priest. He was both the confessor of La Voisin's husband and an employee of hers; she paid him generously to consecrate charms and participate in various magical rituals.[8] La Vosin introduced Father Davot to the magician Lesage, and Davot subsequently served as Lesage's assistant at numerous magical rituals.[9] Davot's neighbors included several members of the magical underworld with whom the renegade priest collaborated on occasion: the palm reader La Bergerot, who lived only a few streets to the north, Maître Jean, a porter at the hospital of Quinze-Vingts and frequent participant in the abbé Cotton's demonic rituals, and a fellow priest named Lemperier, a treasure hunter who boarded with Maître Jean.[10]

Personal ties as well as geographic proximity linked the members of the underworld. They frequently met their compatriots through common acquaintances, as the investigators into the Affair of the Poisons well knew. The web of relationships that connected the members of the city's underworld can be partially reconstructed from the interrogations conducted by La Reynie. During these interrogations La Reynie's first order of business was to establish how the suspect had come to know other members of the underworld.[11] La Reynie thus discovered that Lesage had been introduced to Guibourg by a mutual friend, just as the sorceress La Filastre had come to know Guibourg through a treasure hunter named Odot, a neighbor of La Voisin's.[12] La Voisin, La Bosse, and La Leroux, La Reynie learned, became close friends as well as business associates. Their mutual endeavors included poisoning Monsieur Leféron at the behest of his wife.[13] The priests Huet, Bobie, and Mariette were also friends as well as colleagues, working together for the magician Lesage on occasion.[14] But these relationships, like more legitimate business partnerships, could sometimes sour into intense personal and professional rivalries. La Voisin and Marie Bosse, for example, became bitter adversaries after La Voisin lured La Bosse's lover away from her.

Many members of the criminal magical underworld seem to have conducted their enterprises in well-organized fashion. La Voisin, for example, required her clients to sign receipts that promised payment in return for her services. She may have charged full payment only after the client was satisfied with his or her results. As one such receipt reads, "I, the undersigned Louis Pilliard, tailor, living in Saint-Victoire . . . promise to recognize and satisfy Mme Voisin—if she does that which she has promised. 8 October 1674."[15] Similarly, having contracted to magically bring about a marriage on behalf of a client named De Prade, La Voisin asked him to sign a receipt promising two thousand *livres* upon the successful culmination of the business.[16] The sorceress apparently demanded payment in advance, however, from those who purchased inheritance powders.[17]

Members of the criminal underworld depended upon their network of relationships for client referrals. Sorceresses who offered charms of love magic and the midwives or abortionists who took care of the unwelcome consequences often worked closely together. Such cooperation worked to the financial benefit of both parties, for the sorceresses charged pregnant women for referrals to abortionists or to discreet midwives who would board the women during pregnancy and then dispose of unwanted infants after delivery.[18] La Voisin, infamous even among her colleagues, declared that she regularly sent her clients to abortionists like La Lepère, who "accommodated many girls and women who didn't have husbands."[19] La Voisin, ever eager to turn a profit, would even refer women to La Lepère when she knew perfectly well that they were not in fact pregnant. La Lepère assured her interrogators that she had always found La Voisin's deceptive practice objectionable and had even confronted her about it. La Lepère alleged that La Voisin had responded that such women ought to be taken at their words: "Since they themselves declare that they are whores, she ought to believe it."[20]

Love as well as business affairs connected the denizens of the underworld. The sorceresses La Dodée and La Trianon "lived together as man and wife" and ran their own family business, dispensing various magical charms and assorted poisons to their clients. The renegade priests forged community ties in similar fashion, for it was among the ranks of Paris's sorceresses that they typically found their mistresses. According to Lesage, Abbé Mariette was "the gallant of La Boulard," who was reportedly a member of La Voisin's ring of poisoners.[21] Before he jilted her for the "chubby, forty-ish" La Boulard, La Leroux had been Mariette's mistress.[22] La Lemarchard, a neighbor of La Voisin's, was the priest Davot's lover, and the abbé Cotton maintained a long-standing relationship with La Devaux.[23] Renegade clerics were also known to seize whatever chance arose for a liaison, and some proved to be quite creative in developing these opportunities. Father Gérard persuaded the daughter of a merchant not only to become his mistress but to participate in his demonic rituals as well. He furthermore managed to convince her that her presence at the ceremonies would serve as effective birth control, but his stratagem was uncovered when the young woman became pregnant.[24]

Associations of love and friendship were in fact professionally necessary to the inhabitants of the underworld, for they practiced interdependent occupations. Just like those in legitimate professions, sorceresses and magicians specialized, and they often found that they needed each other's expertise to complete tasks they had been hired to do. The connections between trades were legion. La Voisin and other purveyors of inheritance powders depended upon suppliers such as Galet and Maître Pierre for the active ingredients in their compositions: deadly herbs, arsenic, and toad venom. Abortionists turned to La Voisin to help conceal the evidence of their illegal practices; La Voisin supposedly incinerated fetuses in a little oven located at the back of her garden. Sorceresses in turn relied upon the midwives or abortionists for the cauls and afterbirths needed for a variety of magical charms.[25]

Furthermore, members of the capital's magic network depended on one another for information. They seem to have shared the intelligence gleaned from the spies whom they placed as servants in wealthy households. La Vigoureux, for example, maneuvered to gain a post for her son at the *hôtel* of the marquis de Feuquières. She approached the marquis, claiming a previous relationship with his mother. He later described her attempt: "The only time I ever saw [La Vigoureux] was about two years ago, when she came to my house to tell me that her husband was a lady's tailor, and that he had worked for my late mother, and that I would be doing her a great favor if I would take as a lackey a small boy whom she had with her, whom she claimed to be her son and my mother's godson. But, luckily for me, I thought him too small and refused to employ him."[26] La Vigoureux may have sought to place her son with the marquis because the nobleman frequented magicians in the capital. Palm readers, astrologers, and the like needed to keep abreast of the latest rumors and gossip concerning their clients in order to bolster their credibility as authentic fortune-tellers.[27]

Members of the magical underworld were able to put their gossip networks to good use, particularly when soliciting new business. La Voisin described how she had acquired the comtesse de Soissons as a regular client. When the countess consulted La Voisin for the first time, she decided to test the sorceress by refusing to reveal her identity. La Voisin offered to tell her anonymous visitor's fortune. Peering into the mystery woman's hand, La Voisin declared, "You were once loved by a great prince." As La Voisin already knew perfectly well, the countess had come seeking a means of regaining Louis XIV's love.[28]

The members of the criminal underworld were not necessarily critical to one another's economic survival, however. If La Voisin was unable to purchase arsenic or poisonous toads from La Dodée, she could obtain them fairly easily from someone else. But no sorceress or magician could stay in business very long without access to the services of a priest. The very functioning of the business of magic had a sacral dimension that required priestly cooperation. The magician Lesage, in fact, tried to turn this information to his advantage during his interrogation of November 15, 1680. He protested that he could not possibly have performed a series of conjurations at the home of La Voisin, as she had accused him of doing: "It was easy to see that it wasn't he who said the masses at La Voisin's, and that even had he wanted to, La Voisin . . . well knew that he was married and also knew perfectly well that it was necessary that a priest say the masses in order for them to be effective."[29] The renegade clerics were therefore the linchpin of Paris's magical underworld, for only they possessed the sacerdotal power that was believed necessary to the working of most powerful forms of magic.

Sorceresses consequently hired priests to complete their charms. By celebrating mass over a love charm the priest activated it, just as he "activated" the miracle of the mass. La Voisin, a most prolific sorceress, called upon the assistance of numerous priests, including Davot, Lemeignan, and Guibourg.[30] Magicians, too, needed priests to conduct demonic conjurations. Lesage availed himself of the services of several clerics in addition to his regular partner, the abbé Mariette.[31] The renegade priests were not always hired help, however. They could also act as independent agents and sell their services directly to clients.[32]

While a large proportion of their clients were of modest origins, members of the magical underworld, not unlike the owners of many businesses today, prized a rich and glamorous clientele.[33] In seventeenth-century France, Louis XIV's courtiers fit both categories. Sorceresses therefore solicited business in the *hôtels* of the wealthy, initially gaining access through the legitimate branches of their businesses. La Voisin herself sold cosmetics and perfumes as well as inheritance powders. Even in an era before Avon ladies, pomades that promised a flawless complexion or elixirs that offered perpetual youth opened many doors.[34] Courtiers sought out the denizens of the magical underworld in turn; Louis XIV's court was a permeable establishment that allowed its occupants ready access to the world beyond its borders. Rather than being confined within palace walls, most courtiers in fact enjoyed some freedom to come and go at times when their responsibilities permitted them to do so. When the court was installed in the Louvre, nobles might readily visit friends, frequent shops, and otherwise seek amusement in the city.

Before the Affair of the Poisons, frequenting fortune-tellers and the like enjoyed quite a vogue among the more adventurous nobles of both court and city.[35] As La Fontaine quipped fully a year before the scandal broke, "Lost a hanky? / Have a lover? / Your husband living too long to suit your taste? / A tiresome mother, a jealous wife? / Off you go to the sorceress / To get the news that you want to hear."[36] Not infrequently, titled curiosity seekers who paid their initial visits for entertainment's sake seem to have come away from their encounters with the city's sorceresses convinced of, or at least optimistic about, the efficacy of what they had seen. The widow of a *conseiller du Roi* of the Paris Parlement explained to her interrogators how she had come to visit La Voisin: "She went to La Voisin's out of curiosity, and to know what all the world wanted to know. And as they said that she [La Voisin] was a fortune-teller, she wanted to see what La Voisin would say. . . . She went to see her two or three times, and La Voisin came to see her two or three times. As she didn't want La Voisin to visit her home, she met her in the church of the sisters of Miséricorde. . . . It was out of female curiosity, to know what would happen, and out of folly; it was foolishnesses, stupidities, ridiculous things, and to fall in love."[37]

The comte de Cessac too returned repeatedly to the magician Lesage, but with more serious matters on his mind. According to the magician's testimony, the count initially solicited charms for winning at cards and dice, and then asked for others that would ensure the success of his love affairs. Finally, he commissioned the magician to bring about the death of his brother-in-law and to win for him the affections of his sister-in-law.[38]

## The Magical Best Sellers of Seventeenth-Century Paris

Courtiers or commoners, those who became regular customers of Paris's practitioners of magic sought the fulfillment of their most ardent ambitions—to gain
health, beauty, love, or wealth. Others sought magical assistance to cause harm
to their enemies, believing that if the members of the underworld were able to
cure illnesses, they could also cause them. Those whose aspirations did not fit into
a particular category could even avail themselves of an all-purpose charm that
promised to allow them "to obtain that which you wish for."[39] Finally, Parisians
turned to the sorceresses and magicians of the underworld for the ultimate means
of getting rid of inconvenient spouses, relatives, or rivals: poison.

Clients found that relatively simple charms were readily available from sorceresses or magicians, as were more elaborate (and therefore more costly) spells that
promised greater satisfaction. For those daring or desperate enough to attempt
it, demonic aid could be commissioned, but magicians could not solicit such help
successfully without at least some clerical assistance. Before a *grimoire,* or manual
of magic, that contained instructions for calling forth demons could be employed,
it first had to be consecrated by a priest. Ordained priests, in fact, were believed
to be among the only men able to conduct the most dangerous and powerful of
demonic conjurations. The trade of the city's sorceresses and magicians was therefore largely confined to those potions, spells, and divinations that could be achieved
without recourse to demonic assistance.[40]

The activities of the renegade priests, sorceresses, and magicians of the Affair
of the Poisons attest to a common tradition of magic that had flourished in Europe
for centuries. Like their medieval forebears, the members of Paris's magical underworld exploited the practices, imagery, and sacramentals of the Catholic Church
to increase the efficacy of their magic. The composition of their spells and charms
illustrates that the distinction between superstition and orthodox Christian belief
was still very blurred in seventeenth-century France, despite the post-Tridentine
evangelizing efforts of the Gallican church.[41] The simple spells known as *oraisons*
found in La Voisin's *grimoires,* for example, were made up of a linguistic hodge-
podge of Christian imagery, "debased" holy languages (Latin, Greek, or Hebrew),
and simple alliterative nonsense. One charm for curing toothache entailed writing
"Strigiles falcesque dentate dentium dolorem persanate" on a slip of paper that
was to be worn on a cord around the neck.[42] Another toothache remedy attempted
to harness the power of the Catholic mass. To cure the toothache one was to touch
the painful tooth while repeating "galbes galbat galdes galdat" three times during
mass.[43] Even the invocations of the city's fortune-tellers appropriated holy scripture and prayer. Water diviners allegedly called up visions of the future in a bowl
of water by chanting, "Alpha, Agla, Ley, in the name of the clavicule of Solomon
and the book that God presented to Moses, and you Alpha, and you Agla, and you

Ley, I command you on the part of the great living God, who created the heavens and the earth and the four elements, the Holy Spirit, the sainted Trinity of Paradise, that you appear."[44] The word "Agla" in this spell stands for the Hebrew phrase "Ata Gibor Leolam Adonai," or "Thou art mighty forever, lord."[45]

The spells seized from the sorceresses caught up in the Affair of the Poisons are in fact remarkably similar in content, style, and intent to those in circulation during the Middle Ages. Often identical names were invoked. "Agla," for example, appears frequently in medieval manuals of magic.[46] Other seventeenth-century charms were close paraphrases of earlier incantations.[47] One fourteenth-century method of healing a patient impaled by an iron implement required that the healer address the offending metal object, instructing it to emerge from the patient's body, "just as the spear of Longinus pierced Christ's side and then came out."[48] Seized by La Reynie's police three hundred years later, a charm found in the home of one of Paris's magicians instructed, "To heal a wound," say the words "In the name of the Father and the Son and the Holy Spirit, Sword [or whatever the weapon was], no longer cause harm to NN[49] as did the lance to the adorable body of Jesus Christ on the tree of the cross."[50]

Likewise, the *grimoires* and other collections of spells kept by Paris's sorceresses were bowdlerized editions of medieval books of learned magic. One of the *grimoires* found among La Voisin's papers, entitled *The Book of the Conjurations of Pope Honorius*, bears a close resemblance to the fourteenth-century *Sworn Book of Honorius*. La Voisin possessed another magic manual whose invocations and charms are similar to those of the *Clavicle of Solomon*, a necromancer's manual that circulated in almost every European country since its first appearance in the twelfth century.[51]

If the magic sold in Louis XIV's capital was nothing new, official tolerance of such practices had declined precipitously since the medieval era. Like those who trafficked in poisons, magical practitioners became a target of the Chambre de l'Arsenal. The sorceresses who dispensed love potions and gambling charms were branded a threat not because they were witches who practiced harmful magic or were agents of a demonic conspiracy to destroy Christianity, but because they profaned religion and corrupted the faithful. The simplest of their charms contravened the church's prohibitions against superstition, and the most elaborate of their ceremonies carried idolatry and sacrilege to new heights.

The Affair of the Poisons coincided with the culmination of an intense Catholic drive to eradicate superstition. As Stuart Clark warns, the modern usage of the term "superstition," with its connotations of secular skepticism, can obscure the deep seriousness with which it was regarded in the premodern era. Since the twelfth century, theologians had defined superstition to be no less than religion's opposite. Following the scholastic Thomas Aquinas, Catholic thinkers differentiated between two major categories of superstition. The first, "service to the true God, but in an inappropriate or incorrect manner," was further subdivided into "false worship" and "irrelevant or excess worship." Excess worship was marked by exaggerated piety. It might entail multiplying church rituals beyond what was officially enjoined or assigning baseless meaning to details of Catholic ritual. The second, and more malignant, category of superstition, "service to a false god, but in the manner due to the true," included vain observance, divination, and idolatry (as well as Judaism and Islam), all of which were defined as "perversions of true worship."[52] As a violation of the first commandment, idolatry was the primary transgression committed by Christians, taking second place only to heresy in the hierarchy of spiritual offenses.[53]

The Catholic Church broadened its offensive against the sin of superstition over the course of the early modern period. By the fifteenth century, *maleficia*, or the performance of harmful magic, was classified as a form of idolatry. Witches committed a heinous act of false worship, reasoned such influential theologians as Jean Gerson, when they forged a pact with the devil in exchange for their powers. By the beginning of the sixteenth century, popular magical practices were also branded idolatrous. Wearing magical amulets, engaging in magical healing practices, telling fortunes—all constituted vain observance because they entailed the expectation of unnatural results from natural sources. When God created the universe, Catholic theologians held, he endowed each and every thing in it with particular attributes. If an effect brought about in the natural world exceeded the scope of its God-given properties, that result could only be the consequence of a miracle (regarded as a most unlikely event) or a diabolic pact.[54] Intentions, in this view, were irrelevant. Even if the pact with the devil was only tacit, entered into unknowingly by someone who had no intention of renouncing God, the fault remained. "Those things that cannot naturally bring about the effects for which they are employed are superstitious and belong to a pact entered into by devils," thundered Jacobus Simancas in the widely read inquisitorial manual *Institutiones Catholicae.*[55]

The faithful were repeatedly cautioned against the dangers of superstition throughout the decades of the Catholic Reformation.[56] The catechism published by the Council of Trent in 1566 insisted that "those who give credit to dreams, divination, fortune-telling, and such superstitious illusions" were violators of God's first law.[57] The same sentiment was soon echoed in the teachings of the Gallican church. The most widely used confessional manual in sixteenth-century France charged priests to instruct their congregations that believing that magic, necromancy, and divination were even possible was a sin against the first commandment. The consequences of such activities were dire. As a 1583 church council in Bordeaux tersely ordered, "those who are involved with magic and divination or who place their trust in diviners commit a horrible crime and are excommunicated."[58]

By the eve of the Affair of the Poisons, the church's assault on superstition had reached a positive crescendo. Jean-Baptiste Thiers, a parish priest from Chartres, published his four-volume polemic, *Treatise on Superstitions according to Holy Scripture, Conciliar decrees, and the sentiments of Church Fathers and Theologians*, in 1679. Thiers's work envisioned a purified religion in which the Roman Catholic Church reserved exclusive claim to the realm of the supernatural for its practices, rituals, and personnel. In keeping with the work of earlier theologians, Thiers identified magic, witchcraft, and deviant religious practices as "false and superfluous cults." Those who attempted to divine the future, he continued, always committed a mortal sin. The curé warned of the spiritual dangers posed by popular magical practices. Of particular concern were spells or charms that abused the sacraments, particularly the Eucharist. Offering the most sweeping definition of vain observance to date, Thiers also labeled as superstitious any activity "whose results involve useless or ridiculous ceremonies instituted neither by God or Church."[59]

The Gallican church's mounting crusade against popular superstitions was not simply a matter of doctrinal hair splitting. By proscribing superstition, the church forbade any number of common magical practices that were still considered perfectly licit by their adherents, as those who were summoned by the judges of the Chambre de l'Arsenal attested. Visiting palm readers, carrying one's caul in the belief that it offered preternatural protection, using holy oil as a love potion—all seemed to Louis XIV's subjects, aristocrats as well as artisans, unlikely to compromise their eternal salvation or the public good. As Marie Brissart had explained to her interrogators, her visits to La Voisin were nothing but "foolishnesses, stupidities, ridiculous things."[60] The Sun King's judges, however, disagreed. The members of the Chambre de l'Arsenal considered the city's magicians guilty of the sins of impiety, superstition, and the misuse of holy things. The credulous clients of Paris's sorceresses needed to be shown the error of their sinful ways, and those who led them astray needed to be driven from the kingdom.

Neither the magistrates nor the theologians of the era distinguished between sin and crime.[61] Sinners might violate the laws of God while criminals ignored the laws of God's lieutenant, Louis XIV, but both offenses constituted disobedience to authority—and posed a threat to the divinely ordained social order.[62] Thus both sin and crime were the rightful objects of police attention and state prosecution. From the creation of the police force in 1667, La Reynie's officers were not only directed to attend to matters of public security but were instructed to monitor the morals of the city's inhabitants. To root out blasphemers, gamblers, and those who indulged in "debauchery and riotous living," the police were authorized to pay neighborhood informants a percentage of the fines imposed on convicted offenders. Police agents used the terms "sin" and "crime" interchangeably to describe the misconduct of Parisians under investigation in the weekly reports that they sent to the king.[63] For police as well as parishioners, sin and crime alike risked divine displeasure for the entire community.

Yet, despite the concerted efforts of crown and church to enforce religious orthodoxy, a criminal magical underworld continued to prosper in the French capital.
Sorceresses and magicians offered for sale a cornucopia of cures for a dizzying
variety of ills. They sold remedies to cure headaches, leprosy, pimples, bad breath,
and labor pains.[64] They offered unguents to whiten the complexion, powders
to whiten the teeth, and dyes to cover the white in one's hair. They distributed
charms that bestowed life spans of 166 years.[65] Like their medieval predecessors,
seventeenth-century practitioners of magic also dispensed a substance believed
to be efficacious enough to cure almost any malady. The recipes for *l'or potable,*
or potable gold, found at La Voisin's home are nearly identical to those found
in Latin alchemical and medical treatises from the Middle Ages. The fourteenth-
century *Experimenta* attributed to Raymond Lull, for example, describes potable
gold's ability to "cure illnesses of one month in a day and those of one year's
duration in a month."[66] According to La Voisin's recipes, potable gold could relieve
lethargy, pleurisy, ulcers, gangrene, and rabies, among numerous other afflictions,
simply by altering the liquid in which it had been suspended.[67] La Voisin dispensed
*l'or potable,* at great expense, to her wealthiest clients.[68] The sorceress was not
the exclusive source in the city for this adaptable remedy, however. Recipes involving the use of potable gold can be found in printed medical treatises as late as the
end of the seventeenth century, as well as in manuscript versions of "books of
secrets," such as *L'arsenal des secrets.*[69]
    Sorceresses also provided protective amulets and charms to ensure the health
of their clients. Even the most seemingly innocuous of these violated the Catholic
Church's prohibition against superstition. In this period of almost constant war-
fare, male aristocrats searched avidly for one type of spell in particular that rendered its user invulnerable to sword wounds. According to La Voisin's *grimoire,*
to avoid being wounded by any weapon, one had only to repeat a simple formula
each morning, three times while still in bed and three times after getting out of
bed: "I arise in the name of Jesus Christ, who was crucified for me. Jesus, please
bless me; Jesus, please guide me, Jesus, please govern me well and guide me to
eternal life. In the name of the Father, the Son, and the Holy Spirit."[70] While the
formula above appears licit, its appearance in a magical handbook suggests that
its seventeenth-century users were not drawing a clear distinction between religious and magical practices.[71]
    Paris's magical practitioners also sold items that promised to make their clients
wealthy. The most popular assured success at cards or other games. Gambling was
an enormously popular pastime and magicians peddled hundreds of charms to
noble and commoner alike. The stakes by which courtiers played were so high that
fortunes could literally be made or lost in the course of an evening.[72] According
to the Princess Palatine, the aristocrats at court gambled with abandon, the usual
rules of court politesse suspended. "The stakes are horrendously high here, and the

people act like madmen when they are playing. One bawls, another hits the table with his fist so hard that the whole room shakes, and a third one blasphemes to make one's hair stand on end; in short, they show such despair that one is frightened even to look at them."[73] Courtiers risked enormous sums at the tables. Madame de Montespan, for example, possessed a passion for *hoca* (the latest rage in card games) that was as legendary as her staggering losses. In the winter of 1679, according to the comte de Rebenac, she commonly lost a hundred thousand *écus* a night. Three years later, her luck had not improved. An anonymous source reported, "Madame de Montespan lost, we hear, at *hoca,* more than 500,000 *écus.* The king . . . is very angry with her."[74] A charm that ensured victory at cards could therefore literally be worth a fortune.

Lucky charms provided the simplest means of ensuring that fortune would smile upon one's endeavors at the tables. Louis XIV's subjects did not rely upon mere rabbits' feet for good luck, however. As they believed that cauls brought luck to those born wearing theirs, it seemed logical to conclude that a caul would bring luck to anyone who possessed one, whether or not it had been theirs originally.[75] Paris's sorceresses, who frequently worked as midwives and abortionists, could readily supply cauls to those in need of luck. Marie-Marguerite Montvoisin, for example, claimed that her mother had furnished Mme de Montespan with a consecrated caul.[76] Sorceresses dispensed fetuses, too, which were also thought to bring good fortune. Lesage reported that La Delange had sold a "small stillborn baby no bigger than a thumb" to M. de Bretigny, who had heard such a thing would win him a fortune at the gaming table.[77]

Sorceresses taught their clients verbal spells for the same purpose. These usually consisted of a short formula that called the power of holy things, names, and objects into the gambler's service, thus misappropriating scripture and prayer. La Voisin's copy of the *Book of the Conjurations of Pope Honorius,* seized from her home at the time of her arrest in the winter of 1679, contained several. "To win at cards," instructed one, "pluck a clover of four or five leaves, make the sign of the cross over it, then say: Clover, I pick you in the name of the Father, the Son, and the Holy Spirit, by the virginity of the Sainted Virgin, by the virginity of Saint John the Baptist, by the virginity of Saint John the Evangelist, that you may be of use to me in all sorts of games. It is necessary to say five Paters and five Aves, then continue: El, Agios, Ischyros, Athanatos." The *grimoire* also contained a similar formula for winning at dice. One had only to repeat the words, "Dice, I conjure you in the name of Assizer and of Rassize, that they come make a clean sweep in the name of Assia and of Longrio."[78]

Seventeenth-century sorceresses and magicians, like their medieval predecessors, could also offer those in serious financial straits magical options that promised more than mere luck. The *pistole volant* and the *main de gloire* were among the most sought after, despite the church's injunction that the use of either constituted an offense of vain observance. A *pistole volant* was a magical coin that could be spent repeatedly; no matter how many times the owner exchanged the coin, it would always reappear in his or her pocket.[79] While the magic coin guaranteed that its owner would never want for pocket change, for more substantial gain it was necessary to obtain a *main de gloire*. This powerful item doubled the amount of gold or silver placed beside it. A *main de gloire*, however, was quite expensive. The sénéchale de Rennes had to give La Voisin fifty *louis d'or* as well as an amethyst ring for one.[80]

Fashioning a *main de gloire* was a lengthy and arduous process but, as it did not involve necromancy, anyone acquainted with magic could conceivably create one. The *Grimoire of Pope Honorius the Great* contained detailed instructions. The book directed the magician to begin by stripping the hide, hair, and all, from a mare in heat while chanting, "Dragne, dragne." Once finished, the magician was to conceal the skin in a safe place, and then immediately set off and purchase a new earthenware pot without bargaining over its price. Upon his return, he was to fill the pot with water from the fountain, submerge the hide in it, cover the pot, and place it where no one could see it. Nine days later, at the same hour that he had hidden the pot, the magician was to open it. Inside he would find a small serpent. The magician was then to inform it immediately, "I accept the pact." This done, he was to place the serpent in a new box, again bought without haggling over the price, and never let the box out of his sight for the rest of his days. To activate the *main de gloire*, he was to put either silver or gold into the serpent's box and take the box to bed with him, keeping it next to his body. After three or four hours, the magician would awaken to find that the quantity of gold or silver he had placed in the box had doubled. However, the amount of precious metal produced by the *main de gloire* was limited, for it could generate only a hundred *livres* at a time.[81]

Truly great riches, therefore, were only to be had if one found lost treasure. Searching for lost treasure seems to have been the seventeenth-century equivalent of buying modern-day lottery tickets; innumerable people indulged in the practice despite the overwhelming odds against success. Despite the church's teachings that even believing that one could locate treasure with diabolic assistance was a sin against the first commandment, the enterprise appealed to the many Parisians who believed the persistent rumor that great fortunes had been buried near the Louvre during the Fronde.[82] Spells to locate these princely sums, however, were considered to involve some risk to the participants, for they involved demonic magic. The safest of the charms that promised to reveal the presence of buried treasure required only limited contact with the demonic world. Unfortunately, the spell did not work from afar. The treasure hunter had to stand in the exact place where the treasure had been hidden, strike the ground three times with the left heel, and say, "Sadies satani agir fons toribus: come to me, Seradon, who will be called Sarietur." Then the searcher was to rap three more times, and if any treasure was in the area, the *grimoire* promised, something "will whisper it in your ear."[83]

Because this charm was of use only if one had already determined the location of the hidden treasure, fortune hunters were often willing to turn to potentially perilous forms of magic considered more efficacious: demonic conjurations. Conjurations were a dangerous business because they called up malignant spirits who had to be compelled to cooperate. If a necromancer lacked the will or the ability to control the spirits he summoned, he placed his life as well as his soul at risk.[84] In this, magicians and church officials were in agreement, for necromancy had long been condemned by the Catholic hierarchy as idolatrous.

Necromancers learned how to perform conjurations from *grimoires* that detailed the rituals by which demons could be called forth. According to the *Book of the Conjurations of Pope Honorius,* the conjuration of the demon Baicher, possessor and master of hidden treasures, would bring great riches to those who could effect it. The *grimoire* warned the necromancer to follow its instructions unerringly. This "experiment" could take place only on a Wednesday between midnight and 3:00 A.M. Standing within the safe confines of a large circle traced upon the ground, the necromancer was to present a black crow as payment to the demon when it appeared. Baicher would appear upon hearing the necromancer intone: "I conjure and exorcise Baicher to come to me, by the three names of God, Eloy, Afinay, Agla, Ely lamazabatany, which were written in Hebrew, in Greek, and in Latin, and by all the names which were written in this book and by he who drove you from high in the heavens. I command you by the great living God and by the sainted Eucharist which delivers men from their sins, that without delay you come and put me in possession of the treasure that you own unjustly, without any lateness or delay . . . and that afterwards you leave without causing any noise, nuisance, or terror towards me or towards those who are in my company."[85] If the necromancer and his clients preferred to search for treasure on other days of the week, the *grimoire* included conjurations for summoning the demon Aquiol on Sundays and the demon Acham on Tuesdays.[86]

## Love and Death in the Île de France

Perhaps even greater than Parisians' desire for magical means of acquiring wealth was their demand for love magic. While both men and women commissioned rituals of love magic in order to manipulate others' emotions, the two sexes frequently employed this magic to different ends. Men often turned to love magic to conclude socially or financially advantageous marriages. Thus, like the spells and ceremonies intended to locate buried treasure, much of the love magic commissioned by men seems to have been of the get-rich-quick variety. Sometimes it was intended to bring about equally advantageous benefits; on one occasion the marquis de Valençay, in the midst of a lawsuit with a widow, attempted to buy powders that would cause her to fall in love with him and hence drop her case.[87] No doubt because parental consent was required by law before a marriage could be celebrated, love magic often seems to have been intended to prevail upon the reluctant relatives of the intended bride, rather than the woman herself, to permit the marriage.[88] The marquis de Feuquières, for example, supposedly paid the priest Davot and his accomplices one thousand *pistoles* for a series of demonic rituals intended to secure the marquis an heiress. The steep price of these particular ceremonies was due both to their complexity and to the danger they entailed, according to Lesage, for the agreement included a proviso for removing any relatives of his intended bride who might oppose the marriage. When the demons did not seem to be working quickly enough, the marquis decided to poison his future in-laws instead.[89] Men's recourse to love magic is revealed here to be more concerned with increasing wealth and social standing than with inspiring love for love's sake.

Women, too, used love magic to obtain financial security. One client of La Voisin's was a servant seeking love magic that would inspire her employer to marry her.[90] Another client, a widow, asked La Voisin to help her marry a M. Forne. For forty *écus,* the widow bought a quantity of powdered herb that was supposed to inspire M. Forne to fall in love with her once he came into contact with it (she put it in a drawer through which he was likely to search), as well as a substance she was to rub into her own hands; she was then to touch one of M. Forne's hands. She also purchased two powdered pigeon hearts to slip into his food and finally had a renegade priest say several series of *neuvaines* at various Paris churches. Although the widow may well have been in love with M. Forne, La Voisin attributed her client's persistence to the fact that she had five young children and needed a husband for financial support.[91]

It seems to have been more common, however, for women to direct love magic at men they wanted to marry for love. Marie Miron, for example, hired Lesage and La Voisin at considerable expense to cast a spell over the dashing captain of the guards whom she wanted to marry.[92] Sometimes, too, a woman might approach a sorceress for love magic with which to render a malicious or abusive spouse more amiable. The sénéchale de Rennes came to La Voisin in desperation, asking "to be well loved, to have money, and to be in favor."[93] La Voisin recounted the unfortunate sénéchale's circumstances: "The lady didn't tell [me] anything, except that she was extremely unhappy, that she had been separated from her husband, who kept as his mistress the wife of a *conseiller* or *président* of Rennes, and with whom her husband lived on rue Dauphine. The sénéchale, who had brought four or five hundred thousand *livres* in dowry, had been so reduced by her husband that she no longer had any shoes."[94]

Women's use of love magic during the Affair of the Poisons undermined the social and spiritual order. Love magic, if successful, was intended to bind another's will. The boundary between a client's passion for control and her desire for love, however, was often unclear. Influence over a man's emotions threatened to become command over his reason, which would consequently allow an unruly woman to overturn the natural patriarchal order.[95] Indeed, women did frequently request a love-struck husband in order to render him more malleable. The "wish list" of a client found at the home of La Voisin illustrates this duality. La Voisin's client initially asked "to have in plain power sure, the spirit, the heart, and the goods of my husband." The client, however, does not seem to have wanted to engage her husband's affections merely to increase her domestic bliss, for her list continued, "I ask to have in plain power sure, the heart and the spirit of Monsieur the abbé de Fylla and to be loved by him, I ask to be loved and esteemed by someone of quality . . . I ask to be known by Monsieur de St. Pouange and loved by him."[96] Obtaining her husband's heart, thus moving him to become more pliable and trusting, gave La Voisin's client the ability to engage in other love affairs.[97] Gaining control over his goods granted her greater independence. For this client, the love of her husband was not a goal but the means to an end. Marital happiness sprang from the power over her husband that could be obtained only by manipulating his affections.

The love magic available for purchase in seventeenth-century Paris existed on a broad continuum that ran from the medicinal to the demonic. This spectrum can be divided into three primary, yet frequently overlapping, categories. The many substances believed to possess supernatural properties can be included in an "over-the-counter" category; sorceresses and magicians seem to have maintained an inventory of items that were thought to derive their powers from the principles of natural magic. Materials such as menstrual blood, associated with fertility, were particularly favored in love magic, and potions were often concocted from a combination of reproductive matter. The second category consisted of charms and rituals celebrated by a sorceress or magician. These charms, considered efficacious in their own right, were frequently said over love potions to increase their potency. As simple as a phrase or an *oraison*, they typically called upon heavenly and/or supernatural aid to fulfill a given desire. The final category of love magic encompassed elaborate ceremonies that required the assistance of an ordained priest. The sacrilegious ceremonies of the third category, like those of the second, drew upon the Christian magical tradition of the Middle Ages and co-opted the practices, imagery, and sacramentals of the Catholic Church. In addition, they included elements from the medieval tradition of learned magic, particularly necromancy. The ritual repertory of Paris's renegade priests, though, went far beyond that of their medieval forebears, for they claimed to have developed a uniquely sacrilegious ceremony of love magic. The amatory mass, celebrated over the naked stomach of a living woman, allegedly lured forth the demons of the underworld with the sacrifice of an infant.

First-time clients usually purchased modest "over-the-counter" items of love magic. They bought perfumes or cosmetics guaranteed to render the wearer irresistible or formulated to enhance more than one's visage; La Voisin sold a cream intended to increase a woman's breast size.[98] Sorceresses also did a brisk trade in items such as holy oil that had been used in love magic for centuries. Women bought the oil to rub on their lips, believing that any man kissed by those lips would fall hopelessly in love.

If cosmetics and beauty creams did not bring about the dramatic effects advertised, La Voisin, Lesage, or a competitor might mix up a love potion containing ingredients with more powerful properties derived from natural magic. These potions did not improve the appearance of the client but were intended to change the perceptions of the love object—to capture and thus control his passions. Powdered mole, coxcombs, and human blood were considered among the most useful substances in this regard.[99] Perhaps the most common staple of those love potions, one whose efficacy stemmed from the occult qualities bestowed by natural magic, was the time-honored aphrodisiac Spanish fly. La Reynie's panel of medical experts discovered quantities of *cantharides,* or Spanish fly, among the medicinal and magical wares of several of Paris's sorceresses.[100] Maître Galet, the supplier who furnished La Voisin and other sorceresses with a variety of both medicinal and poisonous herbs, created his own "love powders" from bread and Spanish fly. He claimed to have concocted two sets of potions on behalf of Mme de Montespan that were designed to arouse the ardor of the king. In fact, he told La Reynie, he had "many useful secrets" for exactly such purposes. Galet acknowledged that his customer had complained that the first love potion he sent had had no effect (or rather a misplaced effect, given the king's concurrent attentions to Mme de Soubise), and Galet had been obliged to send a second potion.[101] While Spanish fly was thought to be an effective aphrodisiac in its own right, it could be rendered even more potent when combined with other ingredients that popular tradition had long accorded magical properties.

The blood of a would-be lover was believed to exert a powerful effect over the passions. One recipe for a *philtre pour l'amour* found among La Voisin's papers called for a large quantity of hippomane, *eau de vie,* and "the blood of the one who loves," which were to be combined together and distilled in an alembic.[102] Hippomane too was considered a potent ingredient in love charms.[103] The equivalent of an equine caul, hippomane is a small, black, fleshy mass found on the forehead of a newborn foal. It had been used in love magic since classical times, and its potential as both a love charm and a deadly poison (if ingested in large quantities) was attested to as late as the eighteenth century.[104] La Voisin's own philter of blood and hippomane was considered dangerous enough to merit a warning in her *grimoire:* "Take care not to give too much, because instead of engaging the affections of the one you love, this could cause them to vomit furiously and could even cause death."[105]

During the seventeenth century, there seems to have been a distinct branch of love magic that drew its coercive power from material associated with the reproductive process. Far more powerful than ordinary blood, therefore, was menstrual blood. Used in love magic since the days of the Roman Empire, it was one of the most formidable elements in a sorceress's pharmacy.[106] More than a millennium later, the storerooms of Paris's sorceresses inventoried during the Affair of the Poisons were well stocked with powdered menstrual blood. It not only continued to serve as a powerful sign of femininity or female fertility but was also understood to be the very substance that created children in the womb. Both learned and popular belief in the early modern era held that male sperm provided an infant's essence, but that the mother's menstrual blood was the material out of which the fetus was formed. Menstrual blood can be understood in this view as a uniquely powerful occult substance: it was the basic clay of humankind.[107]

Menstrual blood was only the most common ingredient in a pharmacopoeia of reproductive matter that included cauls, dried afterbirths, breast milk, and the distilled entrails of aborted fetuses. Even parts of newborn infants were put to magical use; one sorceress arrested during the Affair of the Poisons stored desiccated umbilical cords in her medicine chest.[108] Reproductive material was used in a variety of ways. Powdered menstrual blood could be simply added to a meal prepared for a lover, or a client might write down her desires on a sheet of virgin parchment that was then slipped under the chalice during the mass.[109] Virgin parchment was no ordinary paper, but was allegedly manufactured from the skin of a stillborn baby or the caul of a newborn.[110]

The use of consecrated afterbirths in ceremonies held "for love and to acquire the good graces of society" was a logical extension of such beliefs about the potency of reproductive material.[111] According to contemporary medical practitioners, afterbirths were composed of nine months' worth of accumulated menstrual blood. As a treatise by the royal midwife Louise Bourgeois explained, afterbirths were sponges that "receive the menstrual blood collected to feed the fetus" in the womb.[112] An afterbirth therefore concentrated the occult properties of menstrual blood into one powerful, if malodorous, conglomeration. While the vast majority of magical organic material was generated as part of the female reproductive cycle, male reproductive matter was also accorded some magical attributes. Occasionally, the recipe for a particularly elaborate love charm called for the "sperm" of *both* sexes.[113] The most powerful form of love magic available from the sorceresses and magicians of the criminal underworld likewise depended upon reproductive material. The amatory masses discussed in the following chapter combined elements of reproductive magic and necromancy to create a novel, and highly sacrilegious, ritual.

The use of reproductive substances extended beyond love magic. The spell sold by La Voisin that promised "to obtain all that you wish for," for example, called for a client to write the words, "Uriel gariel quriel" with a new quill and "ink mixed with the milk of a woman who has just given birth to her first son."[114] Cauls were perhaps most widely used. Belief in their supernatural properties was prevalent in Europe well into the modern era. Their occult qualities were considered exceptionally adaptable; not only could they be made into magical parchment and bring their possessors good luck; they also ostensibly warded off the evil eye, provided protection in battle, guaranteed lawyers victory in the courtroom, and even rendered a possessor's declaration of love irresistible to whomever heard it.[115]

Certainly less noisome than any bodily product, verbena was also exploited by Paris's sorceresses. Because the herb had to be harvested according to an established ritual, its preparation bridges the first two categories of love magic. La Voisin's *grimoire* instructed that the verbena be gathered on the first Wednesday of the moon, before the sunrise. As the harvester collected the plant, he was instructed to repeat the following charm: "I pluck you, verbena, in the name of the Holy Trinity: Father, Son, Holy Spirit. . . . After which you allow me to possess the love, the soul, the spirit, the heart, the body, the sentiments and control over the natural functions of N., after which she loves no one in the world as much as me, and does not cease to love me or find any repose in any place until she follows my will, in the name of the Father, the Son and the Holy Spirit. Amen. Aglato en te aglata."[116] The *grimoire* instructed that the spell be repeated over and over as the would-be lover collected all the verbena to be found.[117]

If a love-struck client proved unwilling to embark on predawn ritual harvesting or to season her beloved's dinner with powdered insects or menstrual blood, she could avail herself of the rituals and spells available from sorceresses or magicians, which made up the second category of love magic. These ceremonies co-opted the sacramentals of the Catholic Church in order to harness the powers of the holy objects to less licit ends. La Desmaretz, a customer of La Voisin and Lesage seeking to marry the man she wanted, commissioned such a rite. The magician and the sorceress arrived at La Desmaretz's home armed with black candles, white candles, incense, and a wand. The three knelt and recited prayers such as the Veni Creator together (La Desmaretz could not remember exactly which ones they had said), while Lesage gestured with his wand. The ceremony cost La Desmaretz one hundred *écus,* she claimed, but appears to have been worth the price; she later married the man at whom the ceremony had been directed.[118]

Lesage also offered his lovelorn customers ceremonies that employed the powers of sympathetic magic, performing his spells over items intended to represent the hearts of the two lovers. La Voisin witnessed one of the magician's rituals. Lesage, she alleged, struck the earth three times with a wand as he intoned three times, "Per Deum vivum, per Deum sanctum." He continued, "[Name of the intended] I conjure you, on the part of the All-Powerful, to go find [name of the client], that she will entirely possess his body, his heart, and his will, and that he will be able to love no one but her." Then Lesage inscribed the names of the two lovers in wax and tossed the wax into a fire, literally and figuratively melding them together.[119] Members of the magical underworld also supplied clients with wax figures that had been "baptized" with the name of the beloved.[120] The love ritual performed over the baptized figure was intended to work its amorous effect on the body of the loved one. Another such ritual employed the hearts of sacrificed pigeons to symbolize those of the lovers.[121]

The most powerful forms of amatory rituals in seventeenth-century France fall into a third category of love magic: those that were celebrated by, or with the assistance of, an ordained priest. Ordained priests were considered to be among the most forceful magicians of all, for they were able to suffuse spells, charms, and rituals of magic with sacerdotal power. Merely reciting the Gospels, or *evangiles,* over the head of a supplicant was believed to be enough to ensure that that person's prayers would be granted.[122] Furthermore, priests might enhance the effectiveness of an already magical item by celebrating a mass over it, an ability employed to a variety of ends. The abbé Guibourg said masses over a charm for winning at dice, over the dice themselves, over the rope with which a man had been hanged, and over a scrap of paper that, when ground to powder and scattered over someone, would cause him to fall passionately in love and "do all that the other wants."[123] The ritual power of those ordained by the church allowed them to function as mediators between the visible and invisible realms. Both popular and learned tradition thus held that priests could become redoubtable necromancers, able to compel obedience from the demons they invoked.[124]

To arouse love and cause death were often related ambitions in seventeenth-century France, as would-be lovers sought to rid themselves of the rivals or spouses that stood in their way. The spells and rituals of love magic were thus often subverted to malevolent ends. Female customers often sought the freedom to remarry for love, and a second marriage could not be celebrated without an end to the first. Even if a woman was wealthy, determined, and had the support of her family, her divorce suit was unlikely to be granted. If a woman did actually receive a divorce, she was frequently forbidden to marry again.[125] A husband's death might therefore seem the only viable means of ending an unhappy marriage, particularly in cases of abuse. Marie Bosse, for example, claimed that the poison she bought was intended for her husband, who had recently shot and wounded her.[126] Under interrogation, several other sorceresses and magicians averred that numbers of their female clients had sought the means to murder their husbands. Mesdames Leféron, de Dreux, Poulaillon, and Philbert were only among the most prominent of those so accused.

Noble families could not survive if their members formed alliances or squandered family resources for something as ephemeral as love. Sarah Hanley has described how the emerging absolutist state and the robe nobility forged the symbiotic family-state compact, a process that relied upon a legitimate familial lineage to ensure nepotistic succession to office. To secure appropriate marriages, the members of the *noblesse de robe* who sat in the Parlement of Paris enacted a series of regulations that extended their authority over the marriage and inheritance rights of women and children. This expansion of patriarchal control helped establish the networks of robe families that ensured that offices remained within family patrimonies.[127] The wares of love magic sold by the criminal magical underworld promised women like Mme de Virieu the opportunity to defy (or at least attempt to defy) patriarchal authority by ridding themselves of their husbands and marrying lovers of their own choosing. Madame de Virieu, a client of La Voisin, contracted the sorceress to bring about the death of her husband and win the love of "a certain abbé" at the same time.[128] Lethal rituals of love magic could therefore undermine the limits imposed on women's behavior and threaten the institution of the family.

La Voisin herself seems to have believed that widowhood was but a step on the road to a more pleasant union. According to Marie Vertemart, La Voisin generously offered to improve her friend's quality of life, exclaiming, "I want to make you happy, and if I make you a widow, I will marry you off to any man that you choose." La Vertemart protested that she already had a husband and her lover already had a wife. "Don't disturb yourself," responded La Voisin, "there is nothing I can't do. . . . I have made other women happy; only bring the money that I ask, and don't disturb yourself about the matter."[129]

Many of the women who wanted to get rid of their husbands or rivals seem to have first sought out magical means. "Over-the-counter" potions that exploited the powers of natural magic do not seem to have been sufficient for such an undertaking, but Paris's sorceresses and magicians did offer a number of rituals for the purpose that drew their force from the symbolic considerations of sympathetic magic. The pigeon hearts so frequently used in ceremonies of love magic, for example, were also featured in rituals intended to bring death. Lesage performed such a ceremony for the vicomtesse de Polignac, whom he claimed had sought to rid herself of both her husband and her rival for the affections of the king. For a ritual meant to cause the deaths of the vicomte de Polignac and Louise de la Vallière, Lesage instructed the comtesse to bring him the hearts of two pigeons. Reciting a spell that he purported to have learned from a priest, Lesage buried the hearts deep in the Bois de Boulogne. The spell, he assured the countess, would cause her husband and her rival to die within forty days. Unfortunately, from the countess's point of view, the spell had no effect whatsoever.[130] Lesage and La Voisin themselves seem to have believed that such spells were indeed efficacious; the sorceress admitted that she had attempted a similar one against her hapless husband, Antoine. During her love affair with Lesage, La Voisin schemed to do away with Antoine by burying the head of a sheep in the family garden. When he became seriously ill three days later, though, La Voisin relented and dug the head up.[131]

The customers of Paris's sorceresses do not seem to have considered the use of ritual equivalent to the use of poison. While both were apparently considered potentially lethal, clients do seem to have made a clear distinction between the two, turning to poison only when the magic they commissioned failed to bring about the desired result.[132] Ritual magic may in fact have been preferred as a first recourse because the charms acted at a distance and thus did not require a customer's direct involvement.[133] Madame Leféron, like La Voisin and the vicomtesse de Polignac, had first sought to rid herself of her husband through magical means. To that end, she first requested that spells be said over a wax figure of M. Leféron to cause his death. When the spells proved ineffective, she turned to La Leroux to help her poison him instead.[134] Impatient to marry her lover, Mme de Dreux found the task of getting rid of her husband a tricky one.[135] She and La Voisin first considered magical options but rejected them because Mme de Dreux did not think she could obtain any of her husband's linen (it was guarded by his valet, she said), which was necessary for the spell. The two decided that poison was more feasible. It would still be a difficult task, as Mme de Dreux would have little opportunity to administer the poison because she neither slept in the same bed as her husband nor ate many meals with him.[136] The determined Mme de Dreux did, however, eventually succeed in her plan.

Would-be poisoners in seventeenth-century Paris had an abundance of toxins from which to choose. Powdered diamond was reputed to be a lethal poison, but those who tried it found it wanting. According to La Voisin, Mme Leféron bought one hundred *louis d'or* worth of powdered diamond to sprinkle into her husband's food, but to her disappointment, "it hadn't done anything."[137] Sometimes powdered glass was substituted for the powdered diamond, but it too failed to cause death.

Arsenic, by contrast, worked to virulent effect. Contemporary medical practitioners could not determine a poisoning victim's cause of death; it was not until the mid-nineteenth century that the telltale signs of arsenic poisoning were discovered.[138] If given over a period of time, its symptoms were indistinguishable from those of a host of lingering illnesses that caused gradual decline. Administered in large doses, the symptoms of arsenic poisoning resembled those of cholera: destruction of internal organs, inflammation of the throat and intestines, and liver damage. They could also mimic those of dysentery or the plague: fever, diarrhea, vomiting, delirium, and coma.[139] Would-be poisoners did not need to seek out members of the magical underworld in order to buy arsenic, as it was also readily available from apothecaries who sold it in powdered form as *mort-aux-rats*.[140] Powdered arsenic, however, was not as virulent a poison as the liquid arsenical acid supplied by Paris's sorceresses, which had the added benefit of mixing undetectably into wine or water.[141]

The sorceresses taught their clients clandestine ways to administer the arsenic they provided. Madame de Poulaillon apparently availed herself of one such method.[142] Bringing one of M. de Poulaillon's shirts and a quantity of arsenic "as large as an egg," she paid a visit to Marie Bosse. La Bosse treated the bottom half of the garment with a solution of the arsenic, so that when M. de Poulaillon donned the shirt and tucked it into his breeches, "it caused a great inflammation and great pain to his *derrière et aux parties voisines.*"[143] The sores resembled those caused by syphilis. While M. de Poulaillon survived, such an application of poison often proved fatal to the victim.[144] Perhaps an even more surreptitious means of administering arsenic, however, took advantage of the seventeenth-century fashion for enemas. Ensuring that the liquid could not be detected by taste was not a concern with this method, so concentrated solutions of the poison, such as realgar (red arsenic or disulphide of arsenic), orpiment (yellow arsenic or trisulphide of arsenic), or sublimate (mercuric chloride) could be used. The poisons caused the intestine to shrink drastically and the victim soon died from an obstructed bowel.[145]

Herbal poisons were as readily available as arsenic in seventeenth-century Paris.[146] A shepherd known as Maître Pierre furnished many of Paris's sorceresses with a variety of deadly herbs. His customers included La Bosse, La Voisin, La Delaport, and La Trianon, among others. According to Lesage, Pierre's wares included ergot, *droué* ("an herb still more dangerous than ergot"), and mandrake.[147] Sorceresses also purchased sedatives such as opium. When ingested in high doses, the narcotics brought eternal, rather than a single night's, rest. The sorceresses, who distilled their own lethal brews, could avail themselves, too, of hemlock, vitriol or sulfuric acid, *flocely* (a type of poisonous mushroom), aloe, and meadow buttercup, an herb that caused facial contortions, so that its victims died while smiling dementedly.[148] The sorceresses also distilled biting stonecrop (known as *vermiculaire* or *tête-de-souris*) and juniper—poisons that caused the victim to feel that his digestive system was burning up.[149]

The *secret du crapaud* was reputed to be the most lethal and undetectable of toxins as well as the poison used by the marquise de Brinvilliers.[150] It was also perhaps the most costly; La Bosse, herself a manufacturer of the toad poison, claimed that a small vial sold for two hundred *louis d'or.*[151] Recipes for the *secret du crapaud* seem to have been closely guarded trade secrets, but tales about how it could be manufactured circulated among the members of the criminal magical underworld. La Deslauriers described one method of which she had heard tell. A woman named Ménardière, La Deslauriers said, told her that if she took some salt and administered it to a toad, the toad would start to foam at the mouth. If La Deslauriers scraped up the foam and added it to an enema, the person who ingested the poison would die and no one would be able to determine the cause of death.[152] The abbé Guibourg claimed to know another means of manufacturing toad poison. A sorceress named La David, he claimed, had revealed her *secret du crapaud*. She prepared it by placing a live toad in a box that had been pierced with small holes. She would then bury the box in a hole in the ground and ants would enter the box through the tiny holes and kill the toad. Once the toad and the ants were dried and ground up into powder, they "were an excellent poison."[153]

François Belot, a soldier and the son of Marie Bosse, claimed that he had learned how to infuse a silver goblet with toad poison so that whoever drank from the vessel would die. He had been told, he said, that he only needed to "take a toad, whip it, and make it swallow arsenic, and then kill it in the cup or the silver vessel that you want to poison."[154] It was the toad's urine, Belot added, that formed the poison. While this method, by Belot's own admission, never succeeded in actually poisoning anybody, it nonetheless produced a lethal substance. Lucien Nass argues persuasively that in response to such abuse, the toad would have attempted to ward off its tormentors by releasing venom from glands located under its skin. Furthermore, Nass suggests, if the dead toad was left to putrefy in the cup, the liquid from its decomposing body, in combination with its own venomous secretions and the arsenic it had been fed, would have created a highly toxic poison.[155]

A number of counterpoisons had been developed in response to the plethora of poisons available and the considerable anxiety poisoning provoked during the seventeenth century. The French public, including the criminal magical underworld, demonstrated confidence in several. The most popular, orviétan, was sold exclusively by an Italian apothecary named Cristoforo Contugi from his shop on the rue Dauphine.[156] It was a complex concoction calling for more than thirty herbs and apparently proved effectual; François Belot testified that he had taken it himself after being poisoned.[157] Orviétan was similar in composition to a much more expensive counterpoison, reputedly developed in ancient Greece. Known as thériaque de Mithridate, the remedy contained sixty-four ingredients, including opium and viper's flesh.[158]

Other seventeenth-century counterpoisons were less effective than their contemporary reputations suggested. Early modern kings and queens carefully guarded unicorn horns (which in actuality were usually the twisted horns of arctic narwhals) in their treasuries; unicorn horn, it had long been believed, was not only an antidote but reacted in the presence of poison, thus alerting its potential victim.[159] The magician Lesage believed that bezoar, a calcified stone formed in the stomach of an herbivore, could nullify the effects of poison. "Bézoard corrects all," he assured his interrogators.[160] Chardon bénit, or thistle, was also thought to be a counterpoison, as were milk and olive oil. A perhaps more useful antidote was to follow advice similar to that found on household cleaning products today: if swallowed, induce vomiting. La Chéron, for example, testified that when she had believed herself poisoned, she drank her own urine so that she would regurgitate what she had ingested.[161]

Both men and women sought to assure themselves a prosperous and autonomous future in seventeenth-century Paris by locating lost treasure, entering into love

affairs, and physically eliminating the inconvenient people who stood in
of their desires. Members of both sexes purchased deadly rituals and "inhe
powders" from members of the criminal magical underworld—both men and
women, after all, could inherit.[162] While men had other opportunities to acquire
financial independence, women could attain such privileges only through inheritance. It is perhaps not surprising, therefore, that women made up the majority of
the sorceresses' clientele. Their use of magic proved highly subversive of the social
order as well as of religious orthodoxy, however, for it undermined the limits
imposed on women's behavior and thus threatened the institution of the family,
the doctrine of the Catholic Church, and by extension the state itself. By helping
women try to achieve control over men's passions with charms and ceremonies
of love magic, the sorceresses and magicians of Paris symbolically corrupted the
social order. By helping them rid themselves of their husbands, the members of
the criminal magical underworld actively sabotaged it.

# The Renegade Priests of Paris and the Amatory Mass

In an age still saturated with religious values, renegade priests formed the nucleus of the criminal magical underworld of Paris. Their activities placed them at the center of the informal network that linked together practitioners of almost every sort of nefarious activity in the city. The clerics not only acted as sorceresses' suppliers and assistants but functioned as magicians and necromancers in their own right. Like those of the other members of this underworld, their magical practices evolved out of the common tradition of magic that had existed in Europe for centuries. The rogue clerics of the Affair of the Poisons, however, allegedly surpassed the techniques of their medieval forebears as they appropriated the means by which the Catholic Church controlled access to the sacred for their own illicit ends. Their most sacrilegious invention was a unique version of the black mass, a demonic conjuration held over the naked body of a living woman. By performing such ceremonies, they carried the capital crime of "treason against God," or *lèse-majesté divine,* to novel extremes, offering a threat to religious values unmatched by any other Catholic dissidents. This chapter explores the priests' magical activities in the context of the heightened religiosity of Catholic Reformation France, and then turns to an analysis of the priests' most subversive magical ceremony and the challenge it posed to Catholic orthodoxy.

The Affair of the Poisons occurred at the apex of Catholic Reformation conformity in France. By the latter half of the seventeenth century, the efforts of the Gallican church to enforce a comprehensive system of parochial conformity and to promulgate the code of religious practice decreed by the Council of Trent had achieved almost universal success.[1] External observance and devotion were at their apogee as Catholics attended mass each Sunday and holy day as required by canon and state law. Every year the faithful fulfilled their paramount obligation, that of Easter communion, knowing that if they failed in their duty they hazarded excommunication and even privation of Christian burial.[2] French Catholics also received an increased amount of religious instruction as part of the post-Tridentine church's reforming mission. By 1650 parish priests taught almost all children at least a rudimentary catechism, just as the missionaries who crisscrossed the country instructed their parents. Over the course of the seventeenth century, more French men and women than ever before were exposed to the precepts, practices, and priests of the Catholic Church.[3]

Widespread attendance at mass enabled an increasing number of Catholics to witness the weekly miracle performed by the priest as he elevated the host, transforming a simple wafer into the body and blood of Christ. Parishioners understood that priests could perform this sacrament because they had been consecrated by the church and thus had unique access to the divine. Nicolas de la Reynie's investigation into the Affair of the Poisons, however, revealed that many Catholics in late seventeenth-century France believed that the sacerdotal power that allowed priests to perform the miracle of the mass could also be diverted to illicit ends. Priests, they held, could infuse charms with a mystical power that strengthened the charms' inherent magical properties. Furthermore, clerics' cooperation in magical rituals was believed to ensure the efficacy of the ceremonies. While any sorceress or magician could tell one's fortune or create a simple love charm, a serious spell needed the collaboration of a priest. The very functioning of the business of old regime magic, in fact, had a sacral dimension that required priests' participation.[4]

The magical practices of the renegade clerics, although seemingly embraced by scores of Parisians, were sacrilege in the eyes of the Catholic hierarchy. As the lieutenant general of police, the devout La Reynie took the priests' transgressions seriously indeed, not because the priests were involved in "so-called sorcery" but because their actions were so deeply sacrilegious.[5] The divine displeasure hazarded by lay magicians paled in comparison with the dangers risked by the deeply sacrilegious activities of the city's renegade priests. The judges of the Parlement of Paris agreed with La Reynie;[6] while they condemned to death only a handful of people, whether priests or laymen, for *sortilège* between 1625 and 1691, they prosecuted those who committed *sacrilège et profanation* rigorously.[7]

## THE PRIESTS OF THE CLERICAL UNDERWORLD

Priests who dabbled in magic necessarily cloaked their activities in secrecy. The abbé Guibourg was perhaps the most successful in leading the double life his magical endeavors required. He served as curate for a succession of churches in and around Paris over the course of his fifty-year career, including Saint-Jacques-de-l'Hôpital, Saint-Spire in Corbeil, and Saint-Marcel in Saint-Denis.[8] No hint of his illicit activities reached his superiors during that period. Even after Guibourg was arrested in 1679, a *procureur royal* from his town submitted a character reference attesting that the abbé was "a true pillar of the church."[9] According to La Reynie, however, Guibourg was the most reprehensible of those involved in the Affair of the Poisons, a libertine, "a man who could not be compared to any other . . . for his sacrileges and impieties."[10] The abbé's personal appearance must have lent credence to La Reynie's analysis and indeed to early modern beliefs regarding physiognomy, for the seventy-year-old cleric allegedly resembled a debauched vulture. His thick-featured crimson face was disfigured by burst blood vessels and his one good eye leered lasciviously at the world.[11]

Considering the renegade priests' willingness to corrupt the teachings and ceremonies of the church, it is perhaps unsurprising that they led highly irregular personal lives as well. Despite Abbé Guibourg's physical appearance, he did not lack for female companionship. He had several mistresses over the years and fathered a number of children. Guibourg ensured that he would not have to concern himself with his offspring's support; one mistress, La Jeanneton, reportedly told a neighbor, "That devil has debauched me since I was sixteen years old . . . he is the reason I committed massacres."[12] She was apparently referring to the two children she had borne Guibourg; the couple tossed the first child into the river at Marcoussy and exposed the second on the town ramparts of Montlhéry. Guibourg's long-term mistress, Jeanne Chanfrain, bore seven children whose fates may have been even more unfortunate. La Reynie believed that Guibourg had sacrificed several of those infants to the devil during celebrations of the amatory mass.[13]

The police records of the Affair of the Poisons reveal little about the social and economic backgrounds of the forty-six other priests eventually implicated in the scandal. Many renegade clerics served at various churches within Paris—Isaac Gérard at Saint-Saveur, Barthélemy Lemeignan at Saint-Eustache, and Michel Lepreux a *petit bénéficier* at Notre-Dame. As part of the "ecclesiastical proletariat," most held modest positions as sacristans or curates, the ranks of which were traditionally filled by members of artisan or petit-bourgeois families and were often in need of supplementary sources of income. Approximately a third of these religious, however, held benefices that could generate a more comfortable living. Gilles Lefranc is listed in the police records as *prêtre bachelier en theologie de la faculté de Paris*, François Mariette held a position as prior of Sainte-Catherine, and Gilles Davot, chaplain of Notre-Dame de Bonne-Nouvelle in Paris, bore the title *sieur de Barge* as well.[14] While the possession of such benefices probably indicates that they were members of families with higher social status and correspondingly greater income levels than many of their fellow priests, these men were far from wealthy.[15] Consequently, supplementary income may have been the most important reason such men joined the ranks of the clerical underworld, where they could receive sizeable sums of money for their services.[16] Magic could be a lucrative sideline.

Selling the ceremonies of the Catholic Church to customers seeking to sidestep religious rules provided renegade priests with extra income at relatively little risk of exposure. Easter communion, a requirement enforced both legally and socially, created one potential source of revenue. Before Parisians could take communion, they first had to confess their sins. Those unable to repent of their sins, such as the duchesse de Vivonne, found themselves in a quandary. As Easter approached, the duchess recognized that she could not rid her soul of her resentful thoughts toward a Monsieur Duché. Observant Catholic that she was, the duchess knew that to make a false confession would imperil her soul. She resolved to buy a solution instead. According to one witness, Mme de Vivonne paid Father Dussis four *louis d'or* to give her a "white communion," or communion with an unconsecrated host.[17] The duchess thus appeared to fulfill her Easter obligations but did not have to repent of her sins, and Father Dussis probably enjoyed a more bounteous Easter dinner.

Renegade clerics further supplemented their meager incomes by selling church paraphernalia for use in rites of magic. Popular tradition considered Catholic sacramentals to have powerful properties that could be adapted for magical enterprises.[18] While popular religious belief evidently attached a broader meaning to the physical properties of holy things than did orthodox theologians, this misapprehension nonetheless reveals a widespread and profound respect for the power of the objects.[19] Crucifixes, chalices, holy water, candles—all were appropriated for a variety of spells and demonic conjurations. Father Davot, for example, confessed that he had sold Lesage the wax from candles that had been burned at three high masses on Christmas Day.[20] Moreover, magical practitioners exploited the common belief that holy things granted special powers over the passions of others and employed consecrated items in love magic.[21] Lesage went so far as to assure his clients that his love potions (concocted of holy water, salt, sulfur, and incense) were particularly effective because he mixed up his recipes under the shadow of a crucifix containing a fragment of the true cross of Jerusalem.[22]

Paris's renegade priests sold even the most sacred property of the church: the consecrated host. The members of the clerical underworld were of course in an exceptionally privileged position to supply clients with consecrated wafers. In doing so, they committed the most serious type of sacrilege, *lèse-majesté divine*, or treason against God.[23] The Eucharist, considered by Catholics to be the actual flesh and blood of Christ, was far more valuable to magicians than holy water or holy oil, for a consecrated host was believed to possess the most powerful of miraculous properties that could be redirected for illicit use. Europeans had used consecrated wafers in myriad magic spells and ceremonies for centuries, as Jean-Baptiste Thiers's *Traité des superstitions* attests.[24] Shepherds regularly appeared before the Parlement of Rouen during the sixteenth and seventeenth centuries, for example, charged with either stealing the Eucharist to feed to their flocks in the belief that this would protect the sheep from wolves and disease, or for using them "with certain words in order to seduce girls."[25] Consecrated wafers were even put to use in rituals of necromancy, when the power of the central mystery of the mass was used to compel powerful demons to obey the necromancer who had summoned them.[26] Necromancy had long been condemned by the Catholic Church as idolatrous; the use of the Eucharist in demonic ceremonies compounded an already mortal sin. Those convicted of such sacrilegious acts, "the most horrible in the world," were invariably put to death.[27]

The renegade clerics arrested during the Affair of the Poisons procured communion wafers so that they might themselves celebrate rituals of love magic. Abbé Guibourg confessed that he often employed the Eucharist to such amatory ends in the rituals he performed for his clients. On an unconsecrated wafer, he wrote the name of his client and that person's love object. The abbé then celebrated mass with the inscribed host, carefully placing it under a clean wafer to hide it from view. He elevated both during the mass but consumed only the untouched one. Guibourg returned the newly consecrated inscribed host to his client and told her to grind it into fine powder and mix it into her beloved's food.[28]

Renegade priests were frequently commissioned to assist at other magical ceremonies as well. Sorceresses and magicians arranged for priests to consecrate their charms, thus increasing their efficacy. Just as the priest was able to "activate" the miracle of the mass, it was believed, so could he activate magic spells.[29] Lesage regularly sought priestly reinforcement, according to La Voisin. She told her interrogators that a woman named La Desmaretz had requested from the magician a "rod of Aaron," or a spell intended to encourage her lover to marry her.[30] The *verge d'Aaron* called for a branch of hazel that first had to be blessed by a priest wearing his robe and stole. Lesage paid Gilles Davot to do so. Once the hazel had been prepared, Lesage asked La Desmaretz to conduct him to the room in which she and her lover slept. Reciting "per Deum vivum, per Deum verum, per Deum sanctum," he touched the branch to each of the four corners of the bed, and then to each of the four corners of the room. Lesage thus brought the forces of magic and religion to bear upon what his client hoped would become her marriage bed.[31]

Partnerships between Paris's renegade priests and magicians frequently evolved as a result of the interdependence of their professions. Lesage and the abbé Mariette formed perhaps the longest-lasting team, working together for several years before they were arrested in 1668, and reestablishing their association in 1673 after Lesage escaped the galleys. Lesage described one ceremony that, he claimed, he and the abbé Mariette performed for the ambitious vicomtessé de Polignac in 1668.[32] Lesage, Mariette, and their client gathered around a specially prepared altar. Mariette celebrated mass, adding certain amatory conjurations "in between the two elevations, for the designs of the lady Polignac." Next, the abbé blessed two rings "in the name of the king" and then performed a marriage ceremony (ostensibly signifying the creation of a bond between the viscountess and the king). After the mass ended, Mariette gave the viscountess the consecrated host he had used. She placed it in a box that contained a triple conjuration requesting the love of the king, the death of his mistress Louise de la Vallière, and the death of M. de Polignac. The box also contained a piece of paper with verses from the Gospels and a magical star-shaped drawing upon which Mariette had written "Ortus refulget Lucifer."[33] Mariette and Lesage told the viscountess the spell would be completed when she opened the box and read the conjuration aloud.[34]

The cost of the magical ceremonies provided by the renegade clerics and their partners was calculated on a rough sliding scale determined by the wealth of the client, the intricacy of the spell, and the danger of detection. Charms that could be said safely in private were relatively inexpensive: thirty *sols* for a spell over a consecrated host or an *écu* to bless a sprig of hazel to use in a love charm.[35] Spells that risked public exposure bore a higher price. Guibourg claimed he had received forty or fifty *pistoles* to celebrate a mass at his church in Saint-Denis with consecrated wafers upon which had been written the name of the man whom his client wanted to marry. The ceremony was intended to make the man fall hopelessly in love with her.[36] Davot charged a gold *écu* to slip a *billet* onto the altar as he celebrated a public mass at Notre-Dame de Bonne-Nouvelle. The note contained a prayer that his client believed would come true after it had been consecrated: that she might win the heart of a certain abbé and that her husband would die.[37]

Among the many types of love charms that priests were called upon to consecrate were those containing bodily materials that reputedly possessed occult properties. Several priests arrested during the Affair of the Poisons confessed that they had frequently been asked to bless cauls and afterbirths and had even performed rites over fetuses and dead newborns. As was their practice with any magical item, the renegade priests celebrated mass over the reproductive material to intensify its magical powers.[38] Guibourg blessed several afterbirths brought to him by La Voisin and La Pelletier. According to Marie-Marguerite Montvoisin, the abbé placed the afterbirths on the altar during mass at his church in Saint-Denis.[39] Evidently the mass was not a public one.

As priests possessed the ability to infuse magic charms with sacerdotal power, they were also accounted capable of activating personal prayers. If a priest placed the end of his stole on the head of a kneeling supplicant and read part of the liturgy (the Gospel of John was most frequently selected), it was believed that the supplicant's petition to heaven would be granted. The Catholic Church considered the practice licit, as even Thiers admitted, and thus it was commonly used by those seeking relief from illnesses or physical afflictions.[40] The clients of Paris's renegade clerics often requested that the ritual be performed to less creditable ends, however. Court aristocrats such as the princesse de Thianges, the duchesse de Vivonne, and the comtesse de Soissons, all seeking success in love affairs, allegedly had verses from the Gospels said over their heads in this manner.[41] Reading the liturgy over a client's head could sacralize more nefarious purposes as well. Police records contain frequent accounts of women who had the ceremony performed to solicit divine aid in ridding themselves of unwanted spouses.[42] La Vertemart, for example, hired Lesage and Father Davot to help her bring about the death of her husband and that of her lover's wife. La Vertemart described the ceremony for her interrogators: "Davot, having placed his stole on his neck, and wearing his surplice, made her get on her knees. After placing one of the ends of the stole on her head, he recited prayers which she believed were Gospels. . . . Davot came another time to her aunt's house, where he said a mass over her head while wearing his surplice and stole."[43]

Of all the magical ceremonies a priest could be hired to perform in seventeenth-century France, the riskiest were those that involved necromancy. Necromancy, or the practice of learned demonic magic, employs ritual to compel demons to obey the orders of the necromancer. The practice was considered perilous not only because demons were considered beings not to be trifled with, but also because the civil penalty for conducting such sacrilegious ceremonies was death. Conjuring demons required that the necromancer possess a *grimoire,* or magic manual, and great force of will. In circulation since the early medieval era among the members of the clerical underworld, *grimoires* such as *The Clavicule of Solomon,* the *Petit Albert,* and the *Book of the Conjurations of Pope Honorius* described for the necromancer the ritual space and language by which he would be able to call forth demons.[44] Merely following a manual's instructions, however, did not guarantee a successful outcome. Strength of will was necessary to compel the powerful and malignant spirits to comply with the commands of the necromancer. Only if the necromancer triumphed in the contest of wills with the demons he had summoned could he force them to carry out his desires.[45]

By the Middle Ages, both popular and learned tradition held that the majority of necromancers were clerics, a stereotype whose basic accuracy is borne out by judicial records of the period.[46] The number of necromancers involved in the Affair of the Poisons indicates that the association continued into the late seventeenth century, for all but one of the men accused of necromancy were clerics (the exception was Lesage). The renegade priests and abbés of the affair shared several characteristics that may have given them a taste for demonic magic. Like all clerics, they had received some education and thus possessed at least a basic knowledge of Latin and a degree of familiarity with the rites of exorcism. While knowledge of Latin was certainly not limited to the clergy in the seventeenth century, priests did possess both a facility with ritual forms and a command of ritual language that provided them with a sense of ownership over that vocabulary and therefore perhaps an affinity for ritual magic. Their education may also have introduced them to astrological images or other forms of magic. When coupled with access to books of demonic magic, such an education provided all the tools necessary for experimenting with necromancy.[47]

Ordained priests made the most capable necromancers, the French believed, because the unique ritual power of those ordained by the church allowed them to function as mediators between the supernatural and natural worlds.[48] As one of Guibourg's clients explained, "a priest was necessary . . . to make the demon appear."[49] The *Book of the Conjurations of Pope Honorius* also deemed the presence of a priest essential to any ritual of necromancy. This *grimoire* called for "a bold priest without any fear or dread, who is well versed in his religion." Others who attended the ceremony could not affect the priest's contest of wills with the invoked demon "because the entire affair depends absolutely upon the character of the priest; the other persons are merely witnesses."[50]

As many renegade priests involved in the Affair of the Poisons possessed manuals of conjurations and other works of necromancy, they presumably took more than a merely financial interest in their work. While very few of these forty-seven clerics were willing to confess to an abiding interest in the occult arts, several owned copies of the *Enchiridium* [sic] *Leonis Papae,* a *grimoire* that included love spells, demonic ceremonies that would bring about marriages or find hidden treasure, and magical rituals to ensure the death of one's enemies.[51] Such manuscripts were expensive but not prohibitively so; one cleric reported that "a small handwritten book containing several conjurations" had cost him an *écu.*[52] Guibourg owned quite an extensive collection of magical texts. Among the papers seized at his home after his arrest, the Paris police discovered a *Conjuration du miroires magiques ou autrement dit des tenebres,* a manual that offered instructions for creating a magical mirror in which a demon would appear to reveal the future. They also found a document that explained how to fashion a wax effigy to cause death or grievous harm to an enemy, several recipes for love charms, and countless conjurations for summoning the demon Salam to do the necromancer's will.[53]

Before any of the demonic ceremonies described by a *grimoire* could be attempted, the book itself had to be consecrated. The consecration of a *grimoire* was a lengthy process requiring that a priest celebrate mass over the book every morning for a lengthy series of days. The abbé Guibourg described one series that he had conducted: "In a house on the rue de la Pelleterie, at the home of a tailor named La Coudray. . . . Debret and Degennes . . . brought him the necessary ornaments that he needed to celebrate the mass, that he said them in a room during nine days, over a book which he placed under the chalice while saying the mass. And after this he [Guibourg] gave them the book. La Coudray paid for the masses; and for what he was doing, they gave him a cassock and a robe. . . . The masses were said during nine days, at seven in the morning. Between the two elevations, he recited the conjuration that was in the manuscript to make the consecration."[54]

Each *grimoire* included specific instructions concerning its own consecration. The *Book of the Conjurations of Pope Honorius* instructed a priest to recite a series of prayers imploring divine aid for his demonic enterprises. The manual was to be placed "wrapped in linen, under the altar cloth, next to the host during the mass."[55] The priest was then to baptize the manuscript, "wearing his surplice and his stole around his neck, having a sprinkler filled with milfoil, a lit holy candle."[56] The priest was to recite, "All-powerful God, I pray you by your sainted goodness and mercy to bless, consecrate, and sanctify this book . . . and that all the spirits come somewhere where they will obey me and that they do all that is contained in this book each time and when they will please me, without any evil or offense to my body or my soul, by the power of our lord Jesus Christ." After a further series of prayers, the priest was to continue, "I conjure you, O book, that you will be profitable to those who use you in all their affairs, I conjure you by the virtue of the blood of Jesus Christ contained in this chalice, that for all days you will be good to those that read you."[57] Once the priest completed the mass and elevated the host over the *grimoire*, it was ready to be used to summon demons.

To perform these demonic ceremonies, a renegade priest literally cloaked himself in the power of the church. A cleric who conducted such a ritual was required to dress in his priestly vestments, just as anyone performing a professional service in the seventeenth century was expected to dress in the appropriate garments of his or her occupation.[58] As Barthélemy Lemeignan explained, when interrogated as to whether or not he was wearing his surplice and stole during a necromantic ceremony that promised to reveal the location of buried treasure, "One could not accomplish it [the conjuration] without them."[59] Vestments were so critical to the success of the enterprise that Lesage dressed himself as a priest before he attempted his own conjurations. Evidently hoping to deceive the demons, or perhaps impress his clients, he "disguised himself in a black skirt, a white shirt on top of it which was belted with a belt such as priests have."[60] For a layman to appropriate clerical practice successfully, he had to appropriate clerical garb as well.

The priest-necromancer bolstered his strength with the ritual forms and objects of the church as he prepared to do battle with the invoked demon. Wearing his stole around his neck, the cleric clasped a flask of holy water and flourished a branch of hazel as he traced a protective circle on the ground, inscribing in it the appropriate magical words for the particular demon he wished to summon. The cleric began the conjuration on an altar that had been prepared just as if a licit mass were to be held, complete with chalice, pyx, and consecrated host. A consecrated host, as a member of the criminal magical underworld confirmed, "renders conjurations more powerful, and has the power to make the demon appear."[61] The demonic ritual also required that witnesses be present to respond to the mass. When questioned, witnesses consistently described the demonic mass as "the same as an ordinary mass" in which the priest elevated the host and then consumed it.[62]

## A Novel Sacrilege: The Amatory Mass

The culmination of the renegade priests' ability to practice necromancy during this period was the celebration of an amatory mass. Celebrated over the naked body of a living woman, this mass marked the point of convergence between demonic magic and love magic. The logic of popular magical tradition dictated that if a priest could perform the miracle of the mass and exorcize demons, then he could perform the opposites of these rites as well.[63] The ultimate inverse of the Christian rituals was the black mass, in which a priest consecrated the unholy and summoned demons to do his will. The renegade priests of the Affair of the Poisons confessed to performing demonic rituals similar, yet not identical, to black masses. The black mass is a form of Satan worship; the ceremony parodies the licit mass and is intended to culminate in the appearance of the devil in either human or bestial form. These renegade priests, however, followed the framework of the orthodox mass, intending not to parody it but to harness its miraculous powers.[64]

Participation in such sacrilegious ceremonies as the amatory mass speaks profoundly to the religiosity of the renegade clerics' clients. Protestants and other skeptics who did not believe that ordained priests could perform the miracle of transubstantiation would have no reason to concern themselves with ceremonies attempting to harness its power. Nor would they commission ceremonies of love magic that employed Catholic sacramentals, or purchase charms to recite during mass, or hire renegade priests to strengthen the power of their prayers by reciting the Gospels over their heads. Rather than evidence of the failure of the Catholic Reformation to catechize the inhabitants of the Sun King's capital, then, this intense interest in magic can be seen as testimony to the deep religiosity of the age. Neither La Reynie nor his royal master took the travestied masses lightly. Like a majority of devout Catholics of the period, they were genuinely shocked by the revelations of the renegade priests' activities. The police lieutenant and the king understood that these amatory masses not only subverted the teachings of the church but threatened the order of the state that was buttressed by that institution.

While an amatory mass could presumably be celebrated for any purpose, it was too serious a transgression to be performed for trivial reasons. During the Affair of the Poisons, the majority of such masses were said to win love and to cause death. As we have seen, these objectives were often interrelated. Women from all classes allegedly contracted for such diabolical aid. La Voisin accused Mmes Leféron (widow of a *président* of the Parlement) and de Dreux (widow of a *maître des requêtes*) of commissioning masses to cause their husbands' deaths so that they could marry their lovers.[65] Lesage "remembered that Guibourg had also said masses over the stomachs of the comtesse d'Argenton, of La Saint-Pont, and the wife of Baudonin."[66] The cost of the ceremonies, however (Guibourg claimed that he had been offered fifty *pistoles* and an ecclesiastical benefice worth two thousand *livres* for a series of three), was prohibitive enough to restrict the clientele largely to members of the wealthier classes.[67]

Abbé Guibourg claimed to have conducted three amatory masses, in 1667, 1676, and 1679, for Mme de Montespan, who reportedly wished to inflame the love of the king and to vanquish her rivals. The particular importance of Guibourg's client made La Reynie question him extremely carefully, and his descriptions offer some of the most elaborate accounts of such masses found anywhere in the voluminous records of the Affair of the Poisons.[68] The steps of this mass mirrored those of its licit counterpart. It required that the priest be robed in his vestments and employ the usual church paraphernalia: altar, chalice, and pyx to hold the consecrated wafers. Like an orthodox mass, the amatory version required a witness to say the responses. Unlike an ordinary mass, however, it also required candles made of "new yellow wax and the fat of a hanged man," a mattress, and a newborn baby.[69]

According to Abbé Guibourg, an amatory mass was celebrated not over a stone altar but directly over the *ventre,* or stomach, of a living woman.[70] Ideally, but not necessarily, the woman who had commissioned the mass served as the altar during the ceremony. The woman stretched naked on the mattress that had been placed over the altar, her head supported by a pillow held by an overturned chair. A napkin was spread over her stomach, a cross set upon it, and the chalice positioned on her belly. Once everything was in place, Guibourg approached the altar, robed in his alb, stole, and chasuble. He took a sheet of virgin parchment, upon which the client had written her wishes, and placed it under the chalice. Guibourg then said mass "in the ordinary way, as one is accustomed to hear it"[71] but added a crucial change—he read aloud his client's wishes from the virgin parchment as he elevated the host: "Astaroth, Asmodée, princes of love, I conjure you to accept the sacrifice of this infant that I present to you for the things that I ask, which are that the love of the king and the dauphin continues, to be honored by the princes and princesses of the court, and that nothing will be denied to me of all that I will ask of the king, my relatives, and my followers."[72]

As the conjuration summoned the demons to the altar, the blood of an infant enticed them there. Guibourg raised a penknife and slit the throat of the newborn that had been brought for the purpose, then poured its blood into the chalice. Guibourg then "took the infant's body, opened the heart to draw out the curdled blood within it, put it in a vase prepared for that effect," with which he also "placed pieces of the consecrated host, and this was taken away by the woman on whose stomach he had said the mass" to be used as a love philter.[73] At the completion of an amatory mass (although not at the ceremonies reportedly performed over Mme de Montespan herself), Guibourg alleged that he "knew carnally" the woman who had served as his altar.[74]

The amatory masses of the Affair of the Poisons blended the old and the new.

The tale of the ritual sacrifice of infants has a history at least as old as Christianity itself. Over the course of the centuries, the accusation has been leveled against early Christians, medieval Jews, and early modern witches.[75] Historians have often argued that the myth of ritual sacrifice was simply a legend connected only tangentially, if at all, with historical reality, but it is possible that the priests who described these amatory masses were not merely adding lurid details to their confessions. The ring of probability adheres to the richly sacrilegious details, as well as to the court connections of the clients. The infants sacrificed at the masses in order that "the demons would be obliged to appear" may well have been aborted fetuses or prematurely born infants provided by the sorceresses who worked in tandem with the renegade priests, for the sorceresses provided abortion services as well as love magic for their clients. Furthermore, the use of parts of a fetus in magic was not unknown in medieval or early modern Europe. Albertus Magnus wrote during the thirteenth century that women might prevent pregnancy if they wore an amulet containing weasel testicles, a child's teeth, and the finger of a fetus. In *Occult Physique*, the seventeenth-century English author William Williams similarly asserted, "The middle finger of an Abortive, being worn around a woman's neck, will keep her from conceiving."[76]

Statements from those who witnessed the ceremonies corroborate these details. The daughter of La Voisin, for example, described the infant she claimed to have seen sacrificed at Mme de Montespan's amatory mass as "born before term."[77] She also attested that she had seen a priest concoct a love potion with pieces of the body of an infant aborted by La Lepère. These potions were actually made from the distilled corpse or, more commonly, the distilled entrails of a baby. The sorceresses distilled sacrificed infants in order to extract "the purest essences" from their bodies, following alchemical practices outlined in editions of such treatises as Remaclus's *History of All Waters*.[78]

Infants were also supposedly sacrificed in other demonic ceremonies, most commonly rituals intended to solicit supernatural aid in finding treasure or bringing about advantageous marriages.[79] The ceremonies were not said over the womb of a naked woman but were otherwise quite similar to amatory masses. La Reynie's notes include La Joly's description of one ceremony performed by the curé of Saint-Mesmin in Orléans: "He took a new knife and cut the throat of the newborn . . . it was done at night, in the garden, where the curé said the mass wearing new sacerdotal robes. . . . The sacrifice of the infant was to make succeed a marriage that she [La Joly] had arranged, and for which she received 200 *livres,* of which she gave the priest who had performed the sacrifice a share . . . and the curé de Saint-Mesmin placed the blood of the sacrificed infant into the chalice, which he carried off, saying that it could be used for other marriages."[80]

La Reynie did not discount the possibility that the sacrifices of newborns had taken place. In his notes on the case, he recalled an episode three years earlier, when rumors that children were being kidnapped and their throats cut had touched off riots around Paris. He had not been able to locate the source of that rumor at the time. La Reynie mused, "As for the infant sacrifices, the practice is not new; Scripture speaks of this abomination among the Jews. Bodin, one of the most learned men that France has ever had, having applied himself to research the so-called magicians and sorcerers, discovered that they were nothing but poisoners, practicing all sorts of evils, and who, to render these same magical practices more terrible, and to give them more weight, also sacrifice infants to the devil, and perform the same abominations."[81] But as far as La Reynie could ascertain, the infant sacrifices that served as the climaxes of amatory masses were unprecedented. He concluded in a report to the king, "It is difficult to assume that the crimes are possible; they seem so new and so strange that it is painful even to consider them. However, as these villains themselves declare it, and they include so many details and list so many occasions, it is difficult to doubt them."[82]

The use of a woman's body as the altar for the amatory mass, however, was as novel an allegation as the ritual sacrifice of an innocent baby was common. The celebration of the ceremony over a naked woman created a singular form of love magic that was simultaneously spiritual and sexual. The priest, himself both spiritual and sexual, used certain ritual objects during the ceremony: crucifixes, hosts, and altar. The power of the ritual objects was completed by the presence of a sexual object: the body. The naked woman who constituted the altar literally participated in the consecration of the holiest of mysteries. Her body touched the sacrament and thus absorbed more of the priestly magic than could any ordinary communicant. Tellingly, the very center of the ritual took place directly over her *ventre*, her genitals. The ceremony thus infused her sexual organs with the most powerful love magic that could be created.

Renegade priests were the definitive magicians of seventeenth-century France. As no truly powerful magic could be performed without their participation, they stood at the very heart of the criminal underworld of Paris, linking sorceresses, abortionists, poisoners, and a host of other criminals with the usually law-abiding subjects of the crown. Serving the illicit desires of treasure hunters, would-be widows, and aspiring royal mistresses, the renegade priests confessed they had undermined the tenets of the Catholic Church in ways previously undreamed of. Their amatory masses, completely void of theological content yet alarmingly attractive to a wide—and ostensibly devout—audience that included a number of Louis XIV's own courtiers, flouted Catholic orthodoxy. Before the abbé Guibourg and his fellow clerics recounted their deeds to La Reynie, nothing quite like these ceremonies had ever been documented.

The sacrileges the renegade priests carried to such novel extremes were probably never as seditious or powerful as they were during the decade of the 1670s, the chronological center of the Catholic Reformation in France. Protestantism, intellectually decadent and well on its way to legal extinction, was the only viable religiously subversive alternative to Reformation Catholicism was Jansenism.[83] Within this context, Louis XIV and his judges took extremely seriously the physical probability of the illicit masses and other magical ceremonies performed by the city's renegade priests, and considered them a danger to the very core of religious values. As such, these sacrilegious practices threatened the state that relied upon the teachings of the Catholic Church to maintain order.

Consequently, performing amatory masses and other rites of Christian magic proved a risky business for the clerical underworld. While the fate of many of the forty-seven clerics implicated in the Affair of the Poisons remains unknown, the extant judicial records reveal that many of them paid a heavy price for their flamboyant sacrilege. The king and La Reynie considered the disclosures of Étienne Guibourg, Michel Lepreux, and Gilles Lefranc too damning to risk executing these priests publicly; they would have been entitled to make their final confessions at the foot of the scaffold. They spent the remainder of their lives in solitary confinement, chained to the wall of their fortress cells. François Mariette evaded a like fate only by dying in the prison of Vincennes. Because they were not convicted of profaning the Eucharist, Jacques Leroy, Barthélemy Lemeignan, and Jacques Lemaire escaped relatively lightly, each fined fifty *livres* and banished from the kingdom for a period of years.

Jacques Cotton and Gilles Davot, however, received the full measure of ancien régime justice.[84] The hangman's rope dangling around his neck, dressed only in a shirt and holding a heavy candle of white wax, each was forced to beseech the forgiveness of God, the king, and justice for his actions in a public apology performed before the cathedral of Notre-Dame. The priests were then placed in a tumbrel and conducted through the streets to the place de Grève for execution. As perpetrators of the most horrific crimes, they were burned alive in a pyramid of kindling stacked so high that only their heads could be seen. The French criminal code intended such punishment to serve as an example and deterrent; the state's condemnation of the renegade priests who had "insulted God" would not be forgotten by the crowd who witnessed their ashes being cast to the wind.

# The Magic of Mistresses at the Court of Louis XIV

The suspects under investigation during the Affair of the Poisons included a score of Louis XIV's courtiers who had allegedly sought supernatural assistance from members of the criminal magical underworld to further their financial, political, and amatory aspirations. For the majority of these aristocrats, the king was the focus of their ambitions. The most prominent name among them was Louis's official mistress, Athénaïs de Montespan, who had apparently become a regular client of a notorious Parisian sorceress. Madame de Montespan's illicit activities were not unique, however; La Reynie's investigation revealed that many of the highest-ranking women at court had purchased similar magical services as they vied with each other for the heart of the king. In order to understand this phenomenon, it is necessary to examine the role of women within the elaborate structure and ceremonial of Louis XIV's court.

The vogue for ceremonies of illicit love magic exposed by the Affair of the Poisons developed at a time when aristocratic women, despite their exclusion from public political participation, were able to wield unparalleled influence within the circles of Louis XIV's court. By inducing the members of the ancient nobility to neglect their regional power bases in favor of the social and economic rewards of court attendance, the king cultivated the cooperation of his aristocracy.[1] In this way he engendered a court society that, while restrictive of traditionally male forms of power, permitted considerable female influence, based to a great degree upon romantic intrigue. As Mme de Lafayette observed of the court in *The Princesse de Clèves*, "There were countless interests at stake, countless different factions, and women played such a central part in them that love was always entangled with politics and politics with love."[2] The most influential woman at court, therefore, was the one most intimately involved with its most powerful man—Louis XIV.

Inspired by Ernst Kantorowicz's seminal work, scholars such as Ralph Giesey and his students have shown that the central rituals of the French monarchy reveal that the body of the king was understood to be almost the literal embodiment of royal power.[3] As Louis XIV himself remarked, "In France, the nation is not a separate body but resides entirely in the person of the king."[4] Nonetheless, few historians have considered the sexual aspect of the king's mortal body as a source of status and power.[5] Because the king's body was the locus of power at court, access to his person imparted political privilege. This political privilege flowed from any type of access, whether from attending the king at the ritual *lever* or by accompanying him on expeditions to Versailles. The greatest opportunities to earn such political influence, however, were accessible only to the noblewomen at his court; Louis's female courtiers could gain the closest physical proximity possible by means of a sexual relationship with the king.

The years from 1661 to 1683 offered the greatest opportunities for noblewomen to fulfill their political ambitions in this way. Louis XIV's personal rule began in 1661; his morganatic marriage to Françoise de Maintenon in 1683 brought an end to his indulgence in extramarital romances. During this twenty-two-year period, Louis's *maîtresse en titre* became the unofficial or "shadow" queen of the court, wielding a great deal of influence within its networks and cabals. Understandably, becoming Louis's mistress was a goal shared by a number of women at court during this time, and the king granted many of them an opportunity to fulfill their ambitions.[6]

This chapter assesses the official and unofficial functions of women at Louis XIV's court, the heart of the political system of seventeenth-century France.[7] Concentrating on the earlier part of Louis XIV's reign, it first examines how courtiers exercised power and influence and compares the experiences of female and male aristocrats. It then analyzes the role played by Louis's *maîtresse en titre*, the woman who was able to rule the court as its shadow queen. Finally, it turns to a singular, but not unprecedented, means by which would-be royal mistresses attempted to prey upon the affections of the king: love magic.


## Place, Power, and Privilege at Court

Before the court was permanently settled at Versailles, only those men and women who held office lived at court. Nobles saw this type of service to their king as a privilege of their status; serving Louis was a duty that conferred honor equally upon the king and his noble attendants.[8] In addition to such satisfactions, offices provided nobles with opportunities for social advancement, conferred distinction, and often commanded hefty salaries, but could nonetheless entail extremely hard work.[9] While the most prestigious offices were those of the *maison du roi*, as they entailed the closest contact with the king, the sheer number of people required to manage the daily operations of the court meant that there were dozens of other posts as well. Nobles of the sword staffed the majority of offices, the most prestigious of which were reserved for men who held the rank of duke or higher.[10] Louis XIV's court also included the households of the members of the royal family, which were smaller-scale versions of the *maison du roi*. There were several royal households during the first twenty years of Louis's reign, including that of the queen, the queen mother, the king's brother and his wife, and those of the dauphin and dauphine.[11] Consequently, even before its permanent establishment at Versailles in 1682, the court included more than six hundred noblemen and -women, as well as hundreds of servants, guards, officials of the king's government, and officers of the army and of the royal households.[12]

Despite the advantages that accompanied court attendance, Louis's male aristocrats found that life at court restricted the independence of action they had once enjoyed. The great nobles who lived at his court and served in the royal households could no longer maintain the extensive entourages that had traditionally been their prerogative. Thus their clienteles in the provinces gradually declined over the course of Louis XIV's reign, to be replaced by ministerial administrative networks linked to the crown. The crown's creation of a standing army similarly diminished the extent of noble clientage. After 1661 noblemen were required to buy commissions to serve as officers in the royal army, reducing their ability to maintain a military clientage separate from the crown.[13] Male nobles thus found themselves more dependent on royal patronage than they had been during the reign of any previous monarch.[14]

By contrast, the Sun King's court offered noblewomen greater prospects for political power and influence than they would have found in the relative isolation of their provincial estates. Women held significant positions within the administrative and residential complex of the court, serving as officeholders in the queen's household. (Louis, however, controlled appointments to his wife's household as well as his own.)[15] As in the king's household, the most prestigious offices in the *maison de la reine* were those that granted the greatest amount of access to the monarch.[16] The queen's household was composed of approximately the same departments as that of her husband, but with telling differences. It was far smaller than the king's, and unlike the king's *gentilshommes de la chambre,* the queen's maids of honor and attendant ladies received no official salary. The king often intended such appointments to be rewards for fathers, brothers, or husbands rather than for the appointees themselves. Furthermore, the principal officeholders in the queen's household could not purchase their positions, and they possessed no rights over their appointments; Louis could revoke them at will.[17] The holders of these offices were thus more dependent upon the king's favor than their male counterparts in the *maison du roi*.[18]

Female nobles found more significant opportunity to exercise power and influence at court through the back channels of the shadow hierarchy.[19] The shadow hierarchy, the second of two distinct hierarchies at court that together determined a noble's position and privileges, can best be understood as a complement to the fixed, formal hierarchy expressed in the order of precedence at court.[20] The order of the formal hierarchy was dictated by lineage; the more ancient and prestigious the house, the more elevated the rank of its members.[21]

Formal Court Hierarchy

I. Persons of the First Quality / Persons with Rank
King—Queen
Dauphin—Dauphine
Sons and Daughters of France
Grandsons and Granddaughters of France
Princes and Princesses of the Blood—Cardinals
Foreign Princes and Princesses—Royal Bastards
Duke-peers and Duchesses

II. Persons of Quality without Rank
Marquis and Marquises
Counts and Countesses
Viscounts and Viscountesses
Barons and Baronnesses

III. Roturiers / Third Estate[22]

As the chart above indicates, the king stood at the apex of this pyramid of status. Below the monarch, in descending order, stood the queen, the dauphin, and the Children of France, who together formed the *maison royale*. Those of royal blood followed in a precise order, their privileges determined by how closely related they were to the king. After royalty came the nobles of the sword. First among the court nobility stood the *ducs et pairs* and their wives, who were in turn ranked according to the antiquity of their houses.[23] The duke-peers preceded the dukes and duchesses, who were themselves followed by the other members of the *noblesse d'épée*: marquis, counts, and viscounts, all of whom aspired to the title of *duc et pair*.[24] It is important to note that noble rank did not necessarily imply right of access to the king or even bestow the privilege of attending court.[25] While the French nobility as a whole numbered 125,000 individuals in the late seventeenth century, only the 250 men and women who were "people of quality"—princes of the blood, foreign princes, duke-peers, dukes, cardinals, and marshals—were considered worthy to be the close companions of the king.[26]

The nobles of the robe who filled the offices of the royal administration were the final group at court ranked in the formal hierarchy.[27] The position of the nobles of the robe in the official order of precedence was determined by the prestige of the royal offices they had purchased, as was their power at court.[28] The most important were the four secretaries of state: war, foreign affairs, Paris-royal house-marine, and Huguenot affairs.[29] Although they lacked the social rank to move in the highest circles at court, their political influence was nonetheless considerable — as long as they enjoyed the king's good graces.[30] Without the prestige conferred by irreproachable noble descent, they were far more vulnerable to fluctuations of the king's favor than their counterparts among the *noblesse d'épée*. Saint Simon summed up the ministers' position succinctly: "The old maréchal de Villeroy, an old hand at court, used to say jokingly that you had to hold a minister's chamber pot as long as he was in power, and dump it on his head the moment you noticed he was slipping."[31]

In contrast to the fixed formal hierarchy, the shadow hierarchy was fluid, its order determined by qualities less tangible than lineage. It mirrored its official counterpart but was more finely nuanced as well as far less stable, reflecting relative status at a given moment in time. In addition to descent, the shadow hierarchy took into account individual qualities. Physical beauty, great wealth, perfect manners, courageous military exploits, or even a reputation for wit could help to raise a noble to a higher position than his or her lineage earned in the formal hierarchy.[32] The most important factor in determining the relative ranks of the shadow hierarchy, however, was the amount of access to the king an individual courtier possessed. Because the power of the absolute monarchy was invested in the physical body of the king, those privileged enough to have gained proximity to the royal presence secured a great deal of influence over their less fortunate compatriots.[33] Even the appearance of having the king's ear raised one's status in the world of the court.

The shadow hierarchy provided a means for nobles to scale the ranks of the official hierarchy; gains made in the shadow hierarchy could be translated into higher rank in its official counterpart.[34] According to Saint Simon, the duc de Luxembourg waged just such a campaign when he sought to persuade the king that he ought to be granted precedence over the other *ducs et pairs*. "M. de Luxembourg, proud of his successes and the applause of the monde at his triumphs, believed himself strong enough to move from the eighteenth rank of ancientness that he held among his peers to the second, immediately behind M. d'Uzès," wrote the little duke.[35] It was the discrepancy between the courtiers' positions in the official hierarchy and their status in the shadow hierarchy that led to conflict as courtiers competed for the king's favor, the only avenue by which such a promotion within the official hierarchy could be obtained.

Noblewomen, in their capacity as social arbiters, could exert great influence over a courtier's position in the shadow hierarchy.[36] In fact, women headed two of the three major court factions identified by Saint Simon at the end of Louis's reign.[37] The memoirs of Saint Simon are replete with other cases as well. The duchesse de Bourgogne, for example, used her influence with her father-in-law to assuage his displeasure with the duc de Saint Simon; immediately afterward, the duke's *crédit* was restored within the grand dauphin's circle as well as within the wider court.[38] Also of critical importance for ascending the reaches of the unofficial hierarchy were alliances or influence with the powerful individuals who had access to the king, such as his valets, his ministers, or those thought to be his closest advisors.[39]

The formal and shadow hierarchies, taken in conjunction, can be envisioned as a series of narrow staircases leading up to the pinnacle upon which the king majestically perched. There was room for only one person on each step; if someone moved up a step, someone else had to move down.[40] In order to improve their own positions, therefore, courtiers attempted to bring down those above them.[41]

Just as the king's favor dramatically enhanced a noble's position at court, so his displeasure could as rapidly degrade it, for nothing caused a courtier's *crédit* to plummet faster than the king's wrath. Experienced courtiers could consequently take advantage of their superior knowledge of the king and his prejudices to manipulate rivals into embarrassing, if not fatal, faux pas. One such incident served as an object lesson for the entire court. The duc de Lauzun, wishing to disgrace the comte de Tessé, set a trap for the naive count, who knew little of court ceremonial.[42] Lauzun informed the count that *bienséance,* or decorum, bestowed upon a colonel-general of the king's armies (as Tessé was) the privilege of wearing a gray hat while he reviewed his troops. The unwitting man sent off to Paris immediately for a splendid gray hat, trimmed with an enormous feather and an extravagant cockade, to wear the following day when the king was to attend the review of troops. Louis was gravely displeased to see that the count had the temerity to flaunt a hat of such a color when the monarch had made it clear that he disliked it exceedingly. The story immediately circulated at court; Lauzun's intimate knowledge of the king and his habits made Tessé a laughingstock.[43] The ritualized battlefield of the court had claimed another victim.

Thus the single most important consideration in determining a noble's position at court in either hierarchy was the standing she or he had with the king himself. Winning the king's favor was the goal of every courtier, for the king's regard could raise the *crédit* of the most inconsequential.[44] Through his notice, aristocrats improved their places in the hierarchies of the court and gained influence over others who had proved less fortunate in attracting the king's eye.

## The Shadow Queens of the Court

In the heterosexual universe of the court, women seeking to improve their standing possessed an advantage that lay beyond the grasp of male courtiers. Unlike his brother Philippe, Louis XIV had female favorites, and the king was generous with his favors. No courtier achieved greater intimacy with the king than his mistresses, and as physical proximity to the king's body bestowed political power and social prestige, Louis's female courtiers competed to gain access not only to the royal presence but to the royal bed.

The king's bed had long served as the symbolic center of royal authority, as evidenced by the major state ceremonials of the ancien régime. Louis XIII, Louis XIV, and Louis XV were each declared king through an inaugural "bed of justice" before the Parlement of Paris.[45] Their subsequent coronations commenced from another symbolic bed, when two bishops ceremonially awoke the "sleeping" king so that they might lead him into the cathedral proper to be anointed.[46] By the middle of Louis XIV's reign, the focus of royal ceremonial had moved from a metaphorical bed to a literal one when the precisely ordered ceremonies of the *lever*[47] and the *coucher* became the principal rituals of the absolute monarchy.[48] The centrality of the royal bed was made physically manifest in the architecture of the palace of Versailles. The king's bedroom was situated at the heart of the cour de Marbre, the innermost courtyard and the focal point of the approach to the palace. Louis XIV's bed was thus placed at the literal center of his kingdom; palace corridors, garden paths, and even the roads to Versailles all radiated out directly from the *chambre du roi*.[49]

As the king's two beds, mystical and physical, were conflated, so were his two bodies. For the women at court, therefore, access to the king's sexual body could offer unprecedented political advantages. Accordingly, as Primi Visconti observed, "There was not a woman of quality who did not possess an ambition to become the king's mistress."[50] The position of *maîtresse en titre*, in fact, offered the best opportunities to be had since the reign of Henri IV, for Louis XIV's official mistress became the shadow queen of the court and therefore ruled over its shadow hierarchy. Queen Marie-Thérèse, whether out of disinclination or inability (historians usually agree upon the latter; contemporaries considered Louis's wife rather dim-witted) played only a limited role at court. Speaking little French, the queen occupied herself with her devotions and her dwarves and thus left a considerable field of action open to her rivals. Louis's official mistress was consequently accorded far more influence than would have been possible had Marie-Thérèse been able to participate effectively in any of the cabals at court.[51] As Primi Visconti recalled of Athénaïs de Montespan, "Aside from the title, it is certain that Montespan truly reigned and was the real queen."[52] But a *maîtresse en titre* occupied a highly unstable position atop the shadow hierarchy, for her term of office lasted only as long as she could hold the interest of the king.[53]

Sexual intimacy with the king, in the eyes of contemporaries, gave his mistress a unique opportunity to influence the royal will.[54] Madame de Lafayette suggested that the rivalries of the ladies of the court, although always focused on the king, intensified when Louis's personal rule began in 1661: "So a good many people hoped to take part in the government, and a good many ladies, *for reasons not dissimilar,* hoped for an ample share in the King's good graces. They had seen that he was passionately enamored of Mademoiselle de Mancini, and that, to all appearance, she had wielded over him a power as complete as ever a mistress had to sway the heart of a lover. For themselves they hoped that, surpassing her in charms, they might gain at least an equal credit, and many had already chosen for their model the fortunes of the Duchess de Beaufort [Gabrielle d'Estrées, mistress of Henri IV]" (emphasis added).[55]

Louis, unsurprisingly, had quite a different notion about the influence that his mistresses were able to exert over him. In his *Mémoires pour l'an 1667,* he wrote, "One must ensure that the time taken up by one's passions should never be to the prejudice of the work in hand . . . a second, rather more delicate matter to put into practice, which is that, in opening our hearts, we should retain the mastery of our minds, that we should separate our affections as lovers from our decisions as sovereigns, and that the beauty which inspires pleasure in us never has the freedom to interfere in our affairs nor in those of the men who serve us."[56]

Louis seems to have lived up to his first precept and has largely enjoyed the reputation, both contemporary and modern, of having lived up to the second. Certainly he was careful to assure his advisors that he remained in control of his passions, informing Colbert, Lionne, Le Tellier, and Villeroi: "I am young and women generally have considerable influence over those of my age. I enjoin you all, therefore, that should you see that a woman, whoever she may be, has acquired ascendancy over me in the smallest degree, to apprise me immediately of the fact and I shall need only forty-eight hours to rid myself of her and set your minds at rest."[57] In any case, the majority of his courtiers looked upon his affairs with forbearance, perhaps agreeing with Primi Visconti that one "should have some indulgence for this prince if he should fall, surrounded as he is by so many female devils, all seeking to tempt him . . . the worst are the families, fathers, mothers, even husbands" who push their women at him.[58] Louis himself agreed: "The heart of a prince is attacked like a stronghold," he warned his son.[59]

Once attained, a royal mistress's heightened status was rendered visible by court etiquette, which revealed her position to be elevated above all but the queen herself. Louis's mistress subverted the formal hierarchy through her personal relationship to the monarch. As Primi Visconti noted in 1677, "Acting on no other grounds but the general opinion that she was the object of the king's affections, all the princesses and duchesses used to rise to their feet when she approached, even in the presence of the queen, and sat down again only when Mme de Ludres made the appropriate gesture, in exactly the same way as used to happen with Mme de Montespan."[60] Louis XIV was well aware of the ways in which court etiquette made manifest the status of his mistress. When he decided to make his relationship with Louise de la Vallière public, for example, her "coronation" was enacted through the vehicle of etiquette. Louis brought Louise to the queen mother's weekly *appartement* and seated her between Monsieur and Madame, effectively crowning her the shadow queen of the court.[61] Only a few years later he allowed Mme de Montespan privileges that by the rules of court etiquette should have been accorded only to Marie-Thérèse: "She kept a table, where the ladies could eat, as the Queen did in her own apartments; she sat on an armchair, while even princesses and duchesses had only a *tabouret*. The king gave her four horsemen, very nimble [*bien lestes*], who wore the uniform of his own bodyguard, and who accompanied her everywhere."[62]

Interestingly, while court observers watched the king's actions vigilantly for warning signs that his latest love might exert inappropriate influence over his decisions of state, the heightened credit granted his mistress within court society does not seem to have aroused the same level of concern. Louis's mistress was expected to wield influence over her royal lover; her power was an accepted component of the structure of court politics. Courtiers might complain about the inferior pedigree of a mistress, but they did not question the fact that she would occupy the highest reaches of the court hierarchy. Although court society assumed that she would and should forward her own interests, as well as those of her family, *bienséance* required that she exercise a certain degree of restraint. If a mistress failed to take advantage of her position, she was regarded as naive at best. Louise de la Vallière, for example, wasted the favors for which she did ask, squandering her credit with the king because she did not know how to refuse people who importuned her to intercede for them.[63] Madame de Lafayette remarked with some disdain, "La Vallière's lack of wit prevented her making good use of the favor and influence that so great a passion conferred upon her, and that any other mistress of the King would have known how to profit by."[64]

Louise de la Vallière's selfless nature aside, a *maîtresse en titre,* having gained the summit of the shadow hierarchy, enjoyed the most lucrative of material benefits. Athénaïs de Montespan took full advantage of these perquisites, demonstrating a considerable (if socially acceptable) amount of avarice.[65] Louis XIV's most charismatic mistress as well as his longest lasting, Mme de Montespan "reigned" from 1667 to 1679. Although the king had other affairs during her tenure, he always returned to her. She was accounted "as beautiful as the day,"[66] with "blonde hair, large azure eyes, an aquiline but well-formed nose, a small vermilion mouth; in a word, a perfect face." Her physical attractions were enhanced by the *esprit* for which her family was famous; "her greatest charm was a grace, a wit and certain irresistible turn of conversation."[67] Louis XIV built her a magnificent chateau at Clagny designed by Mansart himself,[68] and showered her family with lucrative offices, appointing her brother captain general of the galleys and governor of Champagne, her father governor of Paris, and her sister abbess of Fontevrault. She was able to orchestrate appointments to highly placed offices for her allies at court as well: the duc de Montausier became the dauphin's tutor; the maréchal de d'Albret was named governor of Guyenne; and the king selected her candidate,

La Vienne, to be his first valet of the chamber.[69] Madame de Montespan herself was eventually appointed (albeit as a parting gift) *surintendante* of the queen's household, the highest office at court a woman could attain. Louis also granted Mme de Montespan and her sister several monopolies, including a percentage of all the meat and tobacco sold in Paris.[70] Furthermore, Mme de Montespan had the indefatigable Colbert at her disposal, by order of the king. Louis wrote to his minister in 1675, "Mme de Montespan has written me that you do very well the things that I have ordered you to do [for her], and that you always ask her if there is anything that she wishes. Continue to do this always."[71]

Perhaps a greater prize than the material rewards to be wheedled directly from the king was the considerable influence Louis's mistress could exert within the patron-client networks and cabals of the court. Louis XIV may have prided himself on his ability to segregate his mistresses from his ministers, yet any woman who was even rumored to have attracted his attention found her influence and power at court increased dramatically by sheer virtue of her supposed proximity to the king. Courtiers frequently attributed fluctuations in the king's regard for them to his mistress's influence. The Princess Palatine explicitly attributed the state of her relationship with Louis to the whim of his current mistress: "As for the King, I have been in his good or bad graces according to his mistress's will. At the time of Montespan I was in disgrace, at the time of Ludres things went well for me, when Montespan again had the upper hand they went badly again, when Fontanges came they were better, [but] since the present woman [Mme de Maintenon] holds sway they are always bad."[72]

The king's mistresses, official or otherwise, could use their influence with the king to the detriment of their rivals. Although Louis's relationship with the princesse de Soubise was so discreet that an affair was only suspected rather than confirmed (by contemporaries as well as historians), their continued friendship gave the princess considerable power at court long after any possible amorous liaison had ended.[73] Primi Visconti described the fate that befell one duchess who nettled her in 1681: "One day at Versailles, when [Louis] was about to go on an outing, he asked that the princesse de Soubise should be invited to join him in the queen's carriage, in which he was sitting. The duchesse de la Ferté, who was present, was so overcome with rage against Mme de Soubise that she exclaimed aloud: 'She is too old by now to lay any claim to him.' La Soubise turned to the king and said: 'Your Majesty sees how I was insulted.' The king replied: 'I will remedy it.' And, through the duc de Noailles, he let the maréchal de la Mothe know that his daughter, Mme de la Ferté, wearied him and that she was exiled from the court."[74]

Madame de Montespan, too, was able to maneuver some of her rivals for the king's affections into exile. She often acted indirectly to orchestrate the removal of potential rivals through intermediaries. In 1675 she apparently tired of the king's frequent dalliances with the queen's maids of honor. Madame de Sévigné assessed her response to the situation, "There is no doubt that *Quanto* [Mme de Montespan] found that the quarters of the maids-of-honor bred a hydra-headed monster, and that the only solution was to chop off all of the heads."[75] Madame de Montespan, no doubt suspecting that the king might prove reluctant to dismiss her rivals, did not approach Louis directly but employed an intermediary to bring about the desired result. Using her credit as the king's acknowledged favorite, she reportedly persuaded the duchesse de Richelieu, a confidante of the queen's, to convince Marie-Thérèse that her maids of honor had become a scandal to the court. The pious queen immediately asked the king to order their dismissal.[76]

Moreover, the king's official mistress was not as constrained as other courtiers by the rules of etiquette that ritualized contact with the king. While Louis carefully controlled the access he granted his other courtiers, she enjoyed more private time with him than anyone else did.[77] A mistress did nonetheless have to possess a clear understanding of the etiquette that governed her relationship with the king. One unfortunate woman found her reign as shadow queen brought to an abrupt halt after she broke a cardinal rule. After two years as Louis's unofficial mistress, between 1675 and 1677, Mme de Ludres discovered that the king's interest in her had faded. Louis changed his mind, however, and let it be known through his *premier valet de chambre*, Chamarande, that he sought a reconciliation. Madame de Ludres was eager to accept Louis's overtures but made a fatal error when she failed to employ an intermediary whom the king trusted. Primi Visconti described the incident: "In the end, Mme de Ludres compounded her own destruction. . . . Her confidante was a certain Marianne . . . married to a certain Montataire, a worthless rascal without credit. Marianne, desiring to increase her husband's credit, persuaded Mme de Ludres to use him as an intermediary between herself and the king. His Majesty . . . was so astonished to find himself confronted by Montataire that he immediately broke off relations with Mme de Ludres and sent word to her that she should withdraw to a convent."[78]

Louis's emphasis on etiquette and ceremony was not a matter of personal preference but a deliberate policy of state. As he put it, "There is nothing in this matter that is unimportant or inconsequential. Since our subjects cannot penetrate into things, they usually judge by appearances, and it is most often on amenities and on ranks that they base their respect and their obedience. As important as it is for the public to be governed only by a single person, it is just as important for the one who performs this function to be raised so far above the others that no one else may be confused or compared with him, and one cannot deprive the head of state of the slightest marks of superiority without harming the entire body."[79]

Ceremonial ordered every other courtier's access to Louis XIV and his favors, dictating who rode in the monarch's carriage, who sat in the presence of the royal family, who dined at the same time as the king.[80] Nobles were required to comport themselves according to strict rules of etiquette, and the king followed his own rules. Louis deliberately calibrated his movements, gestures, and expressions for each interlocutor.[81] A ruler, declared Louis, must be "in control of his own looks and words," for only by masking his own thoughts could he "learn the feelings of all while disclosing his own only to those he wished or perhaps even to none at all."[82] The king therefore conducted even the least interactions with his courtiers according to the rules of *politesse*, as Saint Simon famously observed: "There never was a man so naturally polite, nor whose politeness was so sharply measured to the tiniest degree."[83]

As the material and social rewards heaped upon Louis's official mistress and her family demonstrate, the greater the amount of time one spent next to the king, the greater the prospects for profit.[84] While proximity to the monarch had traditionally been beneficial to his favorites, this was never more true than under Louis XIV. Heeding the advice given him by the dying Cardinal Mazarin, Louis declared himself the fount of all royal patronage at the outset of his personal reign: "I announced that all requests for graces of any type had to be made directly to me, and I granted to all my subjects without distinction the privilege of appealing to me at any time, in person or by petition."[85] The king was true to his word; he personally accepted written petitions from all manner of supplicants, noble and commoner alike, throughout his lifetime.[86]

**Fig. 6** *Louis XIV in his coach, accompanied by some ladies in the Bois de Vincennes.* This 1669 engraving by F. van de Meulen depicts Louis XIV as he preferred to travel, in the company of a few privileged noblewomen of the court.

Supplicants found a personal audience with the king more advantageous than handing him a petition that might easily go astray, but most were forced to arrange for a well-placed courtier to act as a broker or go-between within the extensive system of court patronage.[87] As one contemporary noted, "The king's establishment is like a vast market, where there is no choice but to go and bargain, both to maintain one's own existence and to protect the interests of those to whom we are attached by duty or friendship."[88] Petitioners knew that selecting the appropriate intermediary was a matter of critical importance, requiring a finely graded understanding of the unwritten rules that governed Louis's distribution of favors. Brokers traded upon their access to (and presumed influence with) the king or other persons of standing; those who stood closest to the fount of royal patronage became the most sought after and most highly paid.[89] By keeping their ears open for news of opportunities such as new offices or monopolies, court brokers could alert interested parties who would pay handsomely for the information.[90] Those in need of intermediaries sometimes found it possible to comparison shop, as courtiers might charge different fees for their assistance.[91] One petitioner, for example, seeking to obtain a commission as a frigate captain, found that the princesse d'Harcourt underbid the comtesse de Fiesque by five hundred *livres*.[92] Nobles who did not attend court seldom received either material or social reward, regardless of how highly placed their brokers might be. Louis was known to say, when asked a favor on behalf of a noble who was too often absent from court, "I do not know him."[93]

Court noblewomen often proved talented negotiators, their skills used as often to secure pensions or honors or offices as to arrange marriages. Examples are legion. The duchesse de Noailles obtained a treaty for the sale of offices for the manager of her family estates; for a percentage of the bride's dowry, the comtesse de Gramont negotiated the marriage of the son of a wealthy *parlementaire*;[94] and the princesse d'Harcourt, renowned for her cupidity, obtained coveted invitations to Marly for six thousand *livres* apiece.[95] No woman, however, was in a better position to whisper in the king's ear than his mistress, and his mistresses reaped the benefits of their office. Even Louise de la Vallière, the first and least adroit of Louis's mistresses, handed petitions to the king for a fee.

Mistresses, with their exceptional opportunity to speak to the king in private, were of course highly sought after as brokers. Their influence with the king was undoubted, but, as with any other broker, courtiers could never be certain that their causes would be presented favorably. Uncertainty seems to have driven at least one to take an unprecedented risk. The duc de Lauzun boasted that he had been able to discover that Mme de Montespan was doing her utmost to reduce his credit with the king by hiding under the bed in which Louis and his mistress met for their afternoon trysts and listening to their postcoital conversation.[96]

Court brokers might also play a role in obtaining rewards that conferred social distinction without material benefit. The Order of the Holy Spirit brought no income, but it elevated a nobleman's place in the official court hierarchy to a rank immediately below the *ducs et pairs*. Louis found that bestowing this particular honor served a dual purpose. He wrote in his *Mémoires*, "I would have liked to elevate even more people to this honor, since I find that a prince has no greater pleasure than to be able to reward people of quality who have satisfied him without placing any additional burden on the most humble of his subjects. No reward costs the people less and none touches noble hearts more than these distinctions of rank, which are the prime movers of all human actions, especially of the greatest and most noble."[97]

A social distinction just as eagerly sought by noblewomen at court was that of the *tabouret*, which allowed a fortunate few the right to sit on a small folding stool in the presence of the king and queen. While only duchesses and members of the royal family were entitled to this honor, Louis did grant a handful of women the *tabouret* in recognition of extraordinary services or great favor.[98] Louis was well aware that such rewards, however sought after, had no material value. In his *Mémoires*, he gloried in his ability to so manipulate his courtiers; it was "one of the most visible attributes of our power, to be able, if we so wish, to attach an infinite price to something which, in itself, is nothing."[99]

## LOVE MAGIC AND THE KING'S MISTRESSES

Given all the material and social advantages to be gained from becoming Louis XIV's mistress, therefore, it is not surprising that some women at court probably had recourse to magical aid in their quests for the king's attentions. The Affair of the Poisons produced accusations that several of Louis's female courtiers had turned to practitioners of love magic in their attempts to win the heart of the king and gain advantage over their rivals.[100] For court noblewomen, the rewards that could be gained if they won the position of shadow queen may have justified any Machiavellian means they used. The denizens of the criminal underworld offered them a supernatural edge in the intensely competitive world of the court. And, as we have seen, the suspicion that women at court might turn to illicit magic certainly did not defy the seventeenth-century imagination. According to Primi Visconti, "all the courtiers, particularly the women, would have given themselves to the devil for the love of the king."[101]

The visits of Louis XIV's would-be mistresses to the sorceresses and magicians of Paris were by no means unprecedented. Many of the Sun King's nobles allegedly sought out members of the criminal magical underworld for a variety of items that promised to fulfill their most cherished ambitions. Some sought wealth and purchased charms to ensure that they would always win at games of chance; others aspired to political success and dreamed of "secrets" that would supposedly bring them credit with the king; others sought romance and invested in both love charms and spells to vanquish their competitors.[102] Perhaps because a successful love charm could achieve fiscal, political, and amatory ambitions simultaneously if the intended love object were wealthy and powerful enough, spells of love magic were most frequently purchased. Louis XIV, whose sexual body was the locus of ultimate power for women at his court, logically became the target of such charms. As Primi Visconti attested, "Numbers of women, married or not, declared to me that it would offend neither their husbands, their fathers, nor God himself to be loved by that prince."[103] A dozen female courtiers allegedly turned to ceremonies of love magic to fulfill their crowning ambitions—to win not only the love of the king (something he shared rather liberally) but the coveted place of *maîtresse en titre*. In addition to pursuing the social consequence and material advantages that came with the position of shadow queen, these women sought to gain influence over the emotions of the king. They apparently believed that rituals of love magic could ensnare "the body, soul, spirit, heart and mind of Louis de Bourbon."[104] The love magic would provide, or so the women hoped, at least as much control over the king as he had over himself—and Louis was an exceptionally self-controlled man.

According to the suspects in the Affair of the Poisons, men at court, for their part, sought military and thus political advancement through magical means. Male aristocrats did not usually purchase love magic but rather charms that would render them invulnerable to sword wounds or ensure success on the battlefield. The comte de Cessac, claimed the magician Lesage, had bought charms "pour les armes," as had the duc de Luxembourg, marshal of the king's armies.[105] Because victory in battle guaranteed the king's favor and concomitant rewards, it translated easily into political credit.[106] The duc de Luxembourg, claimed Lesage, had also asked him for a book of magic spells and had conjurations performed for various ends. (Luxembourg admitted visiting the magician on two occasions but denied his other charges.)[107] Only a third of the courtiers accused of commissioning magic of any sort were men, however.[108]

Women at court, La Reynie learned, had begun to turn to magic as early as 1667.[109] Madame de Montespan, the comtesse de Gramont, the comtesse de Soissons, and the vicomtesse de Polignac separately commissioned rituals of love magic from La Voisin and her partner, Lesage, during this period. Their timing coincided with the rumors circulating at court that the king's passion for Louise de la Vallière had begun to wane. Lesage described one love charm prepared for Mme de Montespan as a packet of several herbs composed "for love and for the king, and it was to cause love." Lesage recalled that he had made several conjurations over the herbs and had then asked the abbé Mariette to put the finishing touches on the charm by passing the packet under the chalice while he celebrated mass at the church of Saint-Séverin. He assured his interrogators, "That which was done over them they often did together . . . in the last days of the year 1667 and the beginning of 1668."[110]

While Louis's female courtiers commissioned a remarkable assortment of spells and charms, no woman seems to have been as comprehensive or as successful in her magical quest for the king's attention as Athénaïs de Montespan.[111] She embarked on her campaign to win the love of the king during Louise de la Vallière's reign as *maîtresse en titre*, hiring a renegade priest to recite the Gospels over her head. Abbé Mariette, dressed in his surplice and stole, sprinkled holy water over the head of the king's would-be mistress as he recited the "évangile des Rois." Madame de Montespan was nothing if not thorough; at the same time, she commissioned Lesage to make fumigations and burn incense to the same end.[112] The three amatory masses allegedly celebrated by the abbé Guibourg for her were commissioned in 1667, just before her triumph over Louise de la Vallière; in 1676, just as she regained Louis's affections from the princesse de Soubise; and in 1679, as she tried to fend off a new contender, the duchesse de Fontanges.[113] From Mme de Montespan's point of view, only the last failed to fulfill her desires.

After she had won the position of *maîtresse en titre*, Mme de Montespan continued to ply the king with love charms and aphrodisiacs to ensure that his attention did not wander. She was seemingly willing to administer to her lover any potion, no matter how repellent, if it promised to prolong his passion for her. The abbé Guibourg described one particularly elaborate concoction that he prepared for her to slip into the king's food. Guibourg's ritual took place at the home of La Voisin. Dressed in chasuble, stole, and alb, he began the rite in the presence of two witnesses: Mme de Montespan's lady-in-waiting, Claude de Vin des Œillets, and a mysterious Englishman known only as "the Milord." After saying mass, Guibourg recited a conjuration furnished by the English Milord and then began to assemble the ingredients of the charm. The "sperm" of both sexes was called for and promptly provided by the English Milord and Mlle Des Œillets (who substituted menstrual blood but was assured by Guibourg that "it was the same thing"). The sperm and blood were placed in the chalice along with a consecrated host that had been broken into pieces, the blood of a bat, and flour, "to give some body" to the composition. After Guibourg recited a second conjuration over the potion, it was poured into a small bottle and given to Mlle des Œillets to deliver to Mme de Montespan, who was to add it to her royal lover's food.[114] The magical ingredients of the love charm, already considered powerful in their own right, were thus rendered even more so by Guibourg's mass.[115]

The position of shadow queen, however, was difficult to win and even harder to keep. Madame de Montespan occupied the highest reaches of the shadow hierarchy for a dozen years, effectively defending her crown against the onslaughts of countless envious rivals. Perhaps she returned to the sorceresses and magicians of Paris in the late 1670s because their efforts seemed to have helped her to achieve her original success. Despite her fabled beauty and celebrated wit, she evidently felt the vulnerability of her position, particularly after she had borne several children and lost her figure—an occurrence that did not pass unremarked at court. In 1678 Primi Visconti sent a rather catty description of Louis's mistress to a correspondent. He had recently encountered Mme de Montespan, he reported. She "had grown extremely stout and indeed, while she was descending from her carriage one day, I had a glimpse of one of her legs, and I swear it was as broad as my whole body." "But," he added, "I must say, to be just, that I have lost a lot of weight since you have seen me."[116] In moments of crisis, then, Mme de Montespan had recourse to supernatural assistance to maintain her hold over the king.

Through the rituals of love magic provided by the denizens of the magical underworld, Mme de Montespan and other aspiring *maîtresses en titre* sought to climb to the summit of the intricate hierarchy of power and place at court. The competition for royal favor among Louis's courtiers became particularly fierce after the king had successfully centralized court life and the distribution of royal patronage. Louis's courtiers strove mightily for his affections because only a place very close to the king's side—whether in bed or out of it—offered access to the rewards, both material and honorific, that only he could bestow. Thus, what Mme de Montespan attempted to accomplish was far from unusual at Louis XIV's court, where vying for the king's favor had become the preoccupation of every aristocrat. But she succeeded far better than any other female aristocrat who aspired to become the *maîtresse en titre*—and, perhaps not coincidentally, she also stood accused of employing an exceptional range of magical practices to do so.

# Conclusion: The End of Magic?

As Louis XIV drew the investigation into the Affair of the Poisons to a close, he moved to suppress the challenges to royal authority that it had presented. Upon dissolving the Chambre de l'Arsenal on July 21, 1682, Louis launched a final sally against any remaining members of the criminal magical underworld. To ensure that criminals of such magnitude never again disturbed the peace and order of the kingdom, the king ordered the Parlement of Paris to register a royal edict "for the punishment of different crimes, notably for poisoners, fortune-tellers, magicians, and enchanters."[1] Its preamble announced: "The experience of the past has shown how dangerous it is to suffer the least abuses of crimes of this sort, and how difficult it is to root them out. . . . We judge it necessary to renew the ancient ordinances and to add to them new precautions regarding all those who use evil spells [maléfices] and poisons, those who follow the vain professions of fortune-tellers, magicians, or sorcerers or other similar names, who are condemned by divine and human law."[2] Louis XIV proceeded to bring all the forces of ancien régime justice to bear on "all persons practicing divination, or calling themselves fortune-tellers," ordering them to leave the country immediately, on pain of death. The edict similarly forbade "all practices and acts of magic or superstition, in word or speech, either profaning the text of Holy Writ or the Liturgy, or saying or doing things which cannot be explained naturally."[3]

In addition to outlawing the practices of the magicians and sorceresses of the Affair of the Poisons, the edict created a new set of regulations concerning the sale and manufacture of poisons. Arsenic and its most dangerous derivatives were to be delivered only to "those whose professions require them to use it."[4] No longer would any Parisian who requested it be able to obtain mort-aux-rats upon demand; anyone who purchased arsenic or any other poisonous material had to provide his or her name, address, and occupation for the register that was to record every such transaction and be inspected regularly by the government. Only doctors and apothecaries could legally possess poisonous animals or insects, and only doctors, apothecaries, and professors of chemistry might work in their own private laboratories.[5]

The Edict of 1682, however, was intended to accomplish more than the regulation of the sale of poison and the expulsion of every sorceress and magician from France.[6] The testimony heard by the judges of the Chambre de l'Arsenal revealed that belief in magic and witchcraft suffused French society. The crown therefore moved aggressively to extirpate belief in the efficacy of the magic that the members of the criminal magical underworld offered for sale: "These imposters . . . have taken unawares [*surpris*] many ignorant and credulous people who were unwittingly engaged with them." The government declared all magical practices to be false and identified its practitioners to be nothing but "so-called magicians."[7] Sorceresses and the like could not perform feats of magic but only committed sacrilege and blasphemy as they bilked their naive clients.

Counterintuitively, perhaps, the French crown's denial of the reality of witchcraft did not lead to greater leniency. Witchcraft might be a hoax, but even "so-called" sorcery constituted a grave transgression. Echoing the rhetoric of the Gallican church's crusade against superstition, the edict proclaimed that magical practitioners were "condemned by divine and human law," not because they dabbled in the supernatural—for that was declared to be impossible—but because they debased religion itself: "they infect and corrupt the will of our people and . . . profane all that religion holds most sacred." The edict therefore promised the ultimate punishment for "evil-minded persons" who "augment and compound superstition with impiety and sacrilege, under pretext of working so-called acts of magic or other deceptions of a similar nature."[8] Louis XIV and his magistrates, concurring with the fiery sermons of Catholic Reformation preachers, identified sorcery to be not merely sinful but an abomination before God.

The royal edict that in the next century would appear to reflect an enlightened dismissal of witchcraft as "mere superstition" was entirely characteristic of Louis XIV's attempt to legislate a new moral order. Like contemporaneous royal edicts that forbade blasphemy, proscribed impiety, and demanded religious uniformity, it would be policed by agents whose mandate to contain violence and maintain public order did not distinguish between religious and criminal offenses.

Similar logic informed the sentences handed down to those convicted during the Affair of the Poisons. At no point during the affair was a member of the criminal magical underworld executed solely for the performance of *maléfices,* or evil spells. The sternest measures of justice were instead meted out to those whose charms and ceremonies polluted the sacramentals of the Catholic Church.[9] Even those convicted of having used poison, an offense that fell into the category of *crimes énormes* (the gravest of transgressions), received lesser penalties. Poisoners were sentenced to perform public apologies before they were hanged in the public square; hanging was considered the least painful method of execution.[10] Although the members of the magical underworld were most often sentenced for multiple offenses, the crime of sacrilege was apparently the key exacerbating factor for the judges of the Chambre de l'Arsenal. Those convicted of sacrilege, or sacrilege in conjunction with another offense, were forced to make public apologies before the doors of Notre-Dame and then hanged before their bodies were burned. Those convicted of treason against God, the most malignant form of sacrilege, received the harshest and rarest of sentences. They were condemned to make public apologies and were then burned alive at the stake.[11]

France could be safe from such reprobates only if Louis XIV's subjects embraced the practices and teachings of the Catholic Church, as their king had resolved to do. Observers remarked that Louis became increasingly devout following the Affair of the Poisons. The Archbishop of Sens attested, "The slow and hesitant change in the King's attitude and behavior became more clearly marked. . . . He grew less secretive about his newly found virtuousness and no longer feared . . . to replace the amorous intrigues which had amused him hitherto with the sincere practice of religion."[12] For a while, at least, the atmosphere at court changed markedly as a consequence of the king's newfound piety. As Primi Visconti gloomily observed, "All those who compared present-day France to how it had been twenty years ago were stupefied: it seemed that it was no longer the same country. Then, it had been full of balls, festivals, banquets, and concerts . . . now, everyone lived a retired life . . . few people amused themselves, and still circumspection was necessary, particularly at the court. Debauchery, drunkenness, indecent clothing, vices, even swearing put a man in the king's bad graces . . . the realm resembled a seminary."[13]

If the investigation into the Affair of the Poisons marked a bid by the French crown to establish greater control over the souls and the bodies of its subjects, its efforts proved less than successful. Despite the diligent attempts of La Reynie and later ministers to enforce the provisions of the Edict of 1682, Parisians continued to turn to the occult for their financial and amatory pursuits. Eighteenth-century police records indicate that a criminal magical underworld persevered, if not prospered, in the capital. Twenty years after the Affair of the Poisons, Marc-Réné d'Argenson, Nicolas de la Reynie's successor as lieutenant general of the Paris police, urged the crown to allow greater police repression of the "faux sorciers qui abusent de la crédulité publique."[14] D'Argenson's persistent sorceresses apparently continued to employ the same tools of Christian magic as had their predecessors. In a detailed report submitted in 1702, d'Argenson described the "intrigues of the false fortune-tellers and the so-called witches, those who promise to discover treasure, or communicate with genies, who distribute powders, sell talismans, who consecrate bouquets and pentacles." Of particular danger to the public good, he wrote, were the impious priests who conducted sacrilegious rites of demonic magic for clients in search of riches and the love of "people of the first rank."[15]

In fact, the criminal magical underworld of Paris was never successfully abolished. France's shared culture of magic—always shadowed by the state's attempts to extinguish the beliefs and practices that gave rise to it—flourished long past the ancien régime. The Napoleonic Code reiterated Louis XIV's prohibitions against "those who make a profession of divination and prediction," although, in a more skeptical era, self-proclaimed sorceresses and magicians were to be fined or imprisoned rather than banished or executed.[16] Eight successive French regimes, republics and restorations alike, prosecuted fortune-tellers and other occult practitioners as threats to the social order. The practices of Paris's indomitable magical underworld were legalized only by the penal code reform of 1993.[17]

When Louis XIV promulgated his edict against the poisoners, magicians, and sorceresses who had so recently menaced his capital, he moved simultaneously against the second threat to his authority that the Affair of the Poisons had revealed: the machinations of his female courtiers to become his official mistress. Louis's early decision to center royal authority exclusively in his person made physical access the only means by which his courtiers could gain the material and social rewards to which they aspired. In 1666 Louis had noted with evident satisfaction, "[The ruler] alone is the object of all hopes; nothing is pursued, nothing is anticipated, nothing is ever done except through him. His good graces are regarded as the sole source of all favors. The only way to advance oneself is by growing in his personal esteem."[18] Sixteen years later, however, it may have seemed that his decision to hand out all graces personally had had the unfortunate side effect of heightening the already intense competition to become his *maîtresse en titre*.

But by taking aim at the king's bed, the women implicated in the affair (both courtiers and criminals) struck at the very heart of the monarchy. Louis's court was a context in which power was exercised in and through the body, and Louis's bed, around which were enacted the most important rituals of the absolute monarchy, served as the site where the mystical and mortal bodies of the king became one. The king's physical body was therefore the locus of power at court; access to his person, whether at the ritual *lever* or through amorous encounters, imparted political privilege. In attempting to initiate a sexual relationship with the king and thereby command his passions, his would-be mistresses had simultaneously attempted to gain access to the center of royal power.

Louis evidently decided to eliminate the possibility that such forays against his sovereignty might be attempted again. As the Affair of the Poisons drew to a close, the king closed the door to the royal bedroom. The duchesse de Fontanges was to be his last mistress. Madame de Montespan continued to live at court as his favorite in name only; Louis visited the mother of his children daily, but always in the company of a group of other courtiers. Rather amazingly, the king by all accounts remained faithful to Queen Marie-Thérèse until her death in 1683, and then to his morganatic wife, the devout Mme de Maintenon.

Louis XIV's marked religiosity after the Affair of the Poisons is often portrayed as a turning point in his long reign. Its significance lies not in the fact that life at court became less lively than before or that the king himself became more puritanical, but in the impact his enhanced piety had on the twin hierarchies of power and status at court. In the political culture of the old regime, Louis's personal decisions inevitably had political consequences. When the king ceased to take mistresses from among the noblewomen at his court, he closed the only loophole through which courtiers had been able to circumvent the strict ceremonial that governed access to him. All of his courtiers, even those who enjoyed his highest favor, were restricted to the ritualized access dictated by the increasingly intricate etiquette of Versailles. No longer would a *maîtresse en titre* be able to rule over the shadow hierarchy of the court by virtue of her unique access to the king, thus altering the ways in which power was mediated at Louis's court. After the Affair of the Poisons, his female courtiers were no longer able to gain the privileges derived from access to the king's sexual body. Louis XIV's royal touch was once again reserved for the cure of scrofula.

# NOTES

## Introduction

1. Primi Fassiola di San Maiolo, *Mémoires sur la cour de Louis XIV*, ed. and trans. Jean Lemoine (Paris: Calmann-Lévy, 1908), 302.

2. *Edit du Roy pour la punition de différents crimes* (Paris: Jean Baptiste Coignard, 1682), Bibliothèque Nationale (hereafter BN), Collection Delamare, MS 21730, fol. 115. All translations from the French are my own unless otherwise indicated.

3. Even a historian as perceptive as Robin Briggs, for example, refuses to consider the affair at all, noting merely that its "sophisticated imaginings have no equivalent in the village world." Briggs, *Witches and Neighbors: The Social and Cultural Context of European Witchcraft* (New York: Penguin, 1998), 251.

4. Georges Mongrédien, *Madame de Montespan et l'affaire des poisons* (Paris: Hachette, 1953) remains the classic treatment of the Affair of the Poisons. In the most recent scholarly work on the affair, Arlette Lebigre connects the scandal with the French government's decision to regulate the sale of arsenic and other household poisons; see her *L'affaire des poisons* (Brussels: Éditions Complexe, 1989). Other works on the subject include Jean-Christian Petitfils, *L'affaire des poisons: Alchimistes et sorciers sous Louis XIV* (Paris: Albin Michel, 1977); Jean-Christian Petitfils, *Madame de Montespan* (Paris: Fayard, 1988); Jean Lemoine, *Madame de Montespan et la légende des poisons* (Paris, 1908); Lucien Nass, *Les empoisonnements sous Louis XIV, d'après les documents inédits de l'affaire des poisons, 1679–1682* (Paris: Carré et Naud, 1898); and Frantz Funck-Bretano, *Le drame des poisons* (Paris: J. Tallandier, 1977). In addition, Anne Somerset has recently published a popular history on the scandal, *The Affair of the Poisons: Murder, Infanticide, and Satanism at the Court of Louis XIV* (London: Weidenfeld & Nicolson, 2003).

5. See, for example, Brian P. Levack, "The Decline and End of Witchcraft Persecutions," in *Witchcraft and Magic in Europe: The Eighteenth and Nineteenth Centuries,* ed. Begnt Ankarloo and Stuart Clark (Philadelphia: University of Pennsylvania Press, 1999); Alfred Soman, "La décriminalisation de la sorcellerie en France," in *Sorcellerie et justice criminelle: Le Parlement de Paris (16e–18e siècles)* (Brookfield, Vt.: Ashgate, 1992), 179–203; and Robert Mandrou, *Magistrats et sorciers en France au XVIIe siècle: Une analyse de psychologie historique* (Paris: Librairie Plon, 1968).

6. Gossip about the amatory masses performed by renegade priests, for example, was in circulation by the beginning of 1680. Bussy wrote to La Rivière on January 27, "Last Thursday, two priests were arrested, including one named Lesage who claimed that a . . . young woman in love with Rubanstel, had come to him asking to be given secrets to have men fall in love with her. He had told her that an infallible method would be to have him say mass while she stretched naked on the altar, the chalice on her stomach. She agreed to this ritual, but came back to him two weeks later to complain that Rubanstel seemed no more enamored of her than before. He then assured her that it was necessary to add a new element to this ritual, and that if he lay with her after late mass, Rubanstel would be certain to acquire an insatiable passion for her; the lady

performed all the ceremonies." Quoted in Gillette Ziegler, *The Court of Versailles in the Reign of Louis XIV,* trans. Simon Watson Taylor (London: George Allen & Unwin, 1966), 167.

7. See, for example, the letters of the Venetian, Savoyard, and English ambassadors, in François Ravaisson-Mollien, ed., *Les archives de la Bastille: Documents inédits,* 19 vols. (Paris: A. Durand et Pedone-Lauriel, 1866–1904), vols. 4–7, passim.

8. P. J. Yarrow, "Introduction," in Thomas Corneille and Jean Donneau de Visé, *La deviner-esse* (Exeter: University of Exeter Press, 1971), v–xxiii. Corneille and Visé called their play *La devineresse, ou les faux enchantemens* [*sic*]; I have modernized the spelling.

9. The line between entertainment and reality was further obscured when the original en-gravings of the play were recycled to adorn the borders of a new engraving depicting the deeds of La Voisin, the most infamous sorceress arrested in the affair. E. T. Dubois, O. W. Maskell, and P. J. Yarrow, "L'almanach de la devineresse," *Revue d'histoire du théâtre* 32, no. 3 (1980): 216–19.

10. My understanding of the public execution as theater is drawn from Michel Foucault, *Discipline and Punish: The Birth of the Prison,* trans. Alan Sheridan (New York: Vintage Books, 1977), and David Garland, "Punishment and Culture: The Symbolic Dimensions of Criminal Justice," *Studies in Law, Politics, and Society* 11 (1991): 191–222.

11. The judicial documents relating to the Affair of the Poisons are found in several collec-tions. A large proportion of the extant documents have been reprinted in Ravaisson-Mollien, *Archives de la Bastille.* Those documents not included in this collection can be found in Biblio-thèque de l'Arsenal (hereafter BA), 10338–59. BN, Manuscrits français (hereafter MSS fr) 7608 contains documents about the trials and summaries of secret interrogations (although Louis XIV burned the originals in 1709, he was unaware that La Reynie had kept his own notes), and the trial records of La Joly, a sorceress implicated in the affair, are located in BN, MSS fr 7630. La Reynie's personal papers and notes are found in BN, Collection Clairambault 986, fols. 161–463.

12. Natalie Zemon Davis, *Fiction in the Archives: Pardon Tales and Their Tellers in Sixteenth-Century France* (Stanford: Stanford University Press, 1987).

13. Louis XIV permitted Primi's activities at court only because the king had compelled Primi to admit privately that his ability to predict the future was a hoax. The king never betrayed Primi's secret. On the encounter between the two, see Jean Lemoine's introduction to Visconti, *Mémoires sur la cour de Louis XIV,* ix–xi.

14. For example, Mme de Sévigné wrote that the comtesse de Soissons had often regaled her friends with tales of her visits to La Voisin, "as one often does after visiting one of these so-called sorceresses." Mme de Sévigné to the comte de Guitaut, January 30, 1680, in Marie de Rabutin-Chantal, Marquise de Sévigné, *Correspondance,* ed. Roger Duchêne, 3 vols. (Paris: Gal-limard, 1972–78), 2:818.

15. My argument here has been influenced by Brian Levack, *The Witch Hunt in Early Mod-ern Europe,* 2d ed. (London: Longman, 1995).

16. I owe my understanding of the major tenets of medieval magic to Richard Kieckhefer, *Magic in the Middle Ages* (Cambridge: Cambridge University Press, 1989).

17. See, for example, the sixteenth- and seventeenth-century cases analyzed by William Mon-ter in "Toads and Eucharists: The Male Witches of Normandy," *French Historical Studies* 20, no. 4 (1997): 563–95.

18. On this point, see Norman Cohn, *Europe's Inner Demons: An Inquiry Inspired by the Great Witch-Hunt* (New York: Meridian, 1975), 164–73. The maréchal de Villeroi may have had a point, however, when he remarked of the magicians' clients, "These ladies and gentlemen believe in the Devil but not in God." Quoted in Mme de Sévigné to the comte de Guitaut, Jan-uary 30, 1680, in Sévigné, *Correspondance,* 2:818.

19. On the increasing reluctance of the Parlement of Paris to convict for witchcraft over the

course of the seventeenth century, see Monter, "Toads and Eucharists," and the collected articles of Alfred Soman in *Sorcellerie et justice criminelle.*

20. As Michel de Montaigne (himself a retired judge) famously remarked in a 1588 essay, "how much more natural that our mind should be enraptured from its setting by the whirlwind of our own deranged spirit, than that, by a spirit from beyond, one of us humans, flesh and blood, should be sent flying on a broomstick up the flue of his own chimney." Michel de Montaigne, *The Complete Essays,* trans. M. A. Screech (New York: Penguin, 1991), 1168. A majority of Parisian magistrates came to embrace Montaigne's skeptical attitude by the end of the following century. As early as 1610, for example, a sentence handed down by the Parlement of Paris dismissed testimony concerning the witches' sabbat as an illusion. Levack, "Decline and End of Witchcraft Persecutions," 48–53.

21. The Affair of the Poisons lends credence to the premise that elite adoption of a skeptical attitude toward magic and witchcraft was a fashion long before it became a conviction. In "The Decline and End of Witchcraft Persecutions," Brian Levack situates the decline in magical beliefs among members of the upper classes in a larger context of deliberate elite withdrawal from the world of popular culture. Much like adopting courtly manners or following the code of *honnêteté,* deriding magical beliefs served to separate elites from those that they regarded as their inferiors. Thus plays like Corneille and Visé's *La devineresse* and Fontenelle's *La comète* of 1681 (which ridiculed popular fears about comets) appealed to an audience anxious to distinguish itself from beliefs deemed vulgar and ignorant. However, many of the same Parisians who laughed at the shenanigans of fraudulent magicians on stage must have turned to the city's "genuine" sorceresses in moments of personal need. On the use of satire to encourage the upper classes to abandon traditional folk beliefs in astrology, see Sara Schechner Genuth, *Comets, Popular Culture, and the Birth of Modern Cosmology* (Princeton: Princeton University Press, 1997), chapter 4.

22. On the persistence of magical beliefs in modern France, see, among others, Marijke Gijswijt-Hofstra, "Witchcraft After the Witch-Trials," in Ankarloo and Clark, *Witchcraft and Magic in Europe,* 95–188; Tessie P. Liu, "Le Patrimoine Magique: Reassessing the Power of Women in Peasant Households in Nineteenth-Century France," *Gender and History* 6 (1994): 13–36; Marie-Claude Denier, "Sorciers, présages, et croyances magiques en Mayenne aux XVIIIe et XIXe siècles," *Annales de Bretagne et des pays de l'ouest (Anjou, Maine, Touraine)* 97 (1990): 115–32; and David Allen Harvey, "Fortune-Tellers in the French Courts: Antidivination Prosecutions in France in the Nineteenth and Twentieth Centuries," *French Historical Studies* 28, no. 1 (2005): 131–57.

23. Alfred Soman, "Witch Hunting at Juniville," *Natural History* 95, no. 10 (1986): 14–15. Soman expands upon this argument in "Decriminalizing Witchcraft: Does the French Experience Furnish a European Model?" *Criminal Justice History* 10 (1989): 1–30.

24. Brian Levack notes that the French crown's proclamation that magic was "so-called sorcery" did not so much decriminalize magic as reify it, dividing it into its component parts: fraud, superstition, and sacrilege. Levack, "Decline and End of Witchcraft Persecutions," 79–82.

25. The use of poison, before the Affair of the Poisons as after, fell into the legal category of *crimes atroces,* which comprised the gravest capital crimes. Because poisoners committed premeditated murder (*le meutre de guet-à-pens* or *l'assassinat*), they could not receive royal pardons or have their sentences commuted. Neither could their accomplices, who were similarly subject to the death penalty. Richard Mowery Andrews, *Law, Magistracy, and Crime in Old Regime Paris, 1735–1789,* 2 vols. (Cambridge: Cambridge University Press, 1994), 1:548–89.

26. The extent of Louis XIV's power, once seen as the culmination of early modern kingship, has been convincingly demonstrated to have been less extensive than previously thought. Louis's ability to impose his will on his subjects is now held to have been more a matter of consensus than an exercise in absolute rule. See, for example, Pierre Goubert, *Beauvais et le beauvaisis de*

*1600 à 1730* (Paris: Librairie Plon, 1960); William Beik, *Absolutism and Society in Seventeenth-Century France* (New York: Cambridge University Press, 1985); Roger Mettam, *Power and Faction in Louis XIV's France* (New York: Basil Blackwell, 1988); James B. Collins, *The State in Early Modern France* (Cambridge: Cambridge University Press, 1995); David Parker, *Class and State in Ancien-Régime France: The Road to Modernity?* (London: Routledge, 1996); and Jeroen Duindam, *Vienna and Versailles: The Courts of Europe's Dynastic Rivals, 1550–1780* (Cambridge: Cambridge University Press, 2003).

27. Norbert Elias, *The Court Society,* trans. Edmund Jephcott (New York: Pantheon Books, 1983).

28. Mettam, *Power and Faction,* 50–51.

29. Elias, *Court Society,* 243. Elias similarly remarks, "Society under Louis XIII was already a court society characterized by the importance of women—whom the men, bereft of their knightly function, now overshadowed socially far less than before" (194).

30. See Jean-François Solnon, *La cour de France* (Paris: Fayard, 1987), and Jeroen Duindam, *Myths of Power: Norbert Elias and the Early Modern European Court,* trans. Lorri S. Granger and Gerard T. Moran (Amsterdam: Amsterdam University Press, 1996). Duindam does note the importance of women as go-betweens and influence peddlers at court (155–57), but he does not examine their roles in any detail. He concedes that the "amorous domain cannot be neglected," but only briefly considers the place of female courtiers' influence through amorous liaisons in his latest work, *Vienna and Versailles,* 238–39.

31. Ernst Kantorowicz's *The King's Two Bodies: A Study in Mediaeval Political Theology* (Princeton: Princeton University Press, 1957), a study of the political fiction of the king's "two bodies"—one mortal, one sacred—inspired a generation of scholars to examine how the ritual culture of France was structured around the sacralized body of the king. Such scholarship includes, but is not limited to, Ralph Giesey, *The Royal Funeral Ceremony in France* (Geneva: Librairie Droz, 1960); Ralph Giesey, *Cérémonial et puissance souveraine: France, XVe–XVIIe siècles* (Paris: Armand Colin, 1987); Sarah Hanley, *The* Lit de Justice *of the Kings of France: Constitutional Ideology in Legend, Ritual, and Discourse* (Princeton: Princeton University Press, 1983); and Richard A. Jackson, *Vive le Roi! A History of the French Coronation from Charles V to Charles X* (Chapel Hill: University of North Carolina Press, 1984). Emmanuel Le Roy Ladurie only briefly considers the sacrality of the physical royal body and the significance of the intricately calibrated etiquette that dictated who was entitled, for example, to kiss the queen or eat with the king. See his *Saint Simon and the Court of Louis XIV,* trans. Arthur Goldhammer (Chicago: University of Chicago Press, 2001), 52–57. The exception to this general rule is Sergio Bertelli, *The King's Body: Sacred Rituals of Power in Medieval and Early Modern Europe,* trans. R. Burr Litchfield (University Park: Pennsylvania State University Press, 2001).

## Chapter 1

1. Quoted in François Bluche, *Louis XIV,* trans. Mark Greengrass (New York: Basil Blackwell, 1990), 268.

2. Mongrédien, *Madame de Montespan et l'affaire des poisons,* 35.

3. These printed briefs allowed the public to follow the details of court cases that officially took place in private. Although hearings were held behind closed doors in old regime France, lawyers were permitted to publish the briefs submitted to the judges on the case after the beginning of the seventeenth century. Lawyers on both sides of a case published their pleadings, which included evidence presented in court, the client's testimony, and a great deal of extravagant legal rhetoric. Public appetite for *factums* and collections of "notable decisions" only increased over the next two hundred years. Sarah Hanley, "Social Sites of Political Practice in France: Lawsuits,

Civil Rights, and the Separation of Powers in Domestic and State Government, 1500–1800," *American Historical Review* 102 (1997): 27–52. For an analysis of the genre at the peak of public interest during the latter half of the eighteenth century, see Sarah Maza, *Private Lives and Public Affairs: The Causes Célèbres of Prerevolutionary France* (Berkeley and Los Angeles: University of California Press, 1993).

4. The marquise's confessor, Edmé Pirot, a professor of theology at the Sorbonne, described her delicate complexion, chestnut hair, and limpid blue eyes in his lengthy *Relation,* an account of her last days. Ravaisson-Mollien, *Archives de la Bastille,* 3:229–68.

5. Marie-Madeleine was the eldest daughter of Antoine Dreux d'Aubray, seigneur d'Offémont et Villiers, *conseiller d'Etat, maître des requêtes,* and *lieutenant civile de la ville, prevoté et vicomté de Paris.* She brought a dowry of 200,000 *livres* to their marriage, while her husband contributed 30,000 *livres* in *rentes,* estates in Sains, Morainvilliers, and Quesnoy, and the marquisate of Brinvilliers.

6. M. Livelle, *Factum pour Dame Marie Marguerite d'Aubray, Marquise de Brinvilliers, Accusée, Contre Dame Marie Therese Mangot, veuve du Sieur d'Aubray, Lieutenant Civil, Accusatrice; & Monsieur le Procureur General . . .* (Paris: Gilles Tompere, 1676), BN, MSS fr 21727, fols. 217–49.

7. Ibid., 40–43.

8. Petitfils, *Affaire des poisons,* 19–20.

9. A double sexual standard was enforced legally as well as socially. See Hanley, "Social Sites of Political Practice in France," 27–52, for a discussion of the difference between adultery charges brought by husbands and those brought by wives in marital separation suits in early modern France.

10. A *lettre de cachet,* a royal mandate signed by a royal secretary of state, ordered the immediate imprisonment or exile of an individual without recourse to regular judicial processes. *Lettres de cachet* were most commonly used by the head of a household against a recalcitrant member of the family. See Frantz Funck-Bretano, *Les lettres de cachet à Paris: Étude suivie d'une liste des prisonniers de la Bastille (1659–1789)* (Paris: Imprimerie nationale, 1903), ix–xlvi, for an account of the practice.

11. *Mémoire du Proces Extraordinaire d'entre Dame Marie Therese Mangot, veuve de feu Messire Antoine d'Aubray, vivant Lieutenant Civil, demanderesse, accusatrice & appelante . . . ,* BN, Nouvelles Acquisitions Françaises 2447, fol. 219.

12. Anne Somerset suggests that the evidence for Exili's stay in Paris is weak and that the French authorities labeled Exili "an artist of poison" simply because of his nationality. As an Italian, he was readily believed to possess the secrets of poison. Somerset, *Affair of the Poisons,* 10–11.

13. Petitfils, *Affaire des poisons,* 21–22.

14. The original recipe for poison developed by Sainte-Croix and Marie de Brinvilliers was recently on display at the Musée de la Préfecture de la Police, 1 bis, rue des Carmes, Paris. It reads, "Armoise, sabine et cypré blanc, une bonne poignée de chacun, faut faire bouillir dans trois chopines d'eau. Faut le laisser réduire à trois demy costiers, coulez et pressez dans la colature faut mettre une once et demy de sirop d'armoise, et apres avoir bien meslé le tout ensemble en faut faire trois prises qu'il faut avaler trois matins de suite." For other recipes of Sainte-Croix, see Archives de la Bastille (hereafter AB), MS 10338.

15. Petitfils, *Affaire des poisons,* 22–23.

16. Ibid., 23.

17. Mme de Sévigné to Mme de Grignan, May 1, 1676, in Sévigné, *Correspondance,* 2:281.

18. Common seventeenth-century counterpoisons included milk, olive oil, and a complicated brew of more than fifty ingredients known as *orviétan.* Lebigre, *Affaire des poisons,* 11.

19. Mme de Sévigné to Mme de Grignan, April 29, 1676, in Sévigné, *Correspondance,* 2:278.

20. Petitfils, *Affaire des poisons,* 25.

21. Livelle, *Factum pour Dame Marie Marguerite d'Aubray,* fols. 217–19.

22. The Paris police had no jurisdiction over Sainte-Croix's effects at this point. Their authority was limited to placing seals on doors of the deceased's apartment until an official inventory of its contents was made so that his creditors could be satisfied.

23. *Mémoire du Procès Extraordinaire,* BN, Nouvelles Acquisitions Françaises, 2447, fol. 219.

24. Marie and La Chaussée were convicted of murdering her brothers. Marie's murder of her father was unknown at the time.

25. La Chaussée was sentenced to the form of torture known as the *question préalable.* Torture after a guilty verdict was intended to force the criminal to identify his or her accomplices. See Andrews, *Law, Magistracy, and Crime,* for a fuller explication of the uses of judicial torture during this period.

26. See *Extrait du procès-verbal de question,* March 24, 1673, in Ravaisson-Mollien, *Archives de la Bastille,* 3:66–67, for La Chaussée's full confession.

27. Mongrédien, *Madame de Montespan et l'affaire des poisons,* 26–28.

28. Ibid., 30.

29. The presiding judge's sentiments were recorded by Marie's confessor, Edmé Pirot, in his *Relation,* found in Ravaisson-Mollien, *Archives de la Bastille,* 4:229. The extant interrogations of the marquise de Brinvilliers are also reprinted in the same source, 4:176–79, 185–92, and 222–28.

30. Such veneration was not shared by all of the spectators who crowded the route to the scaffold; Mme de Sévigné rather flippantly described the event to her daughter: "Finally, it is done, la Brinvilliers is in the air. Her poor little body was thrown, after her execution, into a raging fire, and her ashes dispersed into the air; so that we will all breathe her spirit in, it will put us into such a poisoning humor that we will all be astonished." Mme de Sévigné to Mme de Grignan, July 17, 1676, in Sévigné, *Correspondance,* 2:342–43.

31. Ravaisson-Mollien, *Archives de la Bastille,* 4:176.

32. Ibid., 226.

33. BN, MSS fr 7608, fol. 129.

34. The band included Vanens's mistress, La Finette, his servants Jean Bartholimat and Jacques Grégoire, his associate the sieur de Clausel, and his valet, François Royal. Also involved were a banker named Cadelan and a Monsieur and Madame Bachimont. At the time of their arrest the Bachimonts were in possession of an assortment of suspicious items, including alembics, furnaces, glass bottles, metal vials, and containers of arsenic, sulfuric acid, and mercury. Lucien Nass has reprinted the entire inventory of the Bachimonts' possessions in *Empoisonnements sous Louis XIV,* 166–79. The original can be found in AB, MS 10339, fols. 609–15.

35. Poison, forgery, and counterfeiting were closely associated crimes in old regime France.

36. François-Michel Le Tellier, marquis de Louvois, served as Louis XIV's minister for war from 1677 to 1691. His rivalry with Colbert was legendary.

37. The correspondence between La Reynie and Louvois and the interrogations and other police documents concerning Vanens and his accomplices are reprinted in Ravaisson-Mollien, *Archives de la Bastille,* vols. 5 and 6, passim. Included in the collection is an account of how Vanens whiled away the time in the Bastille, amusing himself by baptizing a dog and performing other sacrilegious rites.

38. Quoted in Lebigre, *Affaire des poisons,* 23.

39. Ibid.

40. For a discussion of *lèse-majesté* in ancien régime France, as well as Cardinal Richelieu's expansion of the definition of the crime, see William F. Church, *Richelieu and Reason of State* (Princeton: Princeton University Press, 1972), 272–76. Ralph Giesey, Lanny Hardy, and James Millhorn, "Cardinal Le Bret and Lese Majesty," *Law and History* 4 (spring 1986): 23–56, is also useful.

41. Jean-Baptiste Colbert, Louis XIV's minister for more than a quarter-century, held nearly as many posts as he had years in office. He served as intendant of finances, superintendent of royal buildings, controller general, secretary of state for the royal household and the navy, and secretary of state for the marine and the colonies. As minister for Paris, Colbert was responsible for the reorganization of the policing of Paris. In 1665 he began to urge the king to reorganize the administration of the city's policing functions, up until that point divided between the city provost, the Parlement of Paris, and the civil and criminal lieutenants of the Châtelet. His reforms eventually led to the establishment of the lieutenancy of police two years later under Nicolas de la Reynie. Collins, *State in Early Modern France,* 88–91, and Bluche, *Louis XIV,* 152–54.

42. Lebigre, *Affaire des poisons,* 55–68.

43. Confrontation of Marie Vigoureux and Marie Bosse, March 15, 1679, BN, MSS fr 7608, fol. 19.

44. The inventory is found in the *procès-verbal des poudres et al trouvé chez La Bosse,* AB, MS 10342, fols. 42–44.

45. The account of the experiments performed on the powders found in La Bosse's apartment are not extant; the description above is drawn from the tests performed on items found at the home of another sorceress implicated in the Affair of the Poisons. *Procès-verbal de visite sur les drogues et eaux trouvée dans la cassette de la Dame Larcher,* April 28, 1680, AB, MS 10347, fol. 630.

46. *Procès-verbal de visite faite par les experts de drogues de la Voisin,* November 16, 1679, AB, MS 10346, fols. 306–9.

47. For La Bosse's interrogation, see AB, MS 10344, fols. 192–94.

48. See Ravaisson-Mollien, *Archives de la Bastille,* vols. 4–7, passim.

49. Confrontation of Mme de Poulaillon and La Bosse, February 27, 1679, ibid., 5:228.

50. La Bosse described her dealings with Mme de Poulaillon in her interrogations of January 4 and 5, 1680, ibid., 5:157–74.

51. For M. de Poulaillon's suit and its judgment in the Chambre de l'Arsenal, see AB, MS 10359, fols. 47–48 and 61–62. These folios also contain a list of Mme de Poulaillon's accused accomplices in the attempt to kidnap and assassinate her husband. Other documents relating to the case can be found in Ravaisson-Mollien, *Archives de la Bastille,* 5:159–253, and passim.

52. La Bosse had attributed the *eau-forte,* mercury, and hemlock found in her apartment to La Voisin, who had "put all this in her head." AB, MS 10344, fol. 194.

53. Reportedly worth 15,000 *livres,* this costly garment was also known as her "robe d'empereur." Confrontation of La Philbert and La Voisin, March 22, 1679, in Ravaisson-Mollien, *Archives de la Bastille,* 5:315.

54. While she had an assortment of lovers, from the proprietor of her local tavern, the *Bonne Eau,* to the magician Lesage to the comte de la Batie, La Voisin continued to live with and financially support her husband after his jewelry shops failed. She confessed that she had tried to poison Antoine and had arranged to have him killed on a number of occasions but had always changed her mind. Confrontation of La Voisin and La Bosse, March 18, 1679, ibid., 5:268, 317–21, and interrogation of La Voisin, September 12, 1679, ibid., 5:471.

55. One well-to-do client, for example, supposedly paid 6,000 *écus* to bring about a second marriage—a princely sum that allegedly included the poisoning of the woman's first husband. Ibid., 5:269–70, 319–21. For the value of money during the ancien régime, see Frank C. Spooner, *The International Economy and Monetary Movements in France, 1493–1725* (Cambridge: Harvard University Press, 1972).

56. Chiromancy is the art of palm reading; physiognomy, the art of predicting a person's future by reading the lines and features of the face.

57. Interrogation of La Voisin, March 17, 1679, in Ravaisson-Mollien, *Archives de la Bastille,* 5:258.

58. Pilgrims visited the chapel located in the older of the two churches at the abbey. This was also known as "praying to St. Rabonni," because the painting hanging in the chapel was widely misinterpreted. The painting depicted Christ and Mary Magdalene, who had a ribbon of dialogue emerging from her mouth that read "master," or "Rabonni" in Hebrew. The supplicants believed that "Rabonni" was the name of the saint in the picture. Ibid., 5:259n1. In seventeenth-century French, "rabonnir" would have been understood to mean "to make good again."

59. Lebigre, *Affaire des poisons*, 88–89.

60. For a useful guide to the development of the French judicial system and the jurisdictions of its many courts during the ancien régime, see Benoît Garnot, *Justice et société en France aux XVIe, XVIIe et XVIIIe siècles* (Paris: Éditions Ophrys, 2000).

61. Apparently Colbert objected to the creation of the Chambre de l'Arsenal. Primi Visconti wrote, "Colbert was strongly opposed to this tribunal. Apart from the fact that it was costing the King's exchequer a great deal of money, he was alarmed at the scandalous picture of the nation that its revelations were establishing. Louvois, on the contrary, supported it; it was his creation, and he had himself suggested it to the king." Visconti, *Mémoires sur la cour de Louis XIV*, 278.

62. Louis XIV prided himself on having reestablished order at his court, among his nobility, within the church, and in the administration of justice in the country. He also sought to ensure order in his capital, establishing a police force in Paris, installing streetlights, and razing the cour des Miracles. See Louis's comments on the subject of order in *Mémoires for the Instruction of the Dauphin*, trans. and ed. Paul Sonnino (New York: Free Press, 1970), 24–26. On Louis XIV's active promotion of his *gloire* and reputation to both a foreign and domestic audience, see Peter Burke, *The Fabrication of Louis XIV* (New Haven: Yale University Press, 1992), and Joseph Klaits, *Printed Propaganda Under Louis XIV: Absolute Monarchy and Public Opinion* (Princeton: Princeton University Press, 1976).

63. Louis XIV, *Mémoires*, 144–45.

64. Special courts, or *tribunaux d'exception*, also had a precedent in the *Grands Jours d'Auvergne* of Clermont of 1665–66, when, in keeping with a long-standing custom of the Paris Parlement, specially appointed commissioners traveled to trouble spots within their bailiwick during the late summer recess to enforce royal law. See Albert N. Hamscher, *The Parlement of Paris After the Fronde, 1653–1673* (Pittsburgh: University of Pittsburgh Press, 1976), 168–70.

65. As the English ambassador reported, "The least accidents are now attributed to poison and vast numbers of people are quaking with fear over it." Letter to Secretary of State Coventry, April 16, 1679, in Ravaisson-Mollien, *Archives de la Bastille*, 5:335.

66. Members of the robe nobility, or the *noblesse de robe*, acquired their rank through the purchase of royal offices that conferred noble status on their holders. These offices usually ennobled the officeholder himself but not the other members of his family. The entire family might be ennobled if their members held the office for three successive generations or a twenty-year period. The *noblesse d'épée*, or nobility of the sword, considered itself the only "true" nobility, as its families had enjoyed their privileged status since the early Middle Ages. Collins, *State in Early Modern France*, xxvii–xxix.

67. Louis and Louvois had no wish to endure another sensational trial like that of the chevalier de Rohan, in which his attempt to overthrow the monarchy and establish a republic had become public knowledge. See Lebigre, *Affaire des poisons*, 68–70, and Mongrédien, *Madame de Montespan et l'affaire des poisons*, 40–42.

68. Marie Vigoureux reported that the marquis de Feuquières had bought a charm that would protect him from being wounded by any weapon. She reported that the marquis had told her he had been wounded in the previous campaign; he was apparently reluctant to repeat the experience. The marquis had also asked to "speak with the spirits." Interrogation of La Vigoureux, January 4, 1679, in Ravaisson-Mollien, *Archives de la Bastille*, 5:164.

69. The Venetian ambassador asserted, "The *premier président* represented to the king the indignity which the parlement endured by being deprived of its customary jurisdiction and boasted of its irreproachable justice so that the parlement might avoid this stain and affront; the king held fast and did not want to yield to these remonstrances. One of these days, we will learn the unhappy facts uncovered by this new tribunal." Contarini to the doge, April 19, 1679, ibid., 5:339–40.

70. In a letter to La Reynie on March 8, 1679, Louvois communicated Louis's appointments to the panel: "the king has chosen Messieurs de Boucherat, Breteuil, Bezons, Voisin, Fieubet, Pelletier, Pommereuil, and d'Argouges, *conseillers d'Etat;* and you, Messieurs de Fortia, Turgot and d'Ormesson, *maîtres des requêtes;* His Majesty also named Monsieur de Bezons and you as reporters [*rapporteurs chargés de l'instruction*], and M. Robert as the *procureur général* of the commission; would you please organize the project in order that I may take care that it will be expedited." Ibid., 5:237–38.

71. *Lettres patentes du 7 avril 1679*. Reprinted in Archives de la Préfecture de Police (hereafter APP), AA-4, "Notes prises au 18e s. sur l'affaire des poisons par Duval, secrétaire de la lieutenant de police," fols. 103–20.

72. Early modern French law made a distinction between "magic," or *magie,* and "witchcraft," or *sortilège.* Perhaps the most useful explanation of the distinction is offered by Alfred Soman. He defines magic as a science, based on the study of learned ritual magic, which was intended to invoke and compel demons to carry out the wishes of a magician. Witchcraft, he writes, was performed at the behest of and with powers bestowed by the devil. In return for carrying out the devil's orders, a witch was able to exact revenge on his or her enemies. The witch was primarily a rural phenomenon, seen to prey on fellow villagers, while the image of the magician informed the imagination of the city and court. *Magie* was a *cas royaux;* witchcraft was not. Soman, "Décriminalisation de la sorcellerie en France," in *Sorcellerie et justice criminelle,* 187–88. *Cas royaux,* according to the criminal ordinance of 1670, included treason, sacrilege, heresy, resistance to the orders of the king or his officials, unlawful assembly, counterfeiting, forgery, rape, and abortion. Marcel Marion, *Dictionnaire des institutions de la France, XVIIe–XVIIIe siècles* (1923; reprint, Paris: Picard, 1984), 73–74. For a brief discussion of the legal theory underpinning the French judicial system after 1400, see Lisa Silverman, *Tortured Subjects: Pain, Truth, and the Body in Early Modern France* (Chicago: University of Chicago Press, 2001), 39–41.

73. Ravaisson-Mollien, *Archives de la Bastille,* 5:238.

74. Bezons had also served as a magistrate in the 1674 trial of the chevalier de Rohan. Primi Visconti reported, "It is said he was so vicious that, when he fell down in a fit of apoplexy, which happened often to him, for he was small and fat, one had only to say to him: 'Monsieur, the accused has confessed' for him to recover immediately." Visconti, *Mémoires sur la cour de Louis XIV,* 94–95.

75. See "Chambre ardente," in vol. 3 of *Encyclopédie, ou, dictionnaire raisonné des sciences, des arts et des métiers par une société de gens des lettres,* 34 vols., ed. Denis Diderot and Jean Le Rond d'Alembert (Paris, 1751–80).

76. French criminal law was revamped three times during the early modern period. On the changes instituted in the 1670 ordinance, see Marc Boulanger, "Justice et absolutisme: La grande ordonnance criminelle d'août 1670," *Revue d'histoire moderne et contemporaine* 47, no. 1 (2000): 7–36. Louis XIV's 1670 ordinance followed the 1498 Ordinance of Blois and the 1539 Ordinance of Villiers-Cotterets. For a comprehensive account of the changes in French criminal law, see François-André Isambert, ed., *Recueil général des anciennes lois françaises depuis l'an 420 jusqu'à la revolution de 1789,* 29 vols. (Paris, 1821–33).

77. During a *récolement,* the witness was summoned to repeat his statements and asked to swear that they were indeed true. The witness could alter his testimony without incurring a

perjury charge, but only at this point; the second version of the *récolement* was legally binding. See Andrews, *Law, Magistracy, and Crime,* which carefully outlines the legal procedures of French criminal trials in the early modern period.

78. Lebigre, *Affaire des poisons,* 75, and Mongrédien, *Madame de Montespan et l'affaire des poisons,* 40–43.

79. Julius R. Ruff, *Crime, Justice, and Public Order in Old Regime France* (London: Croom Helm, 1984), 53–54.

80. For the history of the role of torture within the medieval and early modern European legal systems, see John H. Langbein, *Torture and the Law of Proof: Europe and England in the Ancien Régime* (Chicago: University of Chicago Press, 1977), and Edward Peters, *Torture* (New York: Basil Blackwell, 1985).

81. Full proofs of guilt, which rendered the *question préparatoire* unnecessary, included the testimony of two disinterested eyewitnesses to the crime and the discovery of certain kinds of written evidence or conclusions drawn from that evidence. Early modern legal scholars wrangled over whether or not the confession of the accused constituted a full or proximate proof. Lisa Silverman, *Tortured Subjects,* 44.

82. Elaine Scarry, *The Body in Pain: The Making and Unmaking of the World* (New York: Oxford University Press, 1985), especially chapter 1.

83. In her compelling study of the use of and meaning ascribed to torture in early modern Toulouse, Lisa Silverman argues that the magistrates of that parlement continued to rely upon torture to coerce confessions because they shared the belief that truth was literally fixed within the body. Only the application of pain, which negated the will, could extort the truth from its physical location. See *Tortured Subjects,* particularly chapter 2.

84. As Silverman argues, "just as modern scholars take it as axiomatic that people lie under torture, early modern Europeans took it as axiomatic that people told the truth under torture." Ibid., 88.

85. Andrews, *Law, Magistracy, and Crime,* vol. 1, chapters 11–15.

86. Albert Soman has demonstrated that only 8.5 percent of those prisoners sentenced to torture by the Parlement of Paris between 1539 and 1542 confessed as a result. "Criminal Jurisprudence in *Ancien Regime* France: The *Parlement* of Paris in the Sixteenth and Seventeenth Centuries," in *Crime and Criminal Justice in Europe and Canada,* ed. Louis A. Knafla (Waterloo, Ontario: Wilfred Laurier University Press, 1981), 45–46. That percentage only declined in the following century, when only 3–7 percent of sentences to torture in the Châtelet de Paris culminated in confession between 1735 and 1749. Andrews, *Law, Magistracy, and Crime,* 1:455, 462.

87. On the persistence of the use of judicial torture during the ancien régime despite its ineffectiveness in extracting confessions, see Silverman, *Tortured Subjects.*

88. There is some discrepancy among the numbers put forth by different historians. Lebigre, for example, maintains that five people were sent to the galleys and twenty-three banished (*Affaire des poisons,* 165), while Petitfils (*Madame de Montespan,* 186) lists four sent to the galleys. The police archives, however, list twenty-one banished and forty-three acquitted. APP, AA-4, fol. 319. See also BN, MSS fr 7608, fols. 380–82, for La Reynie's own count as of April 4, 1682.

89. Lebigre, *Affaire des poisons,* 165.

90. Under French law, the accused was confronted with each witness against him or her in order to verify the witness's testimony. The accused was read aloud the witness's statement and then had the opportunity to challenge it. Alfred Soman, "Anatomy of an Infanticide Trial: The Case of Marie-Jeanne Bartonnet (1742)," in *Changing Identities in Early Modern France,* ed. Michael Wolfe (Durham: Duke University Press, 1997), 261.

91. Confrontation of La Voisin and La Bosse, March 18, 1679, in Ravaisson-Mollien, *Archives de la Bastille,* 5:269–70.

92. Ibid., 270.

93. Ibid., 267–74.
94. Quoted in Mongrédien, *Madame de Montespan et l'affaire des poisons,* 44.
95. APP, AA-4, fol. 303.
96. On the forms of punishment meted out during the ancien régime, see Andrews, *Law, Magistracy, and Crime,* 1:307–93.
97. On the expressive function of punishment, see the work of David Garland, particularly his essay "Punishment and Culture."
98. Soman, "Decriminalizing Witchcraft."
99. James R. Farr, "Death of a Judge: Performance, Honor, and Legitimacy in Seventeenth-Century France," *Journal of Modern History* 75 (March 2003): 1–22.
100. APP, AA-4, fols. 120–71, 303.
101. Lebigre, *Affaire des poisons,* 77.
102. Or so the clerk recorded in the *procès-verbal de la question.*
103. As a viricide, Marie Ferry had her right thumb cut off before her execution and her body was thrown into the fire afterward, as the law demanded for those who murdered their spouses. APP, AA-4, fols. 303–4. The premeditated murder, or *l'assassinat,* of a family member was a *crime atroce* under ancien régime law. To use poison to do so only exacerbated the enormity of the offense. As Richard Mowery Andrews writes, "Murder by design was more than the most aggravated form of homicide. It was also a supreme sin in Catholic doctrine, one for which the penalty in canon law was excommunication. Its essence was evilness of purpose and willful treachery, not the sheer action of killing. . . . Here, there was a perfect conceptual symmetry between criminal law and Catholic morality." Andrews, *Law, Magistracy, and Crime,* 1:549–50.
104. Mme de Poulaillon in fact barely escaped execution. Before her final questioning, the judges had ordered that she be tortured, executed, and all her goods confiscated. However, her appearance *sur la sellette* so moved the Chambre that M. de Fieubet was able to persuade three of his ten fellow judges who had voted for her death to change their minds. The judges were well aware that to commute Mme de Poulaillon's sentence meant that other condemned prisoners would avoid execution as well. Some of the judges may have been motivated to spare Mme de Poulaillon so that Mmes de Dreux and Leféron (already under arrest) would not be put to death. See the *procès-verbal de la Chambre* of June 5, 1679, for an account of the judges' session, in Ravaisson-Mollien, *Archives de la Bastille,* 5:386–87.
105. AAP, AA-4, fols. 288–302. Mme de Dreux's relatives, however, did recuse themselves from hearing her case. *Procès-verbal des séances de la chambre,* April 18, 1679, in Ravaisson-Mollien, *Archives de la Bastille,* 5:337–38.
106. Louvois and the king had little doubt that the women were guilty. La Voisin's and La Bosse's accusations against them were eventually confirmed by a dozen other witnesses. Louvois to Louis, October 8, 1679, in Ravaisson-Mollien, *Archives de la Bastille,* 5:501–2.
107. Ibid., 6:204n1.
108. See Angus McLaren, *Reproductive Rituals: The Perception of Fertility in England from the Sixteenth to the Nineteenth Century* (New York: Methuen, 1984), for an analysis of the various methods of contraception available to women in early modern Europe. Chapter 3 includes a discussion of the availability and use of both herbal and physical methods of restricting fertility, while chapter 4 explores abortion as a means of birth control.
109. Interrogation of La Lepère, April 4, 1679, in Ravaisson-Mollien, *Archives de la Bastille,* 5:328–29.
110. La Lepère described her procedure: "ce n'est que de l'eau, et le tout consiste en la manière de seringuer." Interrogation of La Lepère, May 27, 1679, ibid., 5:379.
111. La Lepère maintained that after she performed an abortion, she was careful to baptize the fetus and then paid a gravedigger to bury it in the consecrated ground of a church cemetery. Confrontation of La Bosse and La Lepère, April 30, 1679, ibid., 5:353–54.

112. See, for example, Lesage's interrogations of November 5, 1679, and January 1, 1680, ibid., 6:37–42.

113. La Dodée, interrogated only once, committed suicide in prison by cutting her own throat in September 1679. Louvois to king, September 16, 1679, ibid., 5:477.

114. In early modern Europe, monks and shepherds, with their traditional knowledge of herbs and plants, were considered likely poisoners. The producers of poison implicated in the affair bear out this stereotype to some degree; the former Capucin Gérard, Brother Martinet of the *Minimes du Palais Royale,* and the shepherds Galet and Maître Pierre supplied poisonous concoctions to many of Paris's sorceresses. Lebigre, *Affaire des poisons,* 65–66.

115. Ravaisson-Mollien, *Archives de la Bastille,* vols. 5–7, passim.

116. The abbé Mariette, arrested at the same time as his partner Lesage, escaped the galleys because his cousin was married to one of the judges of the criminal chamber of the Châtelet. Mariette was sentenced to nine years' banishment from Paris, a period of time he spent at the chateau of the vicomte de Cousserans (another of La Voisin's many lovers), posing as the "prior of Sainte-Catherine." Petitfils, *Affaire de poisons,* 58–60.

117. *Du procès jugé en 1668 et de l'interrogation de Mariette du 30 de Juin de ladict année,* BN, MSS fr 7608, fols. 143–45.

118. A *pistole volant* was a magical coin that reappeared in its owner's pocket no matter how often it was spent. Interrogation of Lesage, March 22, 1679, in Ravaisson-Mollien, *Archives de la Bastille,* 5:285–89.

119. *Du procès jugé en 1668 et de l'interrogation de Mariette du 30 de Juin de ladict annee,* BN, MSS fr 7608, fol. 143.

120. Interrogations of Lesage, May 25, June 23, and September 12, 1679, in Ravaisson-Mollien, *Archives de la Bastille,* 5:376, 420–23, 474.

121. Interrogation of La Voisin, September 12, 1679, ibid., 5:468.

122. Mme de Montespan is the subject of a recent biography by Lisa Hilton, *Athénaïs: The Life of Louis XIV's Mistress, the Real Queen of France* (Boston: Little, Brown, 2002).

123. La Voisin's deposition is no longer extant. Her statements were repeated in a letter sent by Louvois to the king, September 16, 1679, in Ravaisson-Mollien, *Archives de la Bastille,* 5:477.

124. La Vertemart is sometimes referred to as La Lemaire (which was her father's name). See Mongrédien, *Madame de Montespan et l'affaire des poisons,* 49–50.

125. La Reynie's notes, attached to a Declaration by Lesage, September 17, 1679, in Ravaisson-Mollien, *Archives de la Bastille,* 5: 478.

126. Interrogation of La Voisin, September 22, 1679, ibid., 5:483–85. La Voisin consistently denied ever having known Mlle des Œillets. See, for example, her interrogation of January 16, 1680, ibid., 6:101–5.

127. Declaration by Lesage, September 26, 1679, ibid., 5:490.

128. "My intention is that you proceed as soon as possible with the interrogations, and to have written on separate sheets the responses that each of the prisoners make to you." Louis to La Reynie, September 21, 1679, ibid., 5:483.

129. Interrogations of the suspects, conducted by La Reynie, were recorded by the clerk of the commission. Clean (and if the king deemed it necessary, censored) copies of the originals were sent to the judges on the case. The king kept the uncensored statements until La Reynie's death in 1709, when Louis burned them. La Reynie, however, often jotted down his own notes during interrogations and thus historians have been able to piece together some of the missing information.

130. Primi Visconti, in fact, was the only one of the three who wrote that Mme de Montespan had been implicated in the Affair of the Poisons at all. Recounting the affair in his memoirs, he noted, "many [court women] wanted a secret for love, and several the place of Mme de

Montespan; however, La Voisin boasted that it was by her art that Mme de Montespan and Louvois stayed in favor." Visconti, *Mémoires sur la cour de Louis XIV,* 286.

131. Interrogation of October 6, 1679, in Ravaisson-Mollien, *Archives de la Bastille,* 5:495.

132. The bulk of Lesage's accusations against the duc de Luxembourg are contained in his declaration of October 6, 1679, ibid., 5:495–501. Louvois informed the king of the accusations against Luxembourg and Feuquières in his letter of October 8, 1679, ibid., 501–2. After learning of Lesage's accusations, the marquis de Feuquières, present at the ceremony, explained the situation to his father in his letter of March 16, 1680: "The other charge has to do with a note written by the late La Vallière and myself and burnt in the presence of M. de Luxembourg. The fact is that a man known as Lesage told us that he could bring us an answer to any note we wrote, without reading it, in three days; so, treating it as a huge joke, La Vallière filled a sheet of paper with nonsense and then we set fire to it. This villain now claims that the note contained matters of grave importance." Antoine de Pas, marquis de Feuquières, *Lettres inédites des Feuquières,* ed. Étienne Gallois (Paris: LeLeux, 1845), 4:74.

133. Louvois to Louis, October 8, 1679, in Ravaisson-Mollien, *Archives de la Bastille,* 5:502.

134. Ibid., 501–2.

135. Ibid.

136. Ibid. Lesage claimed the two priests present at the mass were his old friend the abbé Mariette and Father Davot. Interrogation of Lesage, November 28, 1679, ibid., 6: 98–100. See also Mongrédien, *Madame de Montespan et l'affaire des poisons,* 55–56. La Voisin's interrogation of January 16, 1680, contains the same accusations against the comtesse de Soissons, the vicomtesse de Polignac, and the duchesse de Bouillon. Ravaisson-Mollien, *Archives de la Bastille,* 6:101–5.

137. Declaration of Lesage, October 14, 1679, ibid., 6:19–20; and interrogation of Lesage, October 28, 1679, ibid., 6:31–36.

138. Confrontation of Lesage and La Voisin, January 16, 1680, ibid., 6:99.

139. This argument was first introduced by Funck-Bretano in *Drame des poisons,* chapter 5. Noémie Courtès, however, finds it less likely, writing, "Il est plus probable que Corneille et plus encore Visé, directeur du *Mercure galant,* aient juste tiré parti d'une idée à la mode." *L'écriture de l'enchantement: Magie et magiciens dans la littérature française du XVIIe siècle* (Paris: Honoré Champion, 2004), 268.

140. Lebigre, *Affaire des poisons,* 82.

141. Corneille and de Visé, *La devineresse.*

142. As Courtès notes, La Voisin's execution coincided with the play's last performance. La Voisin was executed on February 22; the play closed on March 10, 1680. The play was performed 175 times during its initial run and remained popular for decades; it was reprised 128 times before 1739. Courtès, *Écriture de l'enchantement,* 268.

143. Reprinted in Ravaisson-Mollien, *Archives de la Bastille,* 6:67.

144. Of the aristocrats ordered arrested, only the duc de Luxembourg was actually imprisoned. Refusing the advice of friends who urged him to flee Paris, he surrendered himself to the governor of the Bastille on January 24, 1680. Ibid., 6:107.

145. Mme de Sévigné to Mme de Grignan, January 30, 1680, in Sévigné, *Correspondance,* 2:819–22.

146. Bussy to La Rivière, January 27, 1680, in *Correspondance de Roger de Rabutin, comte de Bussy avec sa famille et ses amis, 1666–1693,* ed. Ludovic Lalanne (Paris: Charpentier, 1858), 5:45–46.

147. January 29, 1680, in *Lettres inédites des Feuquières,* 4:72.

148. M. Saville to Secretary of State Coventry, January 25, 1680, in Ravaisson-Mollien, *Archives de la Bastille,* 6:110.

149. The king did make some show of chasing after the comtesse and her friend, ordering

two officers of his guard to arrest the two women. Louvois to M. Boucherat, January 24, 1680, ibid., 6:107.

150. Mme de Sévigné to the comte de Guitaut, January 29, 1680, in Sévigné, *Correspondance,* 2:818.

151. Visconti, *Mémoires sur la cour de Louis XIV,* 277.

152. Mme de Sévigné to the comte de Guitaut, January 29, 1680, in Sévigné, *Correspondance,* 2:818.

153. The English ambassador reported too that the crimes of the accused aristocrats were minor ones. "Tout leur crime se réduit, pense-t-on, à quelques pratiques avec les diseurs de bonne aventure, à propos d'intrigues amoureuses." Saville to Secretary of State Coventry, January 25, 1680. Reprinted and translated in Ravaisson-Mollien, *Archives de la Bastille,* 6:110.

154. Mme de Sévigné to the comte de Guitaut, January 29, 1680, in Sévigné, *Correspondance,* 2:817.

155. Mme de Sévigné to Mme de Grignan, January 30, 1680, ibid., 2:821.

156. Stuart Clark, *Thinking with Demons: The Idea of Witchcraft in Early Modern Europe* (Oxford: Oxford University Press, 1997), 587.

157. Philip K. Riley, "Michel Foucault, Lust, Women, and Sin in Louis XIV's Paris," *Church History* 59 (1990): 40n21.

158. For a fuller explication of this point, see John Bossy, *Christianity in the West, 1400–1700* (Oxford: Oxford University Press, 1985), and James R. Farr, *Authority and Sexuality in Early Modern Burgundy (1550–1730)* (New York: Oxford University Press, 1995).

159. On the influence of the *dévots,* see Alain Tallon, *La compagnie du Saint-Sacrement (1629–1667): Spiritualité et société* (Paris: Éditions du Cerf, 1990).

160. Quoted in Farr, *Authority and Sexuality,* 39–40. Farr notes that the same sentiment was echoed in *L'homme criminel* by the early seventeenth-century Oratorian Jean-François Senault, which stressed a particularly Augustinian vision of original sin that described Adam's disobedience to God as an offense of "criminal man."

161. During the latter half of the seventeenth century, blasphemy was popularly associated with offenses against public order; those accused of blasphemy by their neighbors were usually described as quarrelsome, debauched, and drunken. On this point, and on the history of blasphemy more broadly, see Alain Cabantous, *Blasphemy: Impious Speech in the West from the Seventeenth to the Nineteenth Century,* trans. Eric Rauth (New York: Columbia University Press, 2002).

162. Benoît Garnot, "La législation et la répression des crimes dans la France moderne, XVIe–XVIIIe siècles," *Revue historique* 293, no. 1 (1993): 76.

163. For an extended analysis of Louis XIV's campaign to enforce morality in the capital, see Philip K. Riley, *A Lust for Virtue: Louis XIV's Attack on Sin in Seventeenth-Century France* (Westport, Conn.: Greenwood Press, 2001).

164. February 24, 1680, APP, AA-4, fols. 103–20.

165. The phrase is from the title of Riley's work, *A Lust for Virtue: Louis XIV's Attack on Sin in Seventeenth-Century France.*

166. Louvois to M. Boucherat, February 4, 1680. "Monsieur, le Roi vous a chargé d'expliquer à la chambre que son intention était qu'elle continuât les procédures nécessaires pour la punition des coupables de poison, et qu'elle agît en toute liberté contre tous ceux qui se trouveront convaincus d'un crime si énorme; depuis S.M. ayant été informée des discours qui se sont tenus à Paris à l'occasion des décrets donnés depuis quelques jours par la chambre, elle m'a commandé de vous faire savoir qu'elle désire que vous assuriez les juges de sa protection, et que vous leur fassiez connaître qu'elle s'attend qu'ils continueront à rendre la justice avec la fermeté qu'ils ont commencé, sans s'en laisser détourner par quelque considération que ce puisse être." Ravaisson-Mollien, *Archives de la Bastille,* 6:137.

167. Peers had the traditional right of being heard by the Court of Peers, or the Parlement of Paris sitting together with the peers of the realm. Collins, *State in Early Modern France*, xxix.

168. Interrogation of Mme la Duchesse de Bouillon, January 29, 1680, in Ravaisson-Mollien, *Archives de la Bastille*, 6:117–20.

169. For Mme de Sévigné's account of the duchess's appearance before the Chambre, see her letter of January 30, 1680, to her daughter, in Sévigné, *Correspondance*, 2:822.

170. Ibid., 833, 835.

171. Declaration by Lesage, September 26, 1679, in Ravaisson-Mollien, *Archives de la Bastille*, 5:490.

172. Lebigre, *Affaire des poisons*, 102. La Reynie later reflected in his personal notes: "On ne saurait juger non plus la dame Chappelain, à cause que la Filastre lui a été confrontée: femme d'un grand commerce, appliquée depuis longtemps à la recherche des poisons, ayant travaillée, fait travailler pour cela, suspecte de plusieurs empoisonnements, dans une pratique continuelle d'impiétés, de sacrilèges et de maléfices; accusée par la Filastre de lui avoir enseigné la pratique de ses abominations avec des prêtres, impliquée considérablement dans les affaires de Vanens." BN, MSS fr 7608.

173. The priests included Olivier, Lempérier, Lemeignan, Cotton, and Guibourg. Declaration by La Filastre, August 1, 1680, in Ravaisson-Mollien, *Archives de la Bastille*, 6:273–76.

174. Ibid., 6:19–371, passim.

175. Benoît Robin de la Frasse, a gendarme, confirmed that La Filastre had asked his help in finding a post in the household of the king's new favorite. Interrogation of January 3, 1680, ibid., 6:85–87.

176. The description of Mlle de Fontanges is from the abbé de Choisy. Ziegler, *Court of Versailles in the Reign of Louis XIV*, 173.

177. Interrogation of La Filastre, January 2, 1680, in Ravaisson-Mollien, *Archives de la Bastille*, 6:70–74.

178. La Delaporte said during one of her own interrogations that the majority of those who came to have their palms read weren't long in asking for "something else." Lebigre, *Affaire des poisons*, 94.

179. La Voisin admitted that she knew of such a plot in her interrogation of September 22, 1679. Ravaisson-Mollien, *Archives de la Bastille*, 5:484.

180. For the *procès-verbaux* recorded while La Voisin was under torture, see ibid., 6:150–82. La Reynie's notes on the session are found in BN, MSS fr 7608, fols. 16–18.

181. La Voisin was convicted of "empoisonnements, d'avortements, de séductions, d'impiétés, et profanations." APP, AA-4, fols. 304–5.

182. *Medianoche* was a meal taken after midnight between a fast day and a meat day. Ziegler, *Court of Versailles in the Reign of Louis XIV*, 171.

183. Mme de Sévigné to Mme de Grignan, February 23, 1680, in Sévigné, *Correspondance*, 2:846.

184. Ibid., 2:847.

185. Her first interrogation took place on January 30, 1680. A brief summary of the interrogation indicates that she agreed that her mother had tried to poison Antoine Montvoisin's soup, listed some of her mother's acquaintances, and asserted that Maître Pierre was a poisoner. Ravaisson-Mollien, *Archives de la Bastille*, 6:120.

186. Interrogation of La Fille Voisin, March 28, 1680, ibid., 6:194–98.

187. Interrogation of La Fille Voisin, July 26, 1680, ibid., 6:244.

188. Louis made Mlle de Fontanges a duchess with a pension of 20,000 *livres* in April 1680.

189. Whether or not infusing gloves with poison could kill an intended victim is uncertain, but it was certainly thought possible in the seventeenth century. As Georges Mongrédien explains, "J'ai beaucoup étudié l'affaire des poisons et j'ai, à ce sujet, posé à différents chimistes et médecins

la question de savoir s'ils pensaient possible d'empoisonner soit des gants, soit des chemises, soit du linge de corps, etc. J'ai toujours eu des réponses divergentes et incertaines. Le sûr, c'est qu'à l'époque on y croyait fermement." Quoted in Eglal Henein, "Les poisons dans le roman (1607–1628)," *Madame de Sévigné, Molière et la médecine de son temps: 3e Colloque de Marseille* 95 (October–December 1973): 151–58.

190. Interrogation of La Fille Voisin, July 12, 1680, in Ravaisson-Mollien, *Archives de la Bastille*, 6:241.

191. Interrogation of La Fille Voisin, March 28, 1680, ibid., 6:197.

192. La Voisin had gone to her death maintaining that her petition sought only the release of François Blessis. See her *procès-verbal de question,* February 22, 1680, ibid., 6:178. The plans to poison the duchesse de Fontanges and the king with poison-infused material resemble those of an alleged attempt to poison Elizabeth I of England in 1598. A Jesuit priest supposedly poisoned the pommel of Elizabeth's saddle; when she placed her hand upon it, the poison was to seep into her skin. On this case, see Francis Edwards, S.J. "The Strange Case of the Poisoned Pommel: Richard Walpole, S.J., and the Squire Plot, 1597–1598," *Archivum Historicum Societatis Jesu* 56, no. 111 (1987): 3–82.

193. Interrogation of La Fille Voisin, July 20, 1680, in Ravaisson-Mollien, *Archives de la Bastille*, 6:243.

194. Clagny was the location of the chateau that the king built for Mme de Montespan as a retreat away from the court.

195. Interrogation of La Fille Voisin, July 26, 1680, in Ravaisson-Mollien, *Archives de la Bastille*, 6:244.

196. Interrogation of La Fille Voisin, August 13, 1680, ibid., 6:291.

197. Louvois to La Reynie, June 25, 1680, ibid., 6:229.

198. During July and August 1680, Louis inspected the fortifications of twenty-one towns from Boulogne to Montmédy. Bluche, *Louis XIV,* 288. On Louis XIV's passion for fortifications, see Robert Bornecque, *La France de Vauban* (Paris: Arthaud, 1984).

199. Louvois to La Reynie, July 21, 1680, in Ravaisson-Mollien, *Archives de la Bastille,* 6:262.

200. The prisoners described the ritual of the amatory mass for their interrogators in some detail. The ceremonies, which parodied the Christian mass, were intended to invoke demons who would fulfill the commands of those who had compelled them to appear. The powerful demons were drawn to the mass by an incantation read by the priest and by the blood of an infant sacrificed as part of the ritual. Amatory masses were usually commissioned by fortune hunters seeking the location of buried treasure or by those who sought demonic assistance in matters of the heart.

201. Interrogation of Guibourg, June 26, 1680, in Ravaisson-Mollien, *Archives de la Bastille,* 6:232.

202. The well-informed Lesage added that the women over whom the masses were said were "entirely naked." He also told La Reynie that Guibourg was a member of La Voisin's cabal, an intimate friend of La Filastre, and had said masses over a startling variety of objects: a petition to be handed to the king, an afterbirth, and poisons manufactured from powdered toads. A mass, said by an ordained priest, was believed to infuse these objects with a powerful sacerdotal magic. Interrogation of Lesage, July 18, 1680, ibid., 6:255–60.

203. Interrogation of La Filastre, August 10, 1680, BN, MSS fr 7608, fol. 298.

204. Interrogation of La Fille Voisin, August 20, 1680, in Ravaisson-Mollien, *Archives de la Bastille,* 6:298.

205. Louis to La Reynie, August 2, 1680, ibid., 6:276.

206. Reynie drafted, but never sent, this report to Louvois. He mused, "Parce qu'elle a dit dans tout le reste de la déclaration, il paraît certain air d'ingénuité, ou, si les choses sont fausses, tout le monde peut être trompé; cependant, je ne m'y assurerais pas, et il me paraît, je ne saurais

dire pourquoi, plus de lieu de présumer ces choses horribles fausses que de les croire vraies." *Projet de lettre de M. de la Reynie à Louvois,* September 2, 1680, ibid., 6:306–7.

207. Lebigre, *Affaire des poisons,* 103.

208. The powders were allegedly sent in 1676, when the king embarked on an affair with the princesse de Soubise, and 1677, when Mlle de Fontanges arrived at court and caught the eye of the king. Ravaisson-Mollien, *Archives de la Bastille,* 6:305n1.

209. *Résumé* of the declaration by Galet, September 1, 1680, BN, MSS fr 7608, fols. 302–3.

210. Louvois to M. Robert, September 25, 1680, in Ravaisson-Mollien, *Archives de la Bastille,* 6:315–16.

211. At the foot of the scaffold, La Filastre retracted her statements and said that the poisons were in fact intended for the wife of a friend of whom she was jealous. La Filastre did persist, however, in her statements that Mme de Montespan had purchased love potions for the king (because the amatory masses had been ineffectual) and all that she had said about the amatory masses of the abbé Guibourg. October 1, 1680, ibid., 6:324–26.

212. Louis XIV, *Mémoires,* 144.

213. See the *mémoire* of the clerk, Jean Sagot, on the history of the Chambre's sessions. Ravaisson-Mollien, *Archives de la Bastille,* 6:346–48.

214. Chapter 2 argues that there were two main cultural scripts by which a learned seventeenth-century audience understood the motives of poisoners: the myth of Medea and that of the marquise de Brinvilliers. Medea had long served as the archetypal example of a poisoner. Like Medea, poisoners were held to act out of envy or vengeance toward romantic rivals. The dangerous characteristics of Medea and the marquise—jealousy, illicit sexuality, and greed— were readily mapped onto those women implicated in the Affair of the Poisons.

215. La Filastre, Lesage, and the abbé Cotton claimed that Mme de Vivonne had made a pact with the devil, had amatory masses said, and plotted to poison Mme de Montespan and Colbert. Confrontation of La Filastre with diverse suspects, September 21, 1680, in Ravaisson-Mollien, *Archives de la Bastille,* 6:312.

216. *Projet de lettre de M. de la Reynie à Louvois,* September 2, 1680, and *Compte rendu au roi par M. de la Reynie,* ibid., 6:306–7 and 319–23.

217. Interrogation of Guibourg, October 10, 1680, ibid., 6:335–36.

218. *Projet d'un rapport de M. de la Reynie au Roi,* BN, MSS fr 7608, fol. 354.

219. *Du procès jugé en 1668 et de l'interrogation de Mariette du 30 de Juin de ladict année,* ibid., 7608, fols. 143–45. For La Reynie's conclusions on this point, see his personal notes taken during the November 8, 1680, interrogation of Mariette, ibid., 7608, fol. 251.

220. Mme de Sévigné reported on one such occasion, "What a triumph at Versailles! . . . What a second duchesse de Valentois! . . . Just picture to yourself everything that selfish pride can suggest in its moment of triumph." Mme de Sévigné to Mme de Grignan, June 11, 1677, in Sévigné, *Correspondance,* 2:462.

221. To mollify his *maîtresse en titre,* who had become jealous of Mlle de Fontanges, the king requested in April 1679 that the comtesse de Soissons resign this office in favor of Mme de Montespan. The countess had no choice but to gracefully fulfill the king's request and accept the 200,000 *écus* that sweetened the offer. Mongrédien, *Madame de Montespan et l'affaire des poisons,* 155.

222. Louis XIV granted Louise the title of duchesse de Vaujours and legitimized their daughter in 1667—the year that his affair with Mme de Montespan began. Hilton, *Athénaïs,* 142.

223. The couple, engaged in February 1679, married in October 1680, while the Chambre de l'Arsenal was suspended. Mongrédien, *Madame de Montespan et l'affaire des poisons,* 165. Following Jean Lemoine, some historians have attributed Louvois's influence to the course of the proceedings. Louvois's allies at court (most notably the comte de Gassilly) were not investigated by the Chambre, for example, even though the suspects in the affair lodged accusations against them. On this point, see Somerset, *Affair of the Poisons,* 336–37.

224. Mongrédien, *Madame de Montespan et l'affaire des poisons,* 128–31.

225. So argue most historians who have studied the Affair of the Poisons. See, for example, ibid., 173–82, and Lebigre, *Affaire des poisons,* 123–24.

226. On this point, see Hilton, *Athénaïs,* 213–22.

227. Mongrédien, *Madame de Montespan et l'affaire des poisons,* chapter 5, "Défense de Madame de Montespan." His argument is seconded by Hilton, *Athénaïs,* 214–19.

228. "Guibourg dit un charme pour faire mourir le Roi; prétend que la Des Œillets et l'Anglais était dans le même dessein . . . être exécuté en faisant donner des poudres empoisonnées à madame de Montespan, et en les lui faisant donner comme pour l'amour; on prétendait, en la trompant elle-même, se servir de sa main pour consommer le crime." *Projet de lettre à Louvois,* in Ravaisson-Mollien, *Archives de la Bastille,* 6:393.

229. The young duchess had never recovered from the birth of a stillborn child the year before. Mme de Montespan's remark to that effect may be apocryphal, but it made the rounds of the court. See the letter of Mme de Sévigné to Mme de Grignan, July 14, 1680, in Sévigné, *Correspondance,* 2:1009.

230. *Mémoire* of Sagot, 1681, in Ravaisson-Mollien, *Archives de la Bastille,* 6:346–48.

231. BN, MSS fr 7608, fol. 133.

232. *Mémoire* of La Reynie, in Ravaisson-Mollien, *Archives de la Bastille,* 6:454–59.

233. See the interrogations, *procès-verbaux,* and confrontations found throughout ibid., 6:451–98, 7:1–132.

234. La Reynie would have preferred that the prisoners be tried according to the law. He grumbled, "Il y a encore une grande suite d'autres accusés considérables qui trouvent l'impunité de leurs crimes. La fille de la Voisin ne peut être jugée, non plus que Mariette, quelque chose qui survienne à son égard. Latour, Vautier, sa femme resteront non seulement impunis mais, par les considérations qui feront tenir leurs crimes secrets, leur procès ne pourra être achevé d'instruire." *Mémoire* of La Reynie, BN, MSS fr 7608.

235. Ibid.

236. Louvois to M. Chauvelin, intendant of Franch-Comté, December 16, 1682, in Ravaisson-Mollien, *Archives de la Bastille,* 7:133.

237. The limits placed on Louis XIV's ability to exercise absolute power have been explored in a series of notable studies, including Julian Swann, *Provincial Power and Absolute Monarchy: The Estates General of Burgundy, 1661–1790* (Cambridge: Cambridge University Press, 2003); Duindam, *Vienna and Versailles;* Duindam, *Myths of Power;* Parker, *Class and State in Ancien-Régime France;* Beik, *Absolutism and Society in Seventeenth-Century France;* and Mettam, *Power and Faction.*

238. Ravaisson-Mollien, *Archives de la Bastille,* 4:226.

239. Louis XIV, *Mémoires,* 144–45.

240. In 1665 the king began a reform of the judicial system when he ordered the creation of a special commission to reform its abuses. The recommendations of the commission brought about the reformation of the appeals system and rectified some judicial abuses with the ordinance on justice (1667), streamlined jurisdictional disputes (1669), and revised the criminal code (1670). Collins, *State in Early Modern France,* 113–14.

## Chapter 2

1. During the early modern period, the foreigners associated most closely with poison were Italians. As almost all of the suspects in the Affair of the Poisons were French, this characterization could have little bearing on how the scandal was read by Louis XIV's subjects. After the Affair of the Poisons had come to a close, however, the French government did try to

represent the rash of poisonings as the work of foreigners. See *Edit du Roy pour la punition de différents crimes* (Paris: Jean Baptiste Coignard, 1682), BN, Collection Delamare, MS 21730, fol. 115. That this attempt enjoyed some success can be seen in works that attributed the crime of poison to the instigation of Italians. See, for example, Diderot and d'Alembert, *Encyclopédie* 3:47–48, entry for "Chambre ardente": "On a appelé par la même raison *chambre ardente,* une chambre de justice qui fut établie en 1679, pour la poursuite de ceux qui étoient accusés d'avoir fait ou donné du poison . . . deux Italiens, dont l'un se nommoit Exili, avoient travaillé long-tems [*sic*] à Paris à chercher la pierre philosophale. . . . Ces deux Italiens ayant perdu à cette recherche le peu de bien qu'ils avoient, voulurent réparer leur fortune par le crime, pour cet effet vendirent secrètement des poisons: la marquise de Brinvilliers fut du nombre de ceux qui eurent recours à ce détestable artifice." On the connections made between Italians and poison more generally, see David Gentilcore, *Healers and Healing in Early Modern Italy* (Manchester: Manchester University Press, 1998), 103–9. On the association of servants with the crime, see Stephanie Elizabeth O'Hara, "Tracing Poison: Theater and Society in Seventeenth-Century France" (Ph.D. diss, Duke University, 2003), 32–39, and Frédéric Jacquin, "Un empoisonnement à Paris: L'empoisonnement du sieur de Vaux (1742)," *Histoire, économie et société* 20, no. 1 (2001): 34n91.

2. The sorceress was represented in the visual arts, too. Poussin designed a series of eight tapestries depicting the myth in the middle of the century. Noémie Courtès notes the frequency with which the myth of Medea was retold during the ancien régime: "Il semble donc que Médée soit une figure de référence pour le XVIIe siècle et qu'elle informe l'imaginaire, ce que l'on retrouve dans la fiction où son personnage jouit d'une faveur notable." *Écriture de l'enchantement,* 160.

3. Louis XIV was so taken with Bensarade's effort that he ordered an illustrated edition published. Burke, *Fabrication of Louis XIV,* 195. Le Comte's magisterial compendium was more than a thousand pages long, thirteen of which were dedicated to Medea. The author included a "remède contre la breuvage de Médée" in the work. Courtès, *Écriture de l'enchantement,* 49–50.

4. Thus the anonymous author of *Questions sur les empoisonneurs et autres semblables* found his representative poisoners in both history and myth, among them Jocasta, Medea, Circe, and those executed during the Affair of the Poisons. See the "Sixième question: Pourquoy le crime de poison a tousjours esté plus commun aux femmes qu'aux hommes," BA, MS 2664, fols. 45–50 (c. 1700).

5. On this point, see Erica Harth, *Ideology and Culture in Seventeenth-Century France* (Ithaca: Cornell University Press, 1983), 54–57, as well as Burke, *Fabrication of Louis XIV,* 194–97.

6. For a list of the works, see Courtès, *Écriture de l'enchantement,* 681–84.

7. See the introduction to *Médée,* ed. André de Leyssac (Geneva: Librarie Droz, 1978), 7–16, for a full account of the play's history.

8. Pierre Corneille, *Oeuvres complètes,* ed. Georges Couton (Paris: Gallimard, 1980), 1:1382–84.

9. See Abby E. Zanger, *Scenes from the Marriage of Louis XIV: Nuptial Fictions and the Making of Absolutist Power* (Stanford: Stanford University Press, 1997), 98–130, and Amy Kay Wygant, "Pierre Corneille's Medea-Machine," *Romantic Review* 85, no. 4 (1994): 537–51, for extended discussions of this work.

10. *Thésée*'s popularity stood the test of time; it was revived thirteen times over the course of the next century, most notably in 1677, 1678, and 1679—the years between the execution of the marquise de Brinvilliers and the onset of the Affair of the Poisons. James H. Johnson, *Listening in Paris: A Cultural History* (Berkeley and Los Angeles: University of California Press, 1995), 22–23.

11. *Thésée* was reprised a total of ten times between 1677 and 1768. Courtès, *Écriture de l'enchantement,* 678.

12. Jean Racine, *Phèdre,* in his *Oeuvres complètes,* ed. P. Mesnard (Paris: Hachette, 1885),

396. For a close reading of *Phèdre,* see Amy Kay Wygant, "The Meanings of *Phèdre*" (Ph.D. diss., Johns Hopkins University, 1995), and Amy Kay Wygant, "Medea, Poison, and the Epistemology of Error in *Phèdre,*" *Modern Language Review* 95, no. 1 (2000): 62–71.

13. George Robb has found that Circe, rather than Medea, served as an archetypal figure of the sorceress and poisoner in nineteenth-century England. Others included Morgan Le Fay and Lucrezia Borgia. Robb, "Circe in Crinoline: Domestic Poisonings in Victorian England," *Journal of Family History* 22, no. 2 (1997): 176–90.

14. For example, Donneau de Visé and Thomas Corneille's machine play *Circé* and Alard and Vondrebeck's comedy *Circé en postures* were performed in 1675 and 1678, respectively. Barry Russell, "Années 1675" and "Années 1678" in *Calendrier des spectacles sous Louis XIV,* edition 1996–98. Le théâtre de la foire à Paris: Textes et documents, available online at http://www.foires.net/ (accessed March 20, 2006). For a list of all the productions that featured Circe, see Courtès, *Écriture de l'enchantement,* 682–84.

15. Isaac de Bensarade, *Metamorphoses d'Ovide* (Paris: Imprimerie Royale, 1676), 404.

16. Corneille, *Oeuvres complètes,* 331.

17. Corneille, "Examen," *Médée,* 137.

18. A majority (74 percent) of those executed for the crime of poison during the Affair of the Poisons were women. In general, however, the stereotypical picture of poisoners (as predominantly if not exclusively female) seems not to have had a basis in fact. In his work on the crime of poison in medieval Europe, Franck Collard finds that only 18 percent of those prosecuted for poison were women, while 75 percent were men, and the remaining number were men and women tried together. But because women were more frequently convicted of poison than of murder by any other means, he finds, "la présence féminine parmi les accusés est donc marquée. Néanmoins, elle reste très minoritaire. Plus que la sorcellerie, la *venenatio* est largement commise au masculin." Collard, *Le crime de poison au moyen âge* (Paris: Presses Universitaires de France, 2003), 114. Monique Septon, whose study of criminal and judicial records in French-speaking Belgium begins in the late eighteenth century, writes in "Les femmes et le poison: L'empoisonnement devant les jurisdictions criminelles en Belgique, 1795–1914" (Ph.D. diss., Marquette University, 1996) that only a small majority of the poisoners found in her research were women. The sociological profile of poisoners that emerges from Septon's study indicates that most were of the poorer classes, usually of rural origins, and that poison was used primarily against family members. According to Ann-Louise Shapiro, poison was still considered the female crime par excellence in late nineteenth-century France, despite the rough parity between numbers of men and women convicted for the crime. Between 1886 and 1900, she finds, five women and three men were convicted of poison (270n43). By the end of the nineteenth century, the concept of the born female poisoner, *l'empoisonneuse,* explicitly linked women's use of poison to their moral and physical weakness. There was no male counterpart to the *empoisonneuse.* Beliefs that the crime was feminine in nature led experts to describe the male poisoners as medically degenerate and effeminate. Shapiro, *Breaking the Codes: Female Criminality in Fin-de-Siècle Paris* (Stanford: Stanford University Press, 1996), 70–76. George Robb, studying the crime of poison in Victorian England, also found a rough equity between the sexes. Of those tried for poison, he discovered, 45 percent were men and 55 percent women. However, he notes, poison was the most common means by which wives killed their husbands. Fifty-five percent of women used poison to murder their husbands, but only 5 percent of men who killed their wives used it. See Robb, "Circe in Crinoline."

19. Several other early seventeenth-century plays, far less successful than Corneille's, also emphasized the connection between poison and female jealousy: Rotrou's *Hercule mourant* of 1633–34, Hardy's *Alcméon, ou la vengeance feminine* of 1628, and Monléon's *Thyeste* of 1638. On the dramaturgy of poison during this period, see O'Hara, "Tracing Poison," especially chapter 3.

20. Corneille treated the story of Jason and Medea's theft of the Golden Fleece thirty years later, in the 1660 *La toison d'or.*

21. Ibid., 1.4.229–34.

22. Ibid., 1.5.278.

23. Ibid., 2.4.572.

24. Ibid., 5.2.1340.

25. David Nirenberg, "The Gender of Poison," paper presented at the Gender, Health, and History Conference, Chicago, April 24–25, 1998.

26. Collard, *Crime de poison,* 112.

27. *Questions sur les empoisonneurs et autres semblables,* BA, MS 2664, fol. 45.

28. Furthermore, the German word for poison is *Gift.* Marcel Mauss, *The Gift,* trans. Ian Cunnison (New York: W. W. Norton, 1967).

29. For a critique of Mauss's interpretation of "the law of the gift," see Gloria Goodwin Raheja, *The Poison in the Gift: Ritual, Prestation, and the Dominant Caste in a North Indian Village* (Chicago: University of Chicago Press, 1988).

30. Nirenberg, "Gender of Poison," 11.

31. The ancient Romans connected women, poison, and pharmacology linguistically; the Latin word for "drug" is "venenum," meaning both poison and medicine, and is thought to have been derived from "Venus." Ibid., 3. As Margaret Hallissey has shown in *Venomous Woman* (Westport, Conn.: Greenwood Press, 1987), the trope of the venomous woman runs throughout classical literature as well as the Bible. The trope is given a bizarre twist in an unusually gruesome seventeenth-century pamphlet that described a poison created by a Provençal assassin, the *Discours au vrai de l'étrange cruauté d'un soldat appelé la Planche: Par luy exercée sur une jeune fille pour avoir de son lait empoisonné* . . . (Lyon: Antoine Bessy, 1611). The assassin first seduces a nursing mother, beats her until her milk runs violet and "choleric," and then attaches a toad to her breasts to suck out the bloody milk. He then concocts a toxic brew out of toad venom and the extracted milk. For an extended analysis of this pamphlet, see O'Hara, "Tracing Poison," 50–55.

32. Pliny, *The Historie of the World,* trans. P. Holland (London 1635, S.T.C. 20030a), 163. Quoted in Patricia Crawford, "Attitudes to Menstruation in Seventeenth-Century England," *Past and Present* 91 (1981): 59.

33. Pliny's views on the female affinity for poison circulated in the old regime as well. For example, the anonymous author of *Questions sur les empoisonneurs et autres semblables,* presenting evidence on "Why the crime of poison has always been more common among women than men" averred, "Pliny avowed in good faith that women were in this more skillful than men." BA, MS 2664, fol. 46.

34. Joubert intended his manual to debunk such old wives' tales. He mocked the notion that menstrual blood was poisonous or that it caused dogs to become rabid. Nonetheless, he did maintain that menstrual blood caused plants to die, but noted, "another kind of blood poured on plants will make them wilt just as much." Laurent Joubert, *Erreurs populaires* (1578), trans. Gregory David de Rocher (Tuscaloosa: University of Alabama Press, 1989), 126.

35. [Michael Ettmueller], *Etmullerus Abridg'd: or, A Complete System of the Theory and Practice of Physic* (London, 1699), 634. Quoted in Crawford, "Attitudes to Menstruation," 60.

36. On the use of menstrual blood in love potions in early modern Italy, see Guido Ruggerio, *Binding Passions: Tales of Magic, Marriage, and Power at the End of the Renaissance* (Oxford: Oxford University Press, 1993), especially chapter 3. Ruggerio finds that Venetian love magic derived its power from three areas of the body: the phallus, the heart, and the female genitals and menstrual blood. Menstrual blood served, he argues, as "a primary magical sign of femininity" (118).

37. Joubert, *Erreurs populaires,* 128.

38. See the *procès-verbal de visite sur les drogues et eaux trouvée dans la cassette de la Dame Larcher,* AB, MS 10347, fols. 628–30; *procès-verbal de visite . . . chez Marie Bosse,* AB, MS 10342, fols. 42–44; and *procès-verbal et levée de scelles en presence de la Voisin,* AB, MS 10346, fols. 293–95.

39. The gendering of love magic, unlike the gendering of witchcraft, does seem to be borne out in practice as well as in theory. See Briggs, *Witches and Neighbors,* 321, on this point.

40. Jean de Rotrou, *Hercule mourant,* in *Théâtre complet 2,* ed. B. Louvat, D. Moncond'huy, and A. Riffaud (Paris: STFM, 1999). For a modern translation of the tale, see Ovid, *The Metamorphoses,* trans. Horace Gregory (New York: Viking, 1958), 247–53. A brief version of the story can be found in Jacques Ferrand, *A Treatise on Lovesickness, or Erotic Melancholy* (1610, 1623), ed. and trans. Donald A. Beecher and Massimo Ciavolella (Syracuse: Syracuse University Press, 1990), 349 (for other examples of Ferrand's cautionary tales, see 343–44). Stephanie O'Hara provides a compelling reading of Hardy's play in "Tracing Poison," 171–77.

41. Ferrand, *Treatise on Lovesickness,* 366.

42. Ibid., 340.

43. For examples, see the *résumé* of the declaration of Galet, recorded by La Reynie, September 1, 1680, in Ravaisson-Mollien, *Archives de la Bastille,* 6:305–6; *procès-verbal et levée de scellé en presence de la Trianon,* AB, MS 10346, fols. 301–5, and MS 10347, fols. 628–30; *procès-verbal de visite . . . chez la Trianon,* MS 10348, fols. 254–56; *procès-verbal de visite . . . chez Marie Bosse,* MS 10342, fols. 42–44; and *procès-verbal et levée de scellé en presence de la Voisin,* MS 10346, fols. 293–95. For a detailed account of the substances sold by Paris's sorceresses, see Chapter 4.

44. T. L. Stedman, *Stedman's Shorter Medical Dictionary* (New York: Wilcox & Follett, 1942), 248.

45. Nirenberg, "Gender of Poison," 2. On the association between witchcraft and poison, see, among others, Mandrou, *Magistrats et sorciers en France,* 456–68, and Robin Briggs, *Communities of Belief: Cultural and Social Tension in Early Modern France* (Oxford: Oxford University Press, 1989), 32–36.

46. Corneille, *Médée,* 4.1.975–78.

47. Ibid., 4.1.985–88.

48. Plato, *The Laws,* trans. Trevor J. Saunders (New York: Penguin, 1975), 479. Quoted in Nirenberg, "Gender of Poison," 2.

49. Scot questioned the existence of witchcraft but not the sex of its practitioners. "As women in all ages have been counted most apt to conceive witchcraft . . . so also it appeareth, that they have been the first inventers, and the greatest practisers of poisoning, and more naturallie addicted and given thereunto than men." Scot found that poison, not witchcraft, was the form of female crime to which he could give credence. His treatise continued, "Trulie this poisoning art called Veneficium, of all others is most abhominable; as whereby murthers maie be committed, where no suspicion maie be gathered, nor anie resistance can be made; the strong cannot avoid the weake, the wise cannot prevent the foolish, the godlie cannot be preserved from the hands of the wicked; children maie hereby kill their parents, the servant the maister, the wife hir husband, so privilie, so inevitablie, and so incurablie, that of all other it hath been thought the most odious kind of murther." Reginald Scot, *The Discoverie of Witchcraft* (1584) (London: Centaur, 1964), 112–13. Quoted in Frances E. Dolan, *Dangerous Familiars: Representations of Domestic Crime in England, 1550–1700* (Ithaca: Cornell University Press, 1994), 173.

50. On this point, see Dolan, *Dangerous Familiars,* 173–74.

51. Quoted in Pompa Banerjee, *Burning Women: Widows, Witches, and Early Modern European Travelers in India* (New York: Palgrave Macmillan, 2003), 150.

52. See ibid., 149–62, for numerous examples of such manuals and pamphlets.

53. Legal statutes could be similarly ambiguous. Collard points to the hazy judicial definition

of the crime of poison during the medieval era, writing, "qu'avant l'époque moderne, la *toxicatia* est demeurée dans une sorte d'indistinction formelle." *Crime de poison,* 24. For an analysis of the blurred statutory lines between homicide, sorcery, and poison, see 24–38.

54. David Warren Sabean, *Power in the Blood: Popular Culture and Village Discourse in Early Modern Germany* (Cambridge: Cambridge University Press, 1984), 110.

55. For examples illustrating this point, see Chapter 4.

56. Jean Baptiste du Hamel, *De corporum affectionibus cum manifestis cum occultis libri duo* (Paris, 1670), 427–39, reprinted in Lynn Thorndike, ed., *A History of Magic and Experimental Science,* 8 vols. (New York: Columbia University Press, 1923–58), 8:208.

57. Corneille, *Médée,* 2.1.358–62.

58. Interrogation of Guibourg, November 24, 1680, in Ravaisson-Mollien, *Archives de la Bastille,* 6:383.

59. Quoted in John B. Wolf, *Louis XIV* (New York: W. W. Norton, 1968), 297–98. From Émile Magne, ed. *Lettres inédites à Marie-Louise de Gonzague, reine de Pologne sur la cour de Louis XIV* (Paris, 1920), 330.

60. Madame de Lafayette, *The Princess of Clèves,* trans. Terence Cave (New York: Oxford University Press, 1992), 13.

61. Interrogation of Lesage, October 28, 1679, in Ravaisson-Mollien, *Archives de la Bastille,* 6: 32–33; interrogation of La Voisin, January 16, 1680, ibid., 6:103. See also the *Projet d'un rapport de Monsieur de la Reynie au Roi,* ibid., 6:372–74. The abbé Mariette, however, claimed that Mme de Montespan had asked only for an estrangement between Louis and Louise. *Projet d'un rapport de Monsieur de la Reynie au Roi,* ibid., 6:373.

62. *Projet de lettre de Monsieur de la Reynie à Louvois,* September 2, 1680, ibid., 6:306.

63. Confrontation of Lesage with La Voisin, January 7 and 16, 1680, ibid., 6:91–94 and 98–101. See also the interrogations of La Voisin, October, 9, 1679, and Lesage, November 15, 1680, ibid., 6:4–5 and 359.

64. Confrontation of Lesage and La Voisin, January 16, 1680, ibid., 6:99. Louis XIV seems to have been so convinced that the comtesse de Soissons would be found guilty, in fact, that he warned his former lover of her impending arrest so that she might flee into exile. Lebigre, *Affaire des poisons,* 98–99.

65. Those who sought the assistance of the members of the magical underworld attempted to prevent their rivals from gaining the same supernatural advantage. The vicomtesse de Polignac, after engaging Lesage to advance her campaign for the king, tried to exact a commitment from the magician that he would represent her interests exclusively. She was apprehensive, explained Lesage during his interrogation, that he would be hired by the comtesse de Gramont, whom Mme de Polignac knew to have similar designs. Interrogation of Lesage, October 28, 1679, and confrontation of Lesage with La Voisin, January 7, 1680, in Ravaisson-Mollien, *Archives de la Bastille,* 6:33 and 92. Similarly, the sorceress La Filastre claimed that the duchesse de Vivonne had attempted to discover whether she was also working for Mme de Montespan. *Projet de lettre de Monsieur de la Reynie à Louvois,* September 2, 1680, ibid., 6:306.

66. Ezekiel Spanheim, the Elector Palatine's envoy to Versailles, also revealed that many considered the death of the duchess to have been due to poison, which "widespread rumor, although perhaps baseless, attributed to a beverage which is supposed to have been given her on Mme de Montespan's orders." Spanheim, *Relation de la cour de France en 1690* (Paris: Librairie Renouard, 1882), 16. Madame de Caylus also repeated the gossip in her *Souvenirs de la cour de Louis XIV:* "Many rumors circulated upon that death, to the disadvantage of Mme de Montespan." Quoted in Petitfils, *Madame de Montespan,* 176.

67. "On dit que la Belle Beauté a pensé être empoisonnée, et que cela va droit à demander des gardes." Mme de Sévigné to Mme de Grignan, September 1, 1680, in Sévigné, *Correspondance,* 2:1066. Perhaps in response to the rumors, the king ordered an autopsy performed on

the body, but the doctors found no evidence of poison. Complications from the birth of her child the previous year were the more likely cause of her lingering decline.

68. Quoted in Gilette Zeigler, *The Court of Versailles in the Reign of Louis XIV*, trans. Simon Watson Taylor (London: George Allen & Unwin, 1966), 188.

69. Peter Brown has found that during the fourth to the sixth centuries, a score of courtiers were accused of employing political sorcery in order to increase their power and standing at the imperial court. He argues that the charges were politically motivated, launched by imperial servants against the enemies of the emperor as well as against those courtiers who managed to maintain their positions at court without the favor of the emperor. He attributes the increase in accusations to conflict among the ruling classes and a concomitant political instability. See Brown, "Sorcery, Demons and the Rise of Christianity: From Late Antiquity to the Middle Ages," in *Religion and Society in the Age of Saint Augustine,* ed. Peter Brown (London: Faber & Faber, 1972), 119–46.

70. For an extended discussion of these medieval accusations of political sorcery, see Edward Peters, *The Magician, the Witch, and the Law* (Philadelphia: University of Pennsylvania Press, 1978), especially chapter 5. Those accused in the medieval cases fell into two major groups: low-born favorites, charged by members of the royal family or high-born aristocrats with seeking to oust their rivals from the king's favor, and the women of cadet branches of the royal family, whose possible ambitions to the throne for their children seemed to threaten direct succession. The rumors circulated by the Burgundians against Valentina d'Orléans, accusing her of having magically caused the insanity of King Charles VI, fit neatly into the latter category. On this point, see Jan R. Veenstra, *Magic and Divination at the Courts of Burgundy and France: Text and Context of Laurens Pignon's* Contre les devineurs *(1411)* (New York: Brill, 1998), 81–85. Franck Collard analyzes how the medieval accusations functioned as political propaganda in *Crime de poison,* 257–71.

71. Michel Carmona, *Richelieu: L'ambition et le pouvoir* (Paris, 1986), cited in Jonathan Dewald, "Politics and Personality in Seventeenth-Century France," *French Historical Studies* 16, no. 4 (1990): 907. Less than a century before, similar allegations had been made in a series of pamphlets published by the Catholic League. The pamphlets accused Henri III's favorite, the duc d'Épernon, of bewitching the king: "bloodsucker *mignons* like you have enchanted our kings." Quoted in Charlotte Wells, "Leeches on the Body Politic: Xenophobia and Witchcraft in Early Modern French Political Thought," *French Historical Studies* 22, no. 3 (1999): 372.

72. A detailed version of events can be found in Chapter 1.

73. Mme de Sévigné to Mme de Grignan, May 1, 1676, in Sévigné, *Correspondance,* 2:281.

74. When the marquise was captured and retried in 1676, the *factums* and pamphlets circulated once more. In 1679 the story of the marquise de Brinvilliers was added to François de Rosset's *Histoires tragiques,* a collection of *faits divers* that went through forty editions between 1614 and 1758. Whether her story was added to the collection before or after the Affair of the Poisons began is not known. See Anne de Vaucher Gravili, "Introduction," in François de Rosset, *Histoires tragiques* (Paris: Livre de Poche Classique, 1994). For an analysis of the *factums* that argued for or against the marquise, see O'Hara, "Tracing Poison," chapter 2.

75. The transgressions of the marquise de Brinvilliers seized hold of the English imagination as well. Broadsheets recounting her crimes, capture, and execution were still being published in 1752: *The Female Parricide: or, the History of Mary-Margaret d'Aubray, Marchioness of Brinvillier, who was beheaded and burnt at Paris, for poisoning her Father, her two Brothers, and attempting to kill her Sister in the same Manner.* For a discussion of the early modern broadsheets that highlighted the connections made between women and poison, see Banerjee, *Burning Women,* 155–63.

76. Notes of La Reynie, BN, MSS fr 7608, fol. 127.

77. Mme de Sévigné to Mme de Grignan, April 29, 1676, in Sévigné, *Correspondance,* 2:278.

78. Notes of La Reynie, BN, MSS fr 7608, fol. 127.

79. *Questions sur les empoisonneurs*, BA, MS 2664, fol. 45. The perception that female poisoners were monsters held true in Victorian England as well. See Judith Knelman, "Women Murderers in Victorian Britain," *History Today* 48, no. 8 (1998): 9–15.

80. Bussy to Mlle du P, March 28, 1673, in *Correspondance de Roger de Rabutin*, 3:49.

81. Mme de Sévigné to Mme de Grignan, April 29, 1676, in Sévigné, *Correspondance*, 2:278.

82. "Elle s'était fiche un bâton, devinez où: ce n'est point dans l'oeil, ce n'est pas dans la bouche, ce n'est pas dans l'oreille, ce n'est point dans le nez, ce n'est pas point à la torque; devinez où c'est. Tant y a qu'elle était morte si l'on ne fût promptement couru à son secours." Mme de Sévigné to Mme de Grignan, April 29, 1676, ibid., 2:279.

83. Thus charges of sexual impropriety could often accompany poisoning charges. When Angélique Domaigné and her stepfather, the baron de Divette, were accused of poisoning (her mother and his wife) Mme de Divette, for example, they were also accused of incest. See *Factum en forme de Requête pour Damoiselle Angélique et le Sieur Baron de Divette son Beau-père, accusés de l'Empoisonnement, autres crimes* (Paris: Veuve Dupont, 1681).

84. See, for example, the deep distrust of passion expressed in the 1678 work of Madame de Lafayette, *Princess of Clèves*.

85. The passage is from Vincent Houdry. Quoted in Farr, *Authority and Sexuality*, 21.

86. For this argument, see ibid., 19–23, as well as James R. Farr, "The Pure and Disciplined Body: Hierarchy, Morality, and Symbolism in France During the Catholic Reformation," *Journal of Interdisciplinary History* 21, no. 3 (1991): 391–414.

87. Philippe d'Outreman, *The True Catholic*, 1622. Quoted in Riley, *Lust for Virtue*, 51. Similarly, *The Instructions of Saint Charles Borromeo*, the confessional manual in use in France after 1657, stressed the particularly lustful nature of women. See Riley, *Lust for Virtue*, 52–54, on this point.

88. Antoine Arnauld, *Apologie pour Les Saints Pères*, 1651. Quoted in Riley, *Lust for Virtue*, 52.

89. Ibid., 51.

90. L. Th. Maes, "Empoisonnement, procédure inquisitoriale, et peine de mort au début de XVIIIe siècle," *Revue historique de droit français et étranger* 55, no. 1 (1977): 62–63.

91. *Questions sur les empoisonneurs et autres semblables*, BA, MS 2664, fol. 48. The connection between adultery and poison was made well into the nineteenth century; see Robb, "Circe in Crinoline," 183–85, and Shapiro, *Breaking the Codes*, 74–75. The correlation is found in Jacobean England as well. In the 1616 trial of Frances Howard, countess of Somerset, lawyers for the prosecution argued that Frances's adultery provided the motive for her murder of Sir Thomas Overbury. For detailed analyses of the scandal, see David Lindley, *The Trials of Frances Howard: Fact and Fiction at the Court of King James* (London: Routledge, 1993), and Alistair Bellamy, *The Politics of Court Scandal in Early Modern England: News Culture and the Overbury Affair, 1603–1660* (Cambridge: Cambridge University Press, 2002).

92. Quoted in Nirenberg, "Gender of Poison," 4. This Latin tag is also repeated in *Questions sur les empoisonneurs et autres semblables*, BA, MS 2664, fol. 48. Pompa Banerjee argues convincingly that the close association between adultery and poison informed early modern European responses to the Indian custom of *sati*. European travelers explained that the practice of widow burning had evolved to prevent the husband poisonings that Hindu wives would otherwise commit. See Banerjee, *Burning Women*, 137–73.

93. For the allegations against these courtiers, see interrogation of La Voisin, January 16, 1680; interrogation of Mme la Duchesse de Bouillon, January 29, 1680; *projet de lettre de M. de la Reynie à Louvois*; confrontation of La Filastre, September 21, 1680, in Ravaisson-Mollien, *Archives de la Bastille*, 6:102–4, 118, 306, and 312, respectively.

94. Lafayette, *Princess of Clèves*, 12.

95. M. Saville to Secretary of State Coventry, January 25, 1680, in Ravaisson-Mollien, *Archives de la Bastille*, 6:110.

96. Stephanie O'Hara argues that this belief was articulated in the literary trope of the "duplicitous hand" that described those who poisoned within the household, disguising their murderous intentions with protests of love and loyalty. "Tracing Poison," 133–35. The memoirs of Primi Visconti suggest that domestic poisonings were particular to France and inspired by the Affair of the Poisons itself. He wrote of the beginning of the scandal, "Innumerable people who did not even know what poison was set themselves to studying how to prepare it, with one difference from other nations. There, you poison for vengeance, using it against your enemies, while here, you use poison against fathers, mothers, and relatives out of greed—to gain inheritances or contract new marriages. And there have been many more poisonings since the establishment of the Chambre [de l'Arsenal] than ever before." Visconti, *Mémoires sur la cour de Louis XIV*, 292–93.

97. Dolan, *Dangerous Familiars*, 29. However, in the old regime as now, the number of men accused of homicide far exceeded the number of women. Ruff, *Crime, Justice, and Public Order*, 85–89.

98. For a series of sixteenth-century examples, see Davis, *Fiction in the Archives*, 77–110. Frances Dolan notes that the greatest threats to the patriarchal order of the household were seen to derive from its most intimate relationships—between family members, neighbors, and servants. Women were considered particularly suspect, capable of, if not prone to, infanticide, witchcraft, and even murder by poison. Dolan, *Dangerous Familiars*, 21–58.

99. Interestingly, the early modern concern regarding domestic poisonings accurately reflected a larger trend in criminal violence. Pieter Spierenburg finds that the focus of homicides in the Low Countries shifted between the sixteenth and the eighteenth centuries from "the killing of strangers to the killing of intimates." Spierenburg, "Homicide Trends and Cultural Meanings: Amsterdam, 1431–1816," *Journal of Social History* 27 (1994): 701–16. This is also true of early modern Germany; see Eva Lacour, "Faces of Violence Revisited: A Typology of Violence in Early Modern Rural Germany," *Journal of Social History* 34, no. 3 (2001): 649–81.

100. David Sabean finds that food and food rituals revealed the boundaries of social relationships in early modern Germany. If a married man, for example, accepted food from a woman other than his wife, he was suspected of having an adulterous relationship. Moreover, when relationships within marriage soured, it was not uncommon for spouses to believe that their partner was attempting to poison them. Sabean, *Power in the Blood*, 109–10.

101. Neither husband nor daughter died. If the marquis appeared ill, Sainte-Croix administered a counterpoison, for according to Mme de Sévigné, he "didn't want a wife as wicked as himself." Mme de Sévigné to Mme de Grignan, May 1, 1676, in Sévigné, *Correspondance*, 2:281.

102. The marquise de Brinvilliers attempted to employ an alternative cultural script, that of the servant-poisoner, to her advantage. The *factum* that argued for her innocence declared that La Chaussée, erstwhile servant of Sainte-Croix, had poisoned her brothers and father without her knowledge at the behest of his former master. *Factum pour Dame Magdelaine d'Aubray*, 6.

103. *Questions sur les empoisonneurs*, BA, MS 2664, fol. 48.

104. *Procès-verbal de question* of La Voisin, February 20, 1680, in Ravaisson-Mollien, *Archives de la Bastille*, 6:158–59.

105. Interrogation of Marie-Marguerite Montvoisin, December 6, 1680, ibid., 6:386–88.

106. Interrogation of Guibourg, May 2, 1681, ibid., 6:448–50.

107. Maes notes the contemporary French associations linking female deceit and hypocrisy with poison in "Empoisonnement, procédure inquisitoriale, et peine de mort," 62–63. For an analysis of the connections made in seventeenth-century England between women's capacity for deceit, their use of cosmetics, and poison, see Annette Drew-Bear, "Cosmetics and Attitudes Towards Women in the Seventeenth Century," *Journal of Popular Culture* 9, no. 1 (1975): 31–37.

108. *Questions sur les empoisonneurs,* BA, MS 2664, fol. 47.

109. Eighteenth-century writers agreed. In 1743, for example, Gayot de Pitaval opined that women were poisoners because they "do not have the courage to avenge themselves openly . . . and embrace this means that favors their timidity and hides their malice." Quoted in Shapiro, *Breaking the Codes,* 230.

110. Notes of La Reynie, BN, MSS fr 7608, fol. 127.

111. Quoted in Elias, *Court Society,* 105.

112. Lafayette, *Princess of Clèves,* 25.

113. *Projet de lettre de M. de la Reynie à Louvois,* in Ravaisson-Mollien, *Archives de la Bastille,* 6:396.

114. See Chapter 1 for a brief account of this trial.

115. Liselotte reiterated her accusation frequently as her son struggled with opposing factions at court, recounting the allegation in letters dated November 15, 1715, September 22, 1718, September 14, 1719, and November 19, 1719. Petitfils, *Madame de Montespan,* 176–77. When she failed to repeat the accusation, she otherwise abused Mme de Montespan, writing, for example, "his [the duc du Maine's] mother was the most frivolous, unchristian and villainous person in the world." Liselotte Von der Pfalz, *Letters from Liselotte,* ed. and trans. Maria Kroll (New York: McCall, 1971), 206.

116. Anon., *L'esprit familier du Trianon ou l'apparition de la duchesse de Fontanges, contenant les secrets de ses amours, les pecularités de son empoisonnement et de sa mort* (Paris [Holland]: Chez la Veuve de Jean Felix, 1695), 30. For a discussion of such pamphlets, see Burke, *Fabrication of Louis XIV,* 135–49.

117. François-Marie Arouet de Voltaire, *Mélanges,* ed. J. Van Den Heuvel (Paris: Gallimard, 1961), 1252.

118. For example, Marat wrote on September 16, 1792, "Un mot à la femme Roland . . . Roland n'est qu'un frère coupe-choux, que sa femme mène par l'oreille; c'est elle qui est le ministre de l'intérieur." Marat, *Oeuvres de Jean-Paul Marat,* ed. A. Vermorel (Paris: Décembre-Alonnier, 1869), 230. See also Gita May, *Madame Roland and the Age of Revolution* (New York: Columbia University Press, 1970), 251, on Marat's attacks on Mme Roland.

119. Reprinted in Keith Michael Baker, ed., *The Old Regime and the French Revolution* (Chicago: University of Chicago Press, 1987), 265.

120. Quoted in Chantal Thomas, *The Wicked Queen: The Origins of the Myth of Marie-Antoinette,* trans. Julie Rose (New York: Zone Books, 1999), 132–33. Thomas writes that the theme of Marie-Antoinette as a poisoner queen surfaced repeatedly in prerevolutionary pamphlets. She was accused of having poisoned Maurepas, Vergennes ("I got hold of the recipe of Marie de' Medici"), Mirabeau ("I would say the poison that killed Mirabeau was distilled in her own mortar"), and her own son, the dauphin, who died on June 4, 1789.

## Chapter 3

1. Interrogation of Lesage, June 15, 1680, in Ravaisson-Mollien, *Archives de la Bastille,* 6:222.

2. Ibid.

3. Interrogation of Lesage, July 18, 1680, ibid., 6:256–59.

4. See, for example, the interrogation of La Filastre, March 5, 1680, and the interrogation of La Delaporte, June 23, 1680, ibid., 6:212 and 229. It is necessary to acknowledge that Lesage's testimony, like that of all of the suspects implicated in the Affair of the Poisons, was elicited over the course of a long period of imprisonment and under varying degrees of duress. The truth value of Lesage's statements, however, is of less importance to this argument than the

fact that La Reynie and other authorities perceived his accusations to be credible enough to have offered him "the king's grace" in return for his cooperation. On the agreement struck with Lesage, see Louvois to Louis, October 8, 1679, ibid., 5:501–2.

5. The cour des Miracles ran between rue des Tournelles and rue Jean-Beausire. For the location of Parisian streets during the ancien régime, see Jacques Hillairet, *Dictionnaire historique des rues de Paris*, 2 vols. (Paris: Éditions de Minuit, 1985).

6. Interrogation of La Trianon, May 20, 1679, in Ravaisson-Mollien, *Archives de la Bastille*, 5:373. Rue Bourbon is now known as rue d'Aboukir. Hillairet, *Dictionnaire historique*, 1:704.

7. According to the *procès-verbal de la Chambre* of June 17, 1679, La Chéron told the judges, "the phrase 'soup from the rue Saint-Denis' is a phrase used commonly among the women of her quarter." When asked if the phrase did not signify poison, she said that she didn't know why it was said, and that it was a term she had heard used for the past ten years by women who advised those who complained about their husbands, "Give him a soup from the rue Saint-Denis." Ravaisson-Mollien, *Archives de la Bastille*, 5:411.

8. Declaration and interrogation of La Voisin, November 15, 1679, and June 16, 1679, ibid., 5:408–9 and 6:43–44.

9. Interrogation of Lesage, November 28, 1679, ibid., 6:55.

10. Maître Jean lived "vers Notre-Dame de Bonne-Nouvelle" and La Bergerot was a member of the parish of Saint-Laurent, which adjoined that of Notre-Dame de Bonne-Nouvelle. Interrogation of La Duval, December 14, 1679, ibid., 6:63. According to Guibourg, La Bergerot was a sorceress who proposed that he should say masses over the bones of the dead that she dug up, in order to increase their magical powers. Interrogation of Guibourg, June 23, 1680, ibid., 6:226.

11. At the abbé Guibourg's first interrogation, for example, La Reynie's questions proceeded: Why are you called "M. le Prieur"? What is the name of the priest who lodges with Maître Jean? For whom was the tin chalice that he brought intended? Weren't you in involved in business with Tournet, otherwise known as the prior of the Magdalene? Who introduced you to La David? Do you know a priest named Lefranc? June 23, 1680, ibid., 6:226–27. When La Reynie interrogated La Vigoureux, he asked: Do you know a man named Lesage, and how did you come to meet him? How long has it been since you have seen him? Where does he live? For how long have you known La Delarue? Does Lesage know La Bosse? What is the name of the woman whom La Delarue sent to you? Does La Poulaillon know La Delarue, La Simon, and Lesage? Etc. February 18, 1679, ibid., 5:215–17.

12. Interrogation of La Filastre, June 21, 1680, ibid., 6:225; interrogation of Guibourg, June 26, 1680, ibid., 6:231; and interrogation of Marie-Marguerite Montvoisin, July 5, 1680, ibid., 6:237.

13. Lebigre, *Affaire des poisons*, 87.

14. Interrogation of Lesage, October 14, 1679, in Ravaisson-Mollien, *Archives de la Bastille*, 6:25.

15. AB, MS 10357, fol. 381.

16. Several suspects referred to the receipt. For example, see the interrogation of La Bosse, March 18, 1679, in Ravaisson-Mollien, *Archives de la Bastille*, 5:268–69.

17. See, for example, the interrogation of La Bosse, March 27, 1679, ibid., 5:295.

18. When asked how late in the pregnancy her procedure could be performed, La Lepère replied, "At all times, and when it is people of quality, one must maintain their honor and keep quiet." Interrogation of La Lepère, May 27, 1679, ibid., 5:379–80.

19. Interrogation of La Voisin, April 1, 1679, ibid., 5:324.

20. Confrontation of La Bosse and La Lepère, ibid., 5:353–54. La Voisin described La Lepère's procedure for her interrogators on April 1, 1679, but provided a more detailed description in her *procès-verbal de question* recorded on February 20, 1680, ibid., 5:324 and 6:164.

21. As La Boulard was denounced as a poisoner by Mariette's previous mistress, La Leroux,

this accusation should perhaps be taken with a large grain of salt. *Procès-verbal de question* of La Leroux, April 5, 1680, ibid., 6:199.

22. Interrogation of Lesage, April 9, 1680, ibid., 6:204.

23. Interrogation of Lesage, November 28, 1679 and declaration of La Filastre, August 1, 1680, ibid., 6:57 and 6:273.

24. Interrogation of Lesage, November 28, 1679, ibid., 6:56.

25. Sorceresses such as La Voisin were often accused, for example, of using consecrated afterbirths in their magical rituals. On this issue, see the interrogation of Marie-Marguerite Montvoisin, October 9, 1680, ibid., 6:332–33.

26. The marquis de Feuquières to his father, March 16, 1680, in *Lettres inédites des Feuquières,* 4:108–12. The marquis had been accused of various nefarious acts, such as attempting to make a pact with the devil, by several members of the magical underworld. He wrote to his father to protest his innocence.

27. Lebigre, *Affaire des poisons,* 60. To cite another example, La Bergerot stated that she had worked as a servant in the households of Mme de Mancini and the duchesse de Bouillon, both of whom were alleged to be clients of La Voisin. Interrogation of La Bergerot, June 11, 1679, in Ravaisson-Mollien, *Archives de la Bastille,* 5:399.

28. Interrogation of La Voisin, October 9, 1679, ibid., 6:4–6.

29. Interrogation of Lesage, November 15, 1680, ibid., 6:358.

30. La Voisin also employed Fathers Gabriel and Gérard regularly. Declaration and interrogation of Marie-Marguerite Montvoisin, August 20, 1680, and August 22, 1680, ibid., 6:296, 301.

31. Interrogation of Lesage, November 28, 1679, and *procès-verbal de question* of La Voisin, February 20, 1680, ibid., 6:57, 177.

32. The magical and demonic activities of the renegade priests are discussed fully in Chapter 4.

33. Laundresses, shoemakers, merchants, and artisans purchased magical wares. See APP, AA-4, fols. 120–27, which list names and occupations of those arrested during the affair.

34. La Voisin claimed, for example, that she had traveled to Saint-Cloud "pour faire vendre des eaux pour le teint aux filles de Madame." Confrontation between Lesage and La Voisin, January 16, 1680, in Ravaisson-Mollien, *Archives de la Bastille,* 6:98.

35. Throughout the seventeenth century, nobles consulted astrologers and fortune-tellers to learn what destiny awaited them. Lucien Bély, *La société des princes, XVIe–XVIIIe siècle* (Paris: Fayard, 1999), 108–11.

36. In its entirety, the fable reads: "Une femme à Paris faisait la Pythonisse / On l'allait consulter sur chaque événement / Perdait-on un chiffon, avoit-on un amant, / Un mari vivant trop au gré de son épouse, / Une mère fâcheuse, une femme jalouse, / Chez la devineuse on courait / Se faire annoncer ce que l'on desirer / Son fait consistait en adresse / Quelques termes de l'art, beaucoup de hardiesse, / Du hasard quelquefois, tout cela concourait / Tout cela bien souvent faisait crier miracle." VII.14. La Fontaine, *Oeuvres complètes I: Fables, contes, et nouvelles,* ed. Jean-Pierre Collinet (Paris: Gallimard, 1991), 277.

37. Interrogation of Mme Brissart, August 17, 1679, in Ravaisson-Mollien, *Archives de la Bastille,* 5:453–54.

38. Interrogation of Lesage, October 28, 1679, ibid., 6:34–36. If the count did indeed purchase a magic charm for cards, it was perhaps because his other methods of winning had been discovered. Louis XIV dismissed the count from his post as *maître de la garderobe* in March 1671, after the count had been caught cheating at cards. Mme de Sévigné reported, "It was some time before the king could bring himself to disgrace a man of Cessac's quality, but seeing that everyone who had played with him for the last two months had been ruined, he decided that he could not in conscience do less than bring this roguery to light." Sévigné, *Correspondance,* 1:589.

39. AB, MS 10357, fol. 72. A similar charm is found in MS 10355, fol. 595.

40. Nonetheless, some of Paris's sorceresses built up extensive collections of occult works. When La Trianon was arrested, for example, twenty-five manuscript volumes on the occult sciences were found in her possession. See the letter of M. Brayer to M. de Mazauges, March 1, 1680, reprinted in Ravaisson-Mollien, *Archives de la Bastille,* 6:163–84.

41. On the success of the Catholic Church's efforts to Christianize France during the seventeenth and eighteenth centuries, see Jean Delumeau, *Catholicism Between Luther and Voltaire: A New View of the Counter Reformation,* trans. Jeremy Moiser (Philadelphia: Burns & Oates, 1977), especially chapters 4 and 5.

42. AB, MS 10357, fol. 44.

43. Ibid.

44. Interrogation of La Delaporte, August 4, 1679, in Ravaisson-Mollien, *Archives de la Bastille,* 5:440–41.

45. Kieckhefer, *Magic in the Middle Ages,* 159.

46. See ibid. for a discussion of the presence and persistence of such magical practices from the twelfth to the fifteenth centuries. Kieckhefer demonstrates that blessings and adjurations to Christ or to the saints were often used in conjunction with explicitly magical practices throughout the Middle Ages and the early modern period.

47. Valerie I. J. Flint's analysis of early medieval magic cites many examples of tenth- and eleventh-century love and medicinal charms that are analogous to the seventeenth-century ones listed above. For example, an Anglo-Saxon spell from Aelfric's *Lacnunga,* dated c. 1000, reads, "Sing this prayer upon the black blains nine times; Firstly Paternoster. Tigath tigath tigath calicet aclu cluel ad clocles acre earcre amem nonabiuth aer aernem nidren arcum cunath arcum arctua fligara uflen binchi cutern nicuperam raf afth egal uflen arta arta trauncula trauncula. Seek and ye shall find. I adjure thee by Father, Son and Holy Ghost that thou grow no greater, but that thou dry up. Upon the asp and the basilisk shalt thou tread and upon the lion and the dragon shalt thou trample. Cross Matthew, cross Mark, cross Luke, cross John." Flint, *The Rise of Magic in Early Medieval Europe* (Princeton: Princeton University Press, 1991), 312.

48. Kieckhefer, *Magic in the Middle Ages,* 71.

49. "NN" was used in the early modern period to signify "fill in the blank," much as "X" is today.

50. AB, MS 10355, fol. 595.

51. AB, MS 10357, fols. 38–48 and 166–88. La Voisin's *grimoire* also seems to be closely related to the *Grimoire du Pope Honorius,* which was first printed in 1629 but circulated in manuscript form well before that date. On the content and genealogy of *The Clavicle of Solomon* (or the *Key of Solomon*), *The Sworn Book of Honorius,* and *The Constitution of Pope Honorius,* see E. M. Butler, *Ritual Magic* (Cambridge: Cambridge University Press, 1949), 47–64, 89–94.

52. Clark, *Thinking with Demons,* 474–78.

53. John Bossy, "Moral Arithmetic: Seven Sins into Ten Commandments," in *Conscience and Casuistry in Early Modern Europe,* ed. Edmund Leites (Cambridge: Cambridge University Press, 1985).

54. Clark, *Thinking with Demons,* 480.

55. Quoted in ibid., 481.

56. The Gallican church never formally accepted the decrees of the Council of Trent, but it did adhere to the spirit of the reform the decrees put forward. Farr, *Authority and Sexuality,* 53.

57. Quoted in Clark, *Thinking with Demons,* 500.

58. Ibid., 469.

59. William Monter, *Ritual, Myth, and Magic in Early Modern Europe* (Brighton, Eng.: Harvester Press, 1983), 123.

60. Interrogation of Mme Brissart, August 17, 1679, in Ravaisson-Mollien, *Archives de la Bastille,* 5:453–54.

61. Building upon the work of Heinz Schilling, Farr notes, "There was no meaningful distinction between crime and sin in seventeenth-century France." Farr, *Authority and Sexuality*, 39. The definitions offered in popular dictionaries attest to the ancien régime fusion of the concepts of sin and crime. In his *Dictionnaire français* of 1680, Pierre Richelet asserted that crime "signifies a fault meriting punishment. Enormous fault. Sin." Similarly, *Le Dictionnaire universel d'Antoine Furetière* of 1690 defined "crime" as "an action against natural or civil law . . . there is no crime that will not be punished in this world or the next." Riley, "Michel Foucault, Lust, Women, and Sin," n21.

62. On the link between social order and Reformation Catholicism, see Bossy, *Christianity in the West*.

63. On the policing of the "permeable link between sin and crime," see Riley, *Lust for Virtue*, chapter 1.

64. AB, MS 10357, fol. 488.

65. For some of La Voisin's recipes for such remedies, see ibid., fols. 19–60 and 595–60.

66. *Experimenta*, c. 1300. Attributed to Raymond Lull but speculated to be the work of John of Rupescissa. Quoted in Thorndike, *History of Magic*, 4:59.

67. AB, MS 10357, fol. 488.

68. Wealthy clients who purchased *l'or potable* included the vicomte de Cousserans. Interrogation of La Leroux, September 25, 2679, in Ravaisson-Mollien, *Archives de la Bastille*, 5:487–89.

69. Thorndike, *History of Magic*, 2:777–808.

70. AB, 10357.

71. On this issue, see Kieckhefer, *Magic in the Middle Ages*, 69–73.

72. The next-best thing to a charm that ensured victory at cards was a seat at the queen's table. Marie-Thérèse was reportedly such an abysmal card player that several courtiers were able to support themselves with the money they won from her. Primi Visconti commented, "The Queen . . . is so simple-minded that she loses continuously, and it is the Queen's play that supports the poor princesse d'Elbeuf. This gaming, if it continues at its present intensity, will be the Court's finest source of revenue." Visconti, *Mémoires sur la cour de Louis XIV*, 45–46.

73. Letter to Raugräfin Louise, May 14, 1695, in Elborg Forster, trans. and ed., *A Woman's Life in the Court of the Sun King: Letters of Liselotte von der Pfalz, 1652–1722* (Baltimore: Johns Hopkins University Press, 1984), 88.

74. Pierre Clément, *La police sous Louis XIV* (Geneva: Mégariotis Reprints, 1978), 82–83. Chapter 2 includes a discussion of the court's insatiable appetite for cards and gambling.

75. For a discussion of the powers attributed to cauls from classical times to the eighteenth century, see Thomas R. Forbes, "The Social History of the Caul," *Yale Journal of Biology and Medicine* 25 (1953): 495–508. On the magical uses of cauls in Italy, see Carlo Ginzburg, *The Night Battles: Witchcraft and Agrarian Cults in the Sixteenth and Seventeenth Centuries*, trans. John and Anne Tedeschi (New York: Penguin, 1983), 15–16 and nn. 36 and 37.

76. Interrogation of Marie-Marguerite Montvoisin, August 20, 1680, in Ravaisson-Mollien, *Archives de la Bastille*, 6:297.

77. Interrogation of Lesage, October 14, 1679, ibid., 6:20.

78. For a variety of similar charms, see AB, 10357, passim.

79. One way to create a *pistole volant* was to ask a priest to consecrate the coin. Abbé Guibourg confessed that he had dressed in his surplice and stole, taken a thirty-sou coin, and "baptized it with the secret" for a demoiselle of the court, but to no avail. He admitted wryly that his client had scolded him roundly for his failure in his interrogation of August 4, 1680, in Ravaisson-Mollien, *Archives de la Bastille*, 6:280.

80. Declaration of La Voisin, April 1, 1679, ibid., 5:327–28.

81. *Le livre des conjurations du pape Honorius, avec un recueil des plus rares secrets de l'art*

*magique et des pratiques l'opposant aux maléfices* (n.p., 1670; reprint, Paris: Éditions Perthuis, 1970), 53–56.

82. See the many examples found in Ravaisson-Mollien, *Archives de la Bastille,* vols. 4–7.

83. *Livre des conjurations du pape Honorius,* 114.

84. Richard Kieckhefer, *Forbidden Rites: A Necromancer's Manual of the Fifteenth Century* (University Park: Pennsylvania State University Press, 1998), chapter 1.

85. AB, 10357, fols. 31–32.

86. As the majority of necromancers in early modern Europe were ordained priests, a more complete discussion of necromancy is included in Chapter 4.

87. La Filastre stated that she understood that he wanted love powders. *Récolement* of La Filastre, September 28, 1680, in Ravaisson-Mollien, *Archives de la Bastille,* 6:318.

88. Under a 1639 ordinance, parental consent was required for a legal and binding marriage, regardless of one's age, sex, or marital status. Even a widow, therefore, needed permission from the head of her family before she could remarry. In "Engendering the State: Family Formation and State Building in Early Modern France," *French Historical Studies* 16 (1989): 4–27, Sarah Hanley argues that the 1639 ordinance marked the culmination of the family-state compact that enforced patriarchal and state control over marriage.

89. Interrogation of Lesage, March 6, 1680, in Ravaisson-Mollien, *Archives de la Bastille,* 6:187.

90. *Procès-verbal de question* of La Voisin, February 20, 1680, ibid., 6:161.

91. Interrogation of La Voisin, August 7, 1679, ibid., 5:443–44.

92. Interrogation of Lesage, May 27, 1679, ibid., 5:377–79.

93. Declaration of La Voisin, April 1, 1679, ibid., 5:328.

94. Ibid.

95. On the anxiety provoked by the image of the disorderly woman, see Natalie Zemon Davis's essay "Women on Top," in her *Society and Culture in Early Modern France* (Stanford: Stanford University Press, 1975), 124–51.

96. For good measure, the client also specified, "I ask that I could win at any game that I play, at cards or otherwise." AB, MS 10357, fol. 350.

97. Some clients wishing that their husbands might overlook love affairs asked for the husbands' deaths instead. According to Lesage, Mme de Virieu approached La Voisin for magical assistance to win the love of an abbé as well as assistance in eliminating her husband. Interrogation of Lesage, November 28, 1679, in Ravaisson-Mollien, *Archives de la Bastille,* 6:55–56.

98. At least one client reportedly found La Voisin's breast-enhancement cream ineffectual, according to the rumors circulating during the affair. Bussy Rabutin gleefully reported on the humiliation that the king had unwittingly inflicted upon one of the noblewomen of his court. Upon finding a note from the duchess de Foix among La Voisin's papers, Louis demanded an explanation. The duchess was forced to admit she had bought a cream to increase the size of her bosom but, upon applying it to the site of inadequacy, found it had the opposite effect intended. Bussy to La Rivière, January 27, 1680, in *Correspondance de Roger de Rabutin,* 5:45–46.

99. See, for example, Henricus Cornelius Agrippa, *Three Books of Occult Philosophy,* trans. J. F. London (1651), 81–82. See also the interrogation of abbé Guibourg, November 24, 1680, in Ravaisson-Mollien, *Archives de la Bastille,* 6:383.

100. *Procès-verbal et levée de scellé en presence de la Trianon,* AB, MS 10346, fols. 301–5, MS 10347, fols. 628–30; *procès-verbal de visite . . . chez la Trianon,* MS 10348, fols. 254–56; *procès-verbal de visite . . . chez Marie Bosse,* MS 10342, fols. 42–44; and *procès-verbal et levée de scellé en presence de la Voisin,* MS 10346, fols. 293–95.

101. *Résumé* of the declaration of Galet, recorded by La Reynie, September 1, 1680, in Ravaisson-Mollien, *Archives de la Bastille,* 6:305–6. La Reynie, however, believed that Galet

was lying about Mme de Montespan. The police lieutenant considered it more likely that Galet's customer was actually the duchesse de Vivonne, who was seeking to supplant her sister-in-law in the affections of the king. *Projet de letter de M. de la Reynie à Louvois,* September 2, 1680, ibid., 6:306.

102. During the seventeenth century, distillation was a common means of preparing both medicines and cosmetics. Human blood, for example, "distilled seven times to free it from all water" was considered beneficial for "resolution of the nerves," while distilled puppies were recommended to prevent hair growth on the body. See Remaclus, *Historia omnium acquarium* . . . (Paris, 1542), and Andreas Furnerius, *La décoration d'humaine nature et a ornement des dames* (Paris, 1530), both cited in Thorndike, *History of Magic,* 5:543–44. Also see ibid., 6:220–42, on the continuing influence of alchemical theories on medical practice in the sixteenth and seventeenth centuries.

103. According to witnesses, Lesage provided hippomane to his clients as well. See, for example, the September 1, 1679, interrogation of La Duval, in Ravaisson-Mollien, *Archives de la Bastille,* 5:462–64.

104. Forbes, "Social History of the Caul," 504–5.

105. AB, MS 10357, fol. 44.

106. As Pliny had explained during the second century in his *History of the World,* contact with menstrual blood "turns new wine sour, crops touched with it become barren . . . and to taste it drives dogs mad and infects their bites with poison." Quoted in Crawford, "Attitudes to Menstruation," 63. The belief persisted well into the ancien régime, as evidenced by its popularity in seventeenth-century love potions.

107. This belief persisted well into the eighteenth century, despite the challenges posed to it by the discoveries of scientists such as William Harvey. On the Aristotelian understanding of the formation of children in the womb, see Thomas Laqueur, *Making Sex: Body and Gender from the Greeks to Freud* (Cambridge: Harvard University Press, 1990), 142–48.

108. Interrogation and *levée de scellé* of La Jacob, December 2, 1679, AB, MS 10346, fols. 420–23.

109. Ravaisson-Mollien, *Archives de la Bastille,* 6:372.

110. Virgin parchment was also used in love magic in sixteenth-century Rome. Thomas V. Cohen and Elizabeth S. Cohen, *Words and Deeds in Renaissance Rome: Trials Before the Papal Magistrates* (Toronto: University of Toronto Press, 1993), 293.

111. Interrogation of Guibourg, June 26, 1680, in Ravaisson-Mollien, *Archives de la Bastille,* 6:232. See further examples, ibid., 6:221, 256–57. La Lepère, a midwife and abortionist, claimed that she kept powdered afterbirths to administer to women in labor. Perhaps this was intended to assuage the pains of childbirth. *Procès-verbal de deposition de scellé,* March 18, 1679, AB, MS 10342.

112. Louise Bourgeois, *Observations sur la stérilité perte de fruite fécondité accouchements et maladies des femmes et enfants nouveaux naiz* (Paris, 1626) 1:3. Quoted in Wendy Perkins, *Midwifery and Medicine in Early Modern France: Louise Bourgeois* (Exeter: University of Exeter Press, 1996), 32.

113. Galenists theorized that both men and women produced sperm. Joubert, *Erreurs populaires,* 295n2. For a description of such a love charm, see the interrogation of Guibourg, October 10, 1689, in Ravaisson-Mollien, *Archives de la Bastille,* 6:336. La Reynie's notes from Guibourg's interrogation contain an abbreviated description of the ceremony. See BN, MSS fr 7608, fols. 121–22, 239. See also 7608, fol. 249, for Marie-Marguerite Montvoisin's account in her interrogation of October 9, 1680. She maintained that the potion also contained the blood of a sacrificed infant.

114. AB, MS 10357, fol. 72.

115. Forbes, "Social History of the Caul," 504–9.

116. The final words of the prayer in La Voisin's *grimoire* may have evolved from the medieval magical acronym AGLA. Kieckhefer, *Magic in the Middle Ages,* 159.

117. AB, MS 10357, fols. 47–48.

118. Interrogation of La Desmaretz, May 25, 1679, in Ravaisson-Mollien, *Archives de la Bastille,* 5:375.

119. Declaration of La Voisin, May 25, 1679, ibid., 5:377.

120. Interrogation of La Filastre, June 5, 1680, ibid., 6:217.

121. Interrogation of Lesage, October 28, 1679, and interrogation of Marie-Marguerite Montvoisin, March 28, 1680, ibid., 6:32 and 6:194.

122. Draft of a report from La Reynie to Louvois, ibid., 6:374.

123. Declaration of Abbé Guibourg, July 18, 1680, ibid., 6:246–48.

124. The renegade priests' unique ability to combine necromancy and love magic in a novel ritual known as an amatory mass is the subject of Chapter 4.

125. On women's limited access to divorce in early modern France, see Hanley, "Engendering the State," particularly 13–14, and Hanley, "Social Sites of Political Practice in France."

126. Interrogation of La Bosse, March 12, 1679, in Ravaisson-Mollien, *Archives de la Bastille,* 5:246. Marie-Marguerite Montvoisin reported a similar case of spousal abuse; a client visiting La Voisin said that if the sorceress didn't give her something with which to get rid of her husband, she would murder him in his sleep. Interrogation of August 22, 1680, ibid., 6:303.

127. Hanley, "Engendering the State," 4–27.

128. Interrogation of Lesage, November 28, 1679, in Ravaisson-Mollien, *Archives de la Bastille,* 6:55–57. Similar accusations can be found ibid., 6:310 311, and 479.

129. Interrogation of La Vertemart, December 8, 1680, ibid., 6:388–89.

130. Lesage added that he had been arrested (referring to his first arrest in 1668) before the forty days were up, so he did not know whether his spell had succeeded. In any case, he said, he had received only ten or twelve *pistoles* for his troubles. Interrogation of Lesage, October 28, 1679, ibid., 6:33.

131. La Voisin also admitted that she had twice tried to poison her husband. Confrontation of La Voisin and La Bosse, March 18, 1679, ibid., 5:268–72.

132. Nonetheless, the association between witchcraft and poison was a long-standing one in early modern Europe. In England, even the skeptic Reginald Scot, who scoffed at the existence of witchcraft, argued that women were more likely to turn to the crime of poison than were their male counterparts. On this point, see Dolan, *Dangerous Familiars,* 173–75. On the blurred distinctions between magic and poison in early modern Italy, see Giovanna Fiume, "The Old Vinegar Lady, or the Judicial Modernization of the Crime of Witchcraft," trans. Margaret A. Gallucci, in *History from Crime,* ed. Edward Muir and Guido Ruggerio (Baltimore: Johns Hopkins University Press, 1994), 65–87.

133. Lesage claimed to have lured away La Voisin's client, the vicomtesse de Polignac, by persuading the countess that it would be less hazardous to bring about her husband's death through magic than through La Voisin's "evil ways of poison." "He told her that he could make [her designs] succeed by magical means, without any danger to her." Interrogation of Lesage, November 15, 1680, in Ravaisson-Mollien, *Archives de la Bastille,* 6:359.

134. Confrontation of La Leroux with La Voisin, n.d. [c. January 1680], ibid., 6:68–69. For another case involving the use of wax figures to cause death, see the interrogation of La Joly, October 6, 1682, ibid., 7:41.

135. La Voisin claimed that Mme de Dreux "was accustomed to say on the subject [of her husband's death], 'Hurry up, Madame Voisin!'" Interrogation of La Voisin, September 12, 1679, ibid., 5:470–72.

136. Ibid., and confrontation of La Leroux with La Voisin, n.d. [c. January 1680], ibid., 5:473 and 6:68–69.

137. Interrogation of La Voisin, March 20, 1679, ibid., 5:276–77.

138. James Marsh and Hugo Reinsch developed the first tests to determine the presence of arsenic in the body in 1836 and 1841, respectively. George Robb describes the early tests: "Marsh's test mixed fluid from the deceased's stomach and intestines with dilute sulfuric acid and zinc. If arsenic was present it would react with the zinc producing a white precipitate. Reinsch's test boiled the suspected fluid with hydrochloric acid and copper foil; arsenic would tarnish the copper with a grey film. The tests were complicated by the fact that trace amounts of arsenic occur naturally in the human body. . . . Although these tests were problematic and rather unreliable, they were rarely treated so by scientists and judges." Robb, "Circe in Crinoline," 180.

139. For more on this point, see Fiume, "Old Vinegar Lady," 72.

140. Lebigre, *Affaire des poisons*, 143.

141. Nass, *Empoisonnements sous Louis XIV*, 36. Mme Leféron, claimed La Voisin, added such a solution of arsenic to her husband's soup. Interrogation of September 12, 1679, in Ravaisson-Mollien, *Archives de la Bastille*, 5:470.

142. Mme de Poulaillon availed herself of nearly every known method in her attempts to get rid of her husband. See the interrogation of her servant, Perrine Monstreux, on February 13, 1679, ibid., 5:202–12.

143. Interrogation of Mme de Poulaillon, February 1679, reprinted in Nass, *Empoisonnements sous Louis XIV*, 37.

144. Lucien Nass writes that he performed an experiment to test whether or not it was possible to cause death by administering arsenic in such a fashion. He took a guinea pig, shaved off a small section of its hair, and rubbed arsenic onto the creature's skin. The guinea pig died within two days, but the skin never erupted into sores. See ibid., 38–40, for a description of his experiment. Mid-twentieth-century medical experts, however, offered no consensus as to how fatal such an application would prove. See Henein, "Poisons dans le roman," 156, on this point.

145. Nass, *Empoisonnements sous Louis XIV*, 136. See also p. 57 for an account of his test on a guinea pig. The *procès-verbaux de visites*, the records listing the varieties of poisons found in the homes of several of the sorceresses arrested during the affair, can be seen in AB, mss 10342–52. Some of these *procès-verbaux* (for La Bosse, La Trianon, and the abbé Deshayes, among others) have been reprinted in Nass, *Empoisonnements sous Louis XIV*, 141–79.

146. On the use of mineral, herbal, and vegetable poisons during the Middle Ages, see Collard, *Crime de poison*, 60–83.

147. Interrogation of Lesage, September 13, 1679. Lesage added that La Voisin had told him that the first vial of poison she had furnished to Mme Leféron contained a distillation of mandrake, which was "a dangerous herb capable of causing death by itself." Apparently the poisonous liquid was so thick and so yellow that Mme Leféron returned it, complaining that her husband would be able to discern it. La Voisin then distilled a combination of mandrake and three other herbs for her demanding client, who found the second batch acceptable and promptly added it to her husband's soup. Ravaisson-Mollien, *Archives de la Bastille*, 5:474–75. According to Nass, however, ergot and mandrake are not poisonous. Nass, *Empoisonnements sous Louis XIV*, 66–67.

148. During his interrogation of May 2, 1681, the abbé Guibourg explained the effects of the drug. Ravaisson-Mollien, *Archives de la Bastille*, 6:450–51.

149. Lebigre, *Affaire des poisons*, 64–65.

150. Toads were occasionally available for sale in Paris from herbalists. Anne Petit (known as La Chéron) testified that she had bought a toad for Marie Bosse from an herbalist named Paris who lived close to Les Halles. La Bosse, said La Chéron, bought toads there so often that

she pretended to be picking them up for someone else. Interrogations of La Chéron, February 25 and 26, 1679, in Ravaisson-Mollien, *Archives de la Bastille*, 5:222–28.

151. *Procès-verbal* of La Bosse, June 7, 1679, reprinted in Nass, *Empoisonnements sous Louis XIV*, 48.

152. This was similar to another method described to her by La Chéron, she claimed, which produced poison "by taking a toad and putting salt in its mouth, the salt pulls out the venom, which could cause death." Interrogation of La Deslauriers, May 13, 1681, in Ravaisson-Mollien, *Archives de la Bastille*, 6:452.

153. Interrogation of Guibourg, January 7, 1681, ibid., 6:411. Also reprinted in Nass, *Empoisonnements sous Louis XIV*, 50–52. Because the powder would have given off such a fetid odor that it would have been easily detectable in food, Nass speculates that it would have had to be administered by enema.

154. Interrogation of Belot, June 10, 1679, in Ravaisson-Mollien, *Archives de la Bastille*, 5:392–93.

155. Nass, *Empoisonnements sous Louis XIV*, 47–48.

156. *Orviétan* proved immensely popular in Italy and England as well as France. For a history of its use, see Gentilcore, *Healers and Healing in Early Modern Italy*, 96–99.

157. The recipe has been reprinted in Nass, *Empoisonnements sous Louis XIV*, 96. For Belot's *procès-verbal de question* of June 10, 1679, see Ravaisson-Mollien, *Archives de la Bastille*, 5:395.

158. Theriac was considered so effective against poison during the early modern period that every major Italian city prepared its own supply in elaborate public ceremonies, attended by medical, ecclesiastical, and civic authorities. Gentilcore, *Healers and Healing in Early Modern Italy*, 113–15. For a brief history of the antidote, also known as mithridatium, see Ben Davis, "A History of Forensic Medicine," *Medico-Legal Journal* 53 (1985): 9–23, and Collard, *Crime de poison*, 94.

159. For a brief discussion of the myths surrounding unicorn horns, see Bély, *Société des princes*, 130–31.

160. Quoted in Nass, *Empoisonnements sous Louis XIV*, 97. During the Middle Ages, bezoars were widely held to be valuable antipoisons. Edward I of England, for example, believed that a bezoar had saved his life after he was wounded with a poisoned sword in 1272. Collard, *Crime de poison*, 95.

161. Confrontation of La Bosse and La Chéron, March 17, 1679, in Ravaisson-Mollien, *Archives de la Bastille*, 5:255.

162. The marquise de Brinvilliers, for example, poisoned her father and two brothers in the belief that she would inherit a share of their estates. M. Lottinet, on the other hand, poisoned his two daughters on the eve of their weddings, apparently in order to avoid having to provide dowries for them. Interrogation of Guibourg, May 2, 1681, ibid., 6:448.

## Chapter 4

1. John Bossy, "The Counter-Reformation and the People of Catholic Europe," *Past and Present* 47 (1970): 51–70. Robin Briggs argues that the campaign to instruct the poorer classes in Christian belief sprang from the elites' desire "to combine the salvation of souls with the imposition of order in place of disorder." He continues, "There is no conceivable way of measuring the impact of this educational drive, but it does seem likely that it was considerable." Briggs, *Communities of Belief*, 199–200.

2. See Delumeau, *Catholicism Between Luther and Voltaire*, 214–16, for an account of religious and social sanctions in place in the later seventeenth century to ensure that all church members "who had reached the age of discretion" performed their Easter duties. Following the

figures of G. Le Bras, Delumeau finds "almost total observance" of Easter confession and communion in Paris at the time of the Affair of the Poisons.

3. On the resurgence of devotion in France during the first half of the seventeenth century, see Orest Ranum, *Paris in the Age of Absolutism: An Essay* (University Park: Pennsylvania State University Press, 2002), chapter 7, "A Generation of Saints." On social disciplining during the reign of Louis XIV, see Riley, *Lust for Virtue.*

4. Renegade clerics were not unique to seventeenth-century France; trials and executions of priests accused of magical activities took place throughout the medieval and early modern periods. See Mandrou, *Magistrats et sorciers en France*, 228–29, on this point. On the seventeenth-century drive to correct wayward clergy through better education, increased episcopal control, and visitations, see Farr, *Authority and Sexuality*, 52–58.

5. On the evolution of legislation against secular and religious crimes during the ancien régime, see Garnot, "Législation et la répression."

6. Under the ordinance of 1670, any cleric who violated the criminal code was tried in the royal courts, although ecclesiastical judges had to participate in the judgment. Clerical appeals were heard in the Grand-Chambres of the Parlement, where ecclesiastical judges customarily sat. If found guilty of a secular crime, a cleric was subject to the same penalties as a member of the laity. Andrews, *Law, Magistracy, and Crime*, 1:419.

7. Monter, "Toads and Eucharists," 592. See also Mandrou, *Magistrats et sorciers en France*, 496–97. On the Parisian Parlement's prosecution of the crime of witchcraft during the early modern period, see the collected articles of Soman in *Sorcellerie et justice criminelle.*

8. Interrogation of Guibourg, June 26, 1680, in Ravaisson-Mollien, *Archives de la Bastille*, 6:230.

9. Petitfils, *Affaire des poisons*, 121.

10. Memoirs of La Reynie, undated, in Ravaisson-Mollien, *Archives de la Bastille*, 6:400, 432–33.

11. Petitfils, *Affaire des poisons*, 120–21.

12. Interrogation of Debray, May 30, 1681, in Ravaisson-Mollien, *Archives de la Bastille*, 6:463.

13. Memoirs of La Reynie, undated, ibid., 6:400, 432.

14. *Notes prises par Duval, secrétaire du lieutenant de police*, APP, AA-4, fols. 288–302. The abbé Mariette, in fact, came from a family related by marriage to one of the judges of the Châtelet. When Mariette and his partner Lesage were first arrested in 1668, the abbé's relative transmitted the case to the criminal chamber of the Paris Parlement, the president of which was the brother of Mariette's client the duchesse de Vivonne. Perhaps in return for leniency, Mariette did not identify the members of his clientele. Petitfils, *Affaire des poisons*, 59–60. Mariette thus escaped the galleys to which his partner Lesage was consigned. Banished from Paris, he spent a few years in hiding in the provinces before he returned to the capital. *Du procès jugé en 1668 et de l'interrogation de Mariette du 30 de Juin de ladict année*, BN, MSS fr 7608, fols. 143–45, and *Projet d'un rapport de M. de la Reynie au Roi*, n.d., MSS fr 7608, fol. 354, also reprinted in Ravaisson-Mollien, *Archives de la Bastille*, 6:364–75.

15. Similarly, Robert Mandrou finds that the *prêtres-sorciers* of the demonic possession cases often came from "middling" clergy. *Magistrats et sorciers en France*, 227–31.

16. While Delumeau notes that "in the period of the Counter-Reformation the material situation of the lower clergy increased immeasurably," it seems that these priests may have been excluded from the general increase in the standard of living that many of their fellow religious enjoyed. See Delumeau, *Catholicism Between Luther and Voltaire*, 143. As many of the priests involved in the Affair of the Poisons were older (as far as can be determined, their average age was approximately fifty-five), they may not have had the benefit of a seminary education (which did not become customary until after 1660) and perhaps had fewer opportunities than their younger counterparts.

17. Declaration of La Bergerot, November 18, 1679, in Ravaisson-Mollien, *Archives de la Bastille,* 6:47–48.

18. On this point, see Mandrou, *Magistrats et sorciers en France,* 82–87.

19. Euan Cameron suggests that the insistence of Catholic Reformation theologians on the power of holy things (such as holy water, holy herbs, or making the sign of the cross) and holy rituals (such as exorcism) must have "reinforced popular belief in the power of words and rituals." Cameron, "For Reasoned Faith or Embattled Creed? Religion for the People in Early Modern Europe," *Transactions of the Royal Historical Society* 8 (1998): 185.

20. Declaration of La Voisin, June 16, 1679, in Ravaisson-Mollien, *Archives de la Bastille,* 5:409.

21. For more detailed descriptions of the use of such ingredients in love potions, see ibid., 5:271, 6:186–87, 224–25.

22. Interrogation of La Fille Voisin, March 28, 1680, ibid., 6:194.

23. Robert Muchembled, *Le roi et la sorcière: L'Europe des bûchers, XVe–XVIIIe siècles* (Paris: Desclée, 1993), 57.

24. Jean-Baptiste Thiers, *Traité des superstitions selon l'écriture sainte, les décrets des concils et les sentimens des saints pères et des théologiens* (Paris, 1679), republished as *Traité des superstitions: Croyances populaires et rationalité à l'âge classique,* ed. Jean-Marie Goulemot (Paris: Sycomore, 1984).

25. Monter, "Toads and Eucharists," 529–31. Monter finds that the severity of the capital sentences handed out in these cases involving the magical use of hosts was due not to the sorcery involved but to the fact that the defendants had profaned the Eucharist. See Mandrou, *Magistrats et sorciers en France,* 507–11, for cases in which equally severe sentences (death or life in the galleys) were handed down in 1687, 1692, and 1703.

26. The magician Lesage claimed that he had obtained consecrated hosts from Abbé Mariette for use during rituals of necromancy. Notes of La Reynie, November 25, 1680, in Ravaisson-Mollien, *Archives de la Bastille,* 6:385.

27. Muchembled, *Roi et la sorcière,* 57.

28. See variations on this use of consecrated hosts in Ravaisson-Mollien, *Archives de la Bastille,* 6:307, 408, 468.

29. Priests involved in the Affair of the Poisons often said masses over written charms and wax figures as well as magical potions. See ibid., 6:32, 56, 215–17 for examples.

30. La Desmaretz must have been quite determined to marry the man, for she commissioned several different spells for the purpose. For another example, see her interrogation of May 25, 1679, ibid., 5:375.

31. Declaration of La Voisin, June 16, 1679, ibid., 5:408–10.

32. On the approximate date of the ceremony, see the notes of La Reynie, November 5, 1680, ibid., 6:355–56.

33. Roughly translated, "Let the risen Venus shine forth."

34. Interrogation of Lesage, November 15, 1680, in Ravaisson-Mollien, *Archives de la Bastille,* 6:359.

35. Declaration of La Voisin, June 16, 1679, and interrogation of Guibourg, September 3, 1680, ibid., 5:408 and 6:307.

36. Interrogation of Debray, January 4, 1681, ibid., 6:408.

37. Interrogation of Lesage, November 28, 1679, ibid., 6:56.

38. See, for example, the interrogation of La Fille Voisin, August 22, 1680, ibid., 6:301. Carlo Ginzburg also encountered such practices among seventeenth-century Italians; two *benandanti* confessed to having had their cauls baptized with them (at the behest of their mothers) and masses celebrated over the cauls. Both *benandanti* had been instructed by their mothers to always wear the cauls on their persons for protection. Ginzburg, *Night Battles,* 15.

39. Interrogation of La Fille Voisin, October 9, 1680, in Ravaisson-Mollien, *Archives de la Bastille,* 6:333.

40. On the use of this practice in the context of healing miracles, see François Lebrun, "La place du pèlerinage thérapeutique dans la piété des Bretons aux XVIIe et XVIIIe siècles," *Historiens-Géographes* 78, no. 318 (1988): 15–19.

41. Confrontation of Lesage with La Voisin, January 7 and 16, 1680, in Ravaisson-Mollien, *Archives de la Bastille,* 6:91–94 and 98–101.

42. See, for example, the interrogation of Lesage, November 28, 1679, and the interrogation of La Filastre, January 2, 1680, ibid., 6:56, 72.

43. Interrogation of La Vertemart, September 12, 1679, ibid., 6:58–59.

44. For an extended history of such magic manuals, see Butler, *Ritual Magic,* 47–153.

45. Kieckhefer, *Forbidden Rites,* chapter 1.

46. Kieckhefer, *Magic in the Middle Ages,* 153.

47. Kieckhefer, *Forbidden Rites,* 21n32.

48. See Keith Thomas, *Religion and the Decline of Magic* (New York: Charles Scribner's Sons, 1971), 269–76, on this point.

49. Interrogation of Guibourg, November 24, 1680, in Ravaisson-Mollien, *Archives de la Bastille,* 6:383.

50. AB, 10357. "Livre second concernant les cernes et conjurations pour chasque jour de la semaine à Lucifer," *Livre des conjurations du pape Honorius,* 25.

51. See Ravaisson-Mollien, *Archives de la Bastille,* 6:32, 186, and 194 for examples of spells found in the *Enchiridium.*

52. Declaration of Guibourg, July 8, 1680, ibid., 6:238.

53. *Dossier d'Etienne Guibourg,* AB, MS 10355, fols. 349–61.

54. Declaration of Guibourg, July 8, 1680, in Ravaisson-Mollien, *Archives de la Bastille,* 6:238–39. La Filastre claimed that Cotton, too, had consecrated a *grimoire* in this fashion in her interrogation of August 1, 1680, ibid., 6:275. Under torture, La Voisin asserted that Mariette had also put one under the chalice during a mass. *Procès-verbal de question* of La Voisin, February 20, 1680, ibid., 6:177.

55. AB, MS 10357, fol. 9

56. Ibid.

57. "Livre second concernant les cernes et conjurations pour chasque jour de la semaine à Lucifer," *Livre des conjurations du pape Honorius,* ibid., fols. 9–10.

58. Preparations to be made for a particular conjuration were outlined in each *grimoire.* See, for example, "Livre second concernant les cernes et conjurations pour chasque jour de la semaine à Lucifer," *Livre des conjurations du pape Honorius,* ibid., fol. 25.

59. Interrogation of Lemeignan, July 31, 1680, in Ravaisson-Mollien, *Archives de la Bastille,* 6:272.

60. *Procès-verbal de question* of La Voisin, February 20, 1680, ibid., 6:162–63.

61. Interrogation of La Filastre, June 21, 1680, ibid., 6:225.

62. See, for example, François de Lalande's description of a mass performed by Abbé Cotton in his interrogation of June 15, 1680, ibid., 6:221.

63. See Kieckhefer, *Magic in the Middle Ages,* 151–75, on this point.

64. Butler, *Ritual Magic,* 117.

65. Mme Leféron reportedly purchased some inheritance powders as well. *Procès-verbal de la question* of La Voisin, February 19, 1680, in Ravaisson-Mollien, *Archives de la Bastille,* 6:152–56.

66. Interrogation of Lesage, July 15, 1680, ibid., 6:252.

67. Extract of an interrogation of Guibourg, October 10, 1680, ibid., 6:335–36.

68. The following description is culled from accounts offered by Guibourg during several

different interrogations. See BN, MSS fr 7608, fols. 214–24 and 231–38 for La Reynie's personal notes of these interrogations. La Voisin's daughter, Marie-Marguerite, also described the amatory masses she had witnessed; see her interrogation of October 9, 1680, and La Reynie's notes on the ceremony, in Ravaisson-Mollien, *Archives de la Bastille*, 6:332–33 and 369–74.

69. Interrogation of Guibourg, June 26, 1680, interrogation of La Fille Voisin, October 9, 1680, and *Mémoire* of La Reynie, undated, in Ravaisson-Mollien, *Archives de la Bastille*, 6:232, 332–33, and 369–74.

70. Those interrogated by La Reynie about the steps of the mass explained that the mass was celebrated directly over the client's *ventre*, or stomach. *Ventre* was also used as a polite term for female genitals; the royal midwife Louise Bourgeois, for example, employed the term in her 1609 *Observations diverses*. On this point, see Alison Klairmont-Lingo, "The Fate of Popular Terms for Female Anatomy in the Age of Print," *French Historical Studies* 22, no. 3 (1999): 343.

71. Interrogation of La Fille Voisin, August 22, 1680, in Ravaisson-Mollien, *Archives de la Bastille*, 6:300.

72. BN, MSS fr 7608, fol. 231.

73. *Projet d'un rapport de M. de la Reynie au Roi*, undated, in Ravaisson-Mollien, *Archives de la Bastille*, 6:372.

74. This was allegedly a common occurrence at amatory masses but does not seem to have been a required part of the ritual. See, for example, the interrogation of Lesage, November 28, 1679, ibid., 6:55–57.

75. During the sixteenth century, Jean Bodin asserted in the *Démonomanie des sorciers* that Native Americans too were wont to sacrifice their infants, like Medea. See Corneille, *Oeuvres complètes*, 1:1379, on this point. See R. Po-Chia Hsia, *The Myth of Ritual Murder: Jews and Magic in Reformation Germany* (New Haven: Yale University Press, 1988); Cohn, *Europe's Inner Demons*, 1–59; and Carlo Ginzburg, *Ecstasies: Deciphering the Witches' Sabbath*, trans. John and Anne Tedeschi (New York: Penguin, 1991), for detailed examinations of the persistent myth of ritual murder in European history.

76. See McLaren, *Reproductive Rituals*, 72–73.

77. BN, MSS fr 7608, fol. 249.

78. Remaclus, *Historia omnium acquarium*, cited in Thorndike, *History of Magic*, 5:543–44.

79. It may be that a renegade cleric pledged the baby to the devil or a specific demon before it was even born. See the interrogation of La Fille Voisin, October 9, 1680, in Ravaisson-Mollien, *Archives de la Bastille*, 6:332–33.

80. *Procès-verbal de question* of La Joly, December 19, 1681, ibid., 7:66–67.

81. *Mémoire* of La Reynie, January 26, 1681, ibid., 6:435.

82. Ibid., 6:432. He had also expressed similar sentiments several months earlier, in a draft of a letter to Louvois of August 10, 1680, ibid., 6:287–88.

83. Jansenists were Catholics who adhered to the ascetic ideals and strictly Augustinian theology put forth in Cornelius Jansen's *Augustinus* of 1638. They believed that conversion must take place under grace, embraced predestination, and emphasized the essential corruption of human nature. Strongly represented in the social elite of the country, the Parlement of Paris, and among the theologians of the University of Paris, the Jansenists wrangled with popes and French monarchs throughout the seventeenth and eighteenth centuries. The work of Dale Van Kley in particular has shaped the historical understanding of the pivotal role played by Jansenism during the ancien régime. See Van Kley, *The Jansenists and the Expulsion of the Jesuits from France, 1757–65* (New Haven: Yale University Press, 1975), *The Damiens Affair* (New Haven: Yale University Press, 1984), and *The Religious Origins of the French Revolution: From Calvin to the Civil Constitution, 1560–1791* (New Haven: Yale University Press, 1996).

84. Sentences are listed variously in BN, MSS fr 7608, BN, Collection Clairambault, 986; Ravaisson-Mollien, *Archives de la Bastille*, vols. 5–7; and APP, AA-4, fols. 208–302.

## Chapter 5

1. Norbert Elias contends in his classic work, *The Court Society,* that the presence of the most powerful nobles in the kingdom at court was evidence that Louis XIV had succeeded in domesticating the once independent aristocracy. However, the recent work of Jeroen Duindam convincingly demonstrates that "integration seems to be a more suitable term than domestication, with its connotations of taming and subduing." Duindam, *Vienna and Versailles,* 7. In *Myths of Power,* Duindam maintains that the nobles' attendance at court was the result of a compromise made between the crown and nobility in which the practice of royal authority reconfirmed, rather than enervated, noble authority. Ronald G. Asch, too, notes that the court was marked by a "mutual give and take" between the king and the nobility. See his "Introduction: Court and Household from the Fifteenth to the Seventeenth Centuries," in *Princes, Patronage, and the Nobility: The Court at the Beginning of the Modern Age, c. 1450–1650,* ed. Ronald G. Asch and A. Birke (Oxford: Oxford University Press, 1991), 4. My argument in the following section is largely in agreement with that of Duindam and Asch, but genders their representation of the court and places women at the center of analysis.

2. Lafayette, *Princess of Clèves,* 14.

3. The members of the Iowa school, influenced by Ernst Kantorowicz's *The King's Two Bodies,* have examined the multiple ways in which the political culture of France was structured around the sacralized and symbolized body of the king. On the royal funeral ceremony, see Giesey, *Royal Funeral Ceremony in France;* on the royal court, see Giesey, *Cérémonial et puissance souveraine;* on the royal entries, see Lawrence M. Bryant, *The King and the City in the Parisian Royal Entry Ceremony: Politics, Ritual, and Art in the Renaissance* (Geneva: Librairie Droz, 1986); on the *lit de justice,* see Hanley, Lit de Justice *of the Kings of France;* on the coronation, see Jackson, *Vive le Roi!*

4. Quoted in Sara E. Melzer and Kathryn Norberg, eds., "Introduction," in *From the Royal to the Republican Body: Incorporating the Political in Seventeenth- and Eighteenth-Century France,* ed. Sarah E. Melzer and Kathryn Norberg (Berkeley and Los Angeles: University of California Press, 1998), 3.

5. Abby Zanger has explored the ideological work performed by representations of the king's virility in "Lim(b)inal Images: 'Betwixt and Between' Louis XIV's Martial and Marital Bodies." Thomas E. Kaiser examines the ways in which public perceptions of Louis XIV's overly libidinous behavior contributed to the desacralization of the monarchy in "Louis *le bien-aimé* and the Rhetoric of the Royal Body." Both essays appear in Melzer and Norberg, *From the Royal to the Republican Body,* a collection of articles on the centrality of the body in the political thought of the ancien régime. Sergio Bertelli does examine the premodern rituals celebrating the king as virile progenitor in *The King's Body,* especially chapters 9 and 10.

6. Louis had a succession of mistresses whose tenures frequently overlapped during this period: Louise de la Vallière, Athénaïs de Montespan, Mme de Ludres, the princesse de Soubise, and Marie-Angélique de Fontanges, as well as a series of minor dalliances. While only two women were known as *maîtresses en titre* (Louise de la Vallière and Athénaïs de Montespan), the appellation did not necessarily indicate the true state of a woman's relationship with the king. For example, Louise de la Vallière was Louis's acknowledged mistress from 1661 until she left the court in 1674, but she received the title only in 1666, after Louis's mother, Anne of Austria, died. To further complicate matters, Louis began his affair with Athénaïs de Montespan in 1667. Although she was his favorite by 1668, she was not named *maîtresse en titre* until after she received a legal separation from her husband in 1674. Madame de Montespan remained the *maîtresse en titre* throughout the duration of the king's relationships with Mme de Ludres, the princesse du Soubise, and the duchesse de Fontanges. The devout Françoise de Maintenon, whom the king married secretly in 1683, was never given the title of official mistress.

7. For a wide-ranging comparison of the interplay between court structure and political power over time and place, see Robert Hariman, *Political Style: The Artistry of Power* (Chicago: University of Chicago Press, 1995), especially chapter 3, "No One Is in Charge Here: Ryszard Kapuściński's Anatomy of the Courtly Style."

8. According to Solnon, Louis XIV was able to redirect the nobility's sense of service towards the throne. Solnon, *Cour de France*, 409–10.

9. The offices of Louis XIV's court were divided into four main departments: the chapel, the chamber, the household, and the hunt. The chapel fell under the jurisdiction of the *grand aumônier* or almoner and included the king's confessor and all officiating clergy. The department of the chamber was headed by the grand chamberlain or *premier gentilhomme de la chambre*, who was in charge of all things and activities related to the king's bedroom: his furniture, clothes, personal toilette, and the ceremonial *lever* and *coucher*. Under the direction of the *grand maître de l'hôtel*, the department of the king's household was itself subdivided into three sections, the *paneterie*, the *échansonnerie*, and the *fruiterie*, responsible for bread, wine, and fruit, respectively. The *grand écuyer*, or master of the horse, oversaw the king's messengers and the school for pages and shared responsibility for the royal hunts with the *vénerie* and the *fauconnerie*. The military arm of the royal household included units such as the Hundred Swiss and companies of the Gentlemen of the Household. The *prévôt de l'hôtel* and his staff maintained law and order at court and the Chambre aux deniers managed the court's finances (with the exception of the king's privy purse) under the supervision of the Chambre des Comptes. See Duindam, *Vienna and Versailles*, particularly the second chapter, for a full description of the organization of the seventeenth-century French court. For a comprehensive history of the physical structure of the palace of Versailles and a survey of its inhabitants after 1682, see William R. Newton, *L'espace du roi: La cour de France au château de Versailles, 1682–1789* (Paris: Fayard, 2000).

10. The most important court offices included *grand maître de France, grand chambellan, grand écuyer, grand maître de la garderobe, grand maître des cérémonies, grand aumônier, grand veneur*, and *grand maréchal des logis*. Duindam, *Myths of Power*, 120, and Mettam, *Power and Faction*, 92–93.

11. For a detailed analysis of the queen mother's household, see Ruth Kleinman, "Social Dynamics at the French Court: The Household of Anne of Austria," *French Historical Studies* 16, no. 3 (1992): 517–35. While he did not permit Queen Marie-Thérèse or the dauphine to do so, Louis XIV allowed the queen mother to control her own appointments. Her husband, however, had not granted her the privilege. Solnon, *Cour de France*, 354.

12. The size of the court fluctuated considerably over time and so it is difficult to find reliable figures. Before 1682 it was not yet customary for the great nobles to make their homes at court if they did not hold an official post there, and thus it was more modest in size than it would become after it was settled at Versailles. Sharon Kettering notes that Louis XIV's household numbered 4,000 in 1657, not including guards, but Solnon writes that in 1661 Louis reduced the size of his household to a level smaller than the last Valois. (During Henri III's reign, the number of household officials varied from 1,064 to 1,096.) Kettering, *Patrons, Brokers, and Clients in Seventeenth-Century France* (New York: Oxford University Press, 1986), 220, and Solnon, *Cour de France*, 48. I have based my approximation of the number of nobles at court in 1664 upon the 600 who attended Louis's lavish three-day entertainment at Versailles for Louise de la Vallière, the *Plaisirs de d'île enchantée*. Solnon, *Cour de France*, 300. Duindam calculates that roughly 5,100 people held official posts within the broader court in 1699. See his *Vienna and Versailles* on the calculations he used to reach this figure. By the end of the king's reign more than 10,000 people lived at Versailles, half of whom were noble. Aristocratic attendance at Versailles was on a system of quarters. Service entailed residences of three months, twice a year. Even so, at the peak of noble attendance the 10,000 court nobles (who lived at court, therefore, 5,000 at a time) represented only 5 percent of the entire nobility. Bluche, *Louis XIV*, 354.

13. Kettering also points out that Louis called the *ban-et-arrière ban* (feudal military service) only four times, relying instead upon the standing army created by Louvois in 1661. Kettering, *Patrons, Brokers, and Clients*, 222.

14. On Louis XIV's near-monopoly over the granting of military commissions, see Guy Rowlands, *The Dynastic State and the Army Under Louis XIV: Royal Service and Private Interest, 1661–1701* (Cambridge: Cambridge University Press, 2002).

15. The size of the queen's household varied, encompassing between 425 and 600 persons during the old regime. While women held 20 to 25 percent of appointments within the queen's household during Anne of Austria's reign, fewer than 10 percent of the officeholders in the establishment of Louis XIV's queen, Marie-Thérèse, were women. Duindam, *Vienna and Versailles*, 59–61.

16. The queen's staff was headed by the superintendent of her household and the lady in waiting, and her wardrobe and jewels were managed by the lady of honor. Kleinman, "Social Dynamics at the French Court," 522–23.

17. Ibid.

18. Nevertheless, if Louis wished to replace an important officeholder in the queen's household, he did so with the consent of the present occupant (however reluctantly it might be given) and usually provided her with considerable financial recompense. When he wished to appoint Mme de Montespan *surintendante* of the queen's household in 1679, for example, he asked the comtesse de Soissons to surrender the office as a personal favor to him and gave her 200,000 *livres* in return. For a contemporary account of the exchange, see the letter of Erard du Châtelet, marquis de Trichâteau, to Bussy, April 14, 1679, in *Correspondance de Roger de Rabutin*, 4:467.

19. The term "shadow hierarchy" was coined by Duindam, *Myths of Power*, 153.

20. On the courtiers' understanding of the order of precedence and its privileges, see Emmanuel Le Roy Ladurie, "Rangs et hiérarchie dans la vie de cour," in *The Political Culture of the Old Regime*, vol. 1, *The French Revolution and the Creation of Modern Political Culture*, ed. Keith Michael Baker (New York: Pergamon Press, 1987), 61–76, and Ladurie, *Saint Simon and the Court of Louis XIV*, 23–62.

21. While it drew upon Valois ceremony as well as Spanish and Byzantine custom, the order had been instituted by Henri IV after he ascended the throne just before the turn of the century. Bluche argues that Louis XIV modeled his court protocol and ceremonial after the regulations promulgated by the "'inventor' of this delicate courtly machine, Henry III." Bluche, *Louis XIV*, 188. However, Louis XIV tinkered with the order of precedence throughout his reign. His most controversial innovation was to rank his legitimized children as well as those of Henri IV between the princes of the blood and the *princes étrangers*. Wolf, *Louis XIV*, 270. His decision caused much gnashing of teeth among the members of the aristocracy, according to Saint Simon. See, for example, Saint Simon, *Historical Memoirs of the Duc de Saint Simon: A Shortened Version 1691–1715*, ed. and trans. Lucy Norton, 3 vols. (London: W. W. Norton, 1967), 2:44–48. For the complete French edition of the memoirs, see Saint Simon, *Mémoires de Saint Simon*, ed. Arthur de Boislisle, 43 vols. (Paris: 1879–1928).

22. The chart is taken from Duindam, *Vienna and Versailles*, 120.

23. The title of *duc et pair*, the most prestigious aristocratic hereditary rank in French society, was a relatively recent invention of Louis XIII. It was bestowed by the king and registered by the Paris Parlement. While the title did not confer material benefit, the increase in social status it accorded enabled the recipient to gain ceremonial precedence within the court. See Mettam, *Power and Faction*, 198.

24. The ranks include both women and men; women took their husband's rank upon marriage. These noble titles conferred equal consequence (unlike those of the English nobility, for example, whose titles are hierarchically ranked), but families made claims to precedence based

upon the antiquity of their houses, the illustriousness of the posts and offices held by family members, and the length of time the family had held its title. Duindam, *Myths of Power*, 83.

25. The *généalogiste des ordres du roi* determined who was eligible to attend court. To receive the *honneurs de la cour*, families were required to demonstrate that their noble status had been granted before 1400. Duindam, *Myths of Power*, 152–53.

26. It was these nobles whom Louis sought to draw into his orbit at court. Wolf, *Louis XIV*, 272. On the king's day-to-day activities with his noble attendants, see Jacques Levron, *Daily Life at Versailles in the Seventeenth and Eighteenth Centuries*, trans. Claire Eliane Engel (New York: Macmillan, 1968), chapters 3–5.

27. Most royal offices were venal. Once purchased, they became the property of the holder until his death. Despite their high cost, the offices were greatly sought after by members of leading legal and financier families because they ennobled the officeholder. The office of secretary of the king, for example, cost an exorbitant 250,000 *livres*, but the office ennobled the holder's family as well as himself. Nobility not only increased the family's standing in the social hierarchy but also conferred economic privileges such as exemption from taxes. Considering themselves the only true elite in France, the nobility of the sword were at pains to distinguish themselves from the nobility of the robe. Nobility of birth, they argued, conferred a nobility of ethics and values that could not be simply purchased. Mettam, *Power and Faction*, 55, 74, and Collins, *State in Early Modern France*, xxxii.

28. However, by virtue of the prestige of their offices, some members of the robe nobility outranked some nobles of the sword in the order of precedence at court. The *noblesse de robe* fought for precedence among their own ranks by attempting to prove how long their families had possessed royal office.

29. Collins, *State in Early Modern France*, xxxi.

30. Robe nobles who served Louis XIV faithfully were often rewarded with social promotion, although that promotion was usually granted indirectly, to their children. Louis married three of Colbert's granddaughters, for example, into prestigious ducal families. Mettam, *Power and Faction*, 95.

31. Saint Simon, *Mémoires de Saint Simon*, 12:124.

32. Duindam is in agreement with Elias's analysis on this point. See Duindam, *Myths of Power*, 90, and Elias, *Court Society*, 100.

33. On this point, see Melzer and Norberg, "Introduction," 2, as well as Hariman, *Political Style*, 58–59. A courtier who was granted the privilege of additional access to the king found that his or her *crédit* at court rose as soon as the news had circulated. The duc de Saint Simon, for example, already numbered among the favored by virtue of the frequent invitations he had received to accompany the king to Marly, accepted the congratulations of the entire court once it became known that the coveted *pour* (a mark of distinction meted out sparingly by the king) had been written on his door there. Duindam, *Myths of Power*, 120.

34. Duindam and Elias are in agreement on this result of the "status dissonance" at court. See Elias, *Court Society*, 90–91, and Duindam, *Myths of Power*, 153–54.

35. Quoted in Elias, *Court Society*, 91.

36. Jean-Marie Constant, *La vie quotidienne de la noblesse française aux XVIe–XVIIe siècles* (Paris: Hachette, 1985), 52.

37. For an analysis of these three factions, see Emmanuel Le Roy Ladurie, "Versailles Observed: The Court of Louis XIV in 1709," in *The Mind and Method of the Historian*, trans. Siân Reynolds and Ben Reynolds (Chicago: University of Chicago Press, 1981), 149–73. Ladurie expands his analysis in *Saint Simon and the Court of Louis XIV*, chapter 4, "Cabals, Lineages, and Power." Duindam, however, finds that Ladurie's precise chart of the court factions confers "a false sense of precision." Duindam emphasizes instead the "changeable panorama of loyalties and conflicts" at court. Duindam, *Vienna and Versailles*, 248.

38. *Crédit* had several related meanings in seventeenth-century France. It could refer to one's reputation and credibility, to one's influence with the king, or to political influence derived from one's relationship with powerful individuals. Sharon Kettering, "Brokerage at the Court of Louis XIV," *Historical Journal* 36, no. 1 (1993): 80. Primi Visconti used the term to mean "favor with [the king]": "Le crédit de la duchesse de la Vallière était alors fort diminué et la marquise de Montespan en pleine faveur." Visconti, *Mémoires sur la cour de Louis XIV*, 9–10.

39. Louis was secretive about who his closest advisors were, but ever watchful courtiers often had a shrewd idea of who had gained the king's confidence. See Mettam, *Power and Faction*, 87–92, on this point. However, while courtiers could guess who the king's advisors were, they could rarely be absolutely certain. It proved advantageous for Louis's nobles to cultivate relationships with a number of different candidates who were likely to have gained the king's affections. Those who had sustained personal contact with the monarch, such as his mistresses, were therefore assiduously courted.

40. This analogy is similar to that offered by Henri Brocher in *À la cour de Louis XIV: Le rang et l'étiquette sous l'ancien régime* (Paris: Alcan, 1934), 41.

41. Elias describes the court as a stock exchange in which everyone's worth was relative to everyone else's. *Court Society*, 90–92. The king's favor was understood to be finite, a view consistent with the early modern understanding of how the economy as a whole functioned. Because the amount of material wealth in the world was believed to be fixed, if one person became rich, logic dictated that somebody else must therefore be impoverished by the same amount.

42. The comte de Tessé might have benefited from reading Nicolas Faret's *Honneste-Homme ou l'art de plaire à la cour*, a manual written in 1630 (reprinted regularly until 1681) that advised its readers on the proper code of conduct at court. A newcomer's first step, Faret instructed, was to find "a friend who is faithful, judicious and of experience, who may give us good directions and let us see, as in a picture, the customs which are observed, the powers which reign, the factions and parties which are honored, the manners and fashions which are in course, and generally all the things which cannot be learned but upon the place." Quoted in Jorge Arditi, *A Genealogy of Manners: Transformations of Social Relations in France and England from the Fourteenth to the Eighteenth Century* (Chicago: University of Chicago Press, 1998), 134.

43. The anecdote is from Saint Simon, *Mémoires de Saint Simon*, 5:361–64.

44. This argument regarding the importance of access to the king and its impact on an individual's position in the court hierarchy takes the middle ground between Norbert Elias, who argues that ancestry became far less important than the king's favor in determining status at court, and Ellery Schalk, *From Valor to Pedigree: Ideas of Nobility in France in the Sixteenth and Seventeenth Centuries* (Princeton: Princeton University Press, 1986), who suggests that lineage had become the more important factor by Louis XIV's reign. Certainly the nobles who attended Louis were of ancient descent and the king was usually quite careful to grant his favorites only those rewards that were commensurate with their rank. See Mettam, *Power and Faction*, 86–88, on this point. Nonetheless, the king's favor (whether real or imagined by the remaining courtiers) could and did elevate the relative status of nobles of impeccable descent. In 1679, for example, Louis raised that of the duc de la Rouchefoucauld when he appointed him *grand veneur*, an office traditionally reserved for princes. Mettam, *Power and Faction*, 92.

45. On the *lit de justice*, see Hanley, Lit de Justice *of the Kings of France*.

46. On the royal coronation from the Middle Ages to the nineteenth century, see Jackson, *Vive le Roi!* On Louis XIII's coronation, see Ralph Giesey, "La Crise du cérémoniale en 1610," in *Cérémonial et puissance souveraine*.

47. For detailed descriptions of the *lever*, see Elias, *Court Society*, 83–84, Levron, *Daily Life at Versailles*, 39–44, or Solnon, *Cour de France*, 356–539.

48. Although the court was not permanently established at Versailles until 1682, the king's apartments at the palace (site of the performance of the *lever* and *coucher*) were in use by 1673.

Tellingly, Ralph Giesey finds that 1673 marked the point at which court ritual replaced state ceremonial (royal funerals, coronations, *entrées, lits de justice*) as a means of representing royal power. He notes that Louis XIV performed no state ceremonials during the last half of his reign. His last royal entry, into Paris, took place as part of his marriage festivities in 1660 and his final *lit de justice* in 1673. Giesey, "The King Imagined," in Baker, *French Revolution and the Creation of Modern Political Culture.*

49. I am grateful to Sheila ffolliott for this observation. For the architectural plans of Versailles, see Newton, *Espace du roi,* passim.

50. Visconti, *Mémoires sur la cour de Louis XIV,* 57.

51. Had Marie-Thérèse remained at the Spanish court, her piety might have translated into greater power than she was able to wield at the French one. Studying three royal Habsburg women in the early seventeenth century, Magdalena S. Sánchez argues that Margaret of Austria, the Empress María, and Margaret of the Cross were able to exercise political power by consciously manipulating their reputations for religious devotion. See Sánchez, *The Empress, the Queen, and the Nun: Women and Power at the Court of Philip III of Spain* (Baltimore: Johns Hopkins University Press, 1998), especially chapter 6. After 1683, however, Mme de Maintenon's piety helped her maintain her position despite her undistinguished birth. But Louis cared little for *dévotes* while his official queen was alive.

52. Visconti, *Mémoires sur la cour de Louis XIV,* 304.

53. Duindam describes the position of royal mistress—with its privileges and pitfalls—as akin to royal favorite in *Vienna and Versailles,* 242.

54. See Kaiser, "Louis *le bien-aimé* and the Rhetoric of the Royal Body," 148, on this point.

55. Madame de Lafayette, *The Secret History of Henrietta, Princess of England First Wife of Philippe, Duc d'Orléans, Together with Memoirs of the Court of France for the Years 1688–1689,* trans. J. M. Shelmerdine (New York: Howard Fertig, 1993), 8.

56. Quoted in Bluche, *Louis XIV,* 265. These comments, however, were not included in the final version of the king's memoirs.

57. Quoted in Wolf, *Louis XIV,* 308.

58. Visconti, *Mémoires sur la cour de Louis XIV,* 294. Spanheim penned a similar analysis of family ambition when he described the origins of Louis's affair with Mlle de Fontanges: "It was Mlle de Fontanges, daughter of the comte de Roussille, a distinguished gentleman of Auvergne, who came to the court in the year 1679 to take up a post as one of Madame's maids of honor, and with the conscious determination, abetted by her own family, to make the king her lover." Spanheim, *Relation de la cour de France,* 13.

59. Louis XIV, *Mémoires,* 247. On its authenticity, see Paul Sonnino, "The Dating and Authorship of Louis XIV's *Mémoires,*" *French Historical Studies* 3, no. 3 (1964): 303–37.

60. Visconti, *Mémoires sur la cour de Louis XIV,* 186–87.

61. Wolf, *Louis XIV,* 294.

62. Visconti, *Mémoires sur la cour de Louis XIV,* 304.

63. Wolf, *Louis XIV,* 293.

64. Lafayette, *Secret History of Henrietta, Princess of England,* 53. After Louise was replaced by Athénaïs de Montespan as *maîtresse et titre,* however, the shy Louise was held up as a paragon of royal mistresses; she was remembered as a graceful woman who had treated the queen with great respect, proved incapable of dabbling in affairs of state, been rightfully ashamed of her adulterous relationship with the king, and taken the veil in order to atone for her sinful life. Extolling Louise's many virtues served of course as a useful means of criticizing the excesses of the current mistress.

65. Madame de Sévigné, however, gave Mme de Montespan the nickname "Quanto" or "How much?" a reference to both a popular card game and to Mme de Montespan's love of spending money. Petitfils, *Madame de Montespan,* 296n2.

66. Quoted in Wolf, *Louis XIV*, 304.

67. Visconti, *Mémoires sur la cour de Louis XIV*, 10. Saint Simon, on the other hand, described Mme de Montespan as "cross, capricious, ill-tempered, and of a haughtiness in everything which reached to the clouds, and from the effects of which nobody, not even the king, was exempt. . . . With that she loved her family and her relatives, and did not fail to serve people for whom she had conceived friendship." Saint Simon, *Memoirs of the Duke of Saint Simon*, 237.

68. Jules Hardouin-Mansart (1646–1708) was the chief architect of Versailles. He oversaw the final enlargement of Louis XIV's palace and the adjacent buildings that would eventually house 5,000 courtiers and as many government officials, guards, and servants. It was he who designed the legendary Hall of Mirrors. Madame de Sévigné rhapsodized over Mansart's chateau at Clagny: "The palace of Apollidonus and the gardens of Armida combined may give some faint indication of the splendor of this place." Mme de Sévigné to Mme de Grignan, July 3, 1675, in Sévigné, *Correspondance*, 1:1081.

69. Hilton, *Athénaïs*, 129.

70. Mongrédien, *Madame de Montespan et l'affaire des poisons*, 50–52.

71. *Oeuvres de Louis XIV*, ed. Grimoard and Grouvelle (Paris, 1806), 5:536–37, quoted in Wolf, *Louis XIV*, 640n11.

72. Letter to Electress Sophie, May 2, 1679, in Forster, *Woman's Life in the Court of the Sun King*, 100.

73. Bluche, *Louis XIV*, 266. Saint Simon wrote, "Her charms had made it possible for her to gain a close insight into the king's secret thoughts, and she was able to make use most advantageously of this knowledge as a result of the close relationship which still existed between them . . . she was content to enjoy his favor when his devotion [to Mme de Montespan] resolved him to repudiate her, knowing well how to put the king at his ease and even to make use of his devotion to the other to improve her own position." Saint Simon, *Historical Memoirs of the Duc de Saint-Simon*, 1:412.

74. Visconti, *Mémoires sur la cour de Louis XIV*, 305.

75. Mme de Sévigné to Mme de Grignan, December 1, 1675, in Sévigné, *Correspondance*, 2:174–75.

76. Visconti, *Mémoires sur la cour de Louis XIV*, 43.

77. Etiquette and ceremony ritualized courtiers' interactions with each other as well. As Solnon notes, "Etiquette remained, however, at the center of the mechanism of the court . . . it marked the ranks, underlined everyone's place." Solnon, *Cour de France*, 363.

78. Visconti, *Mémoires sur la cour de Louis XIV*, 187–88.

79. Louis XIV, *Mémoires*, 144.

80. Duindam, *Myths of Power*, 103.

81. Primi Visconti described the king in an unguarded moment: "In public, he is full of gravity and quite different than he is in private. Finding myself in his chamber with several other courtiers, I noticed several times, if by chance the door to his room happened to be open, that he would immediately compose his expression before he left, as though before a theater." Visconti, *Mémoires sur la cour de Louis XIV*, 33.

82. Louis XIV, *Mémoires*, 200.

83. Quoted in Duidam, *Myths of Power*, 119.

84. J. Russell Major, *From Renaissance Monarchy to Absolute Monarchy: French Kings, Nobles, and Estates* (Baltimore: Johns Hopkins University Press, 1994), 335–66. The bounty distributed by the king and negotiated through court brokers included pensions, gifts of money, estates, and royal offices. His gifts were carefully distributed among the various factions so that none could become powerful enough to pose a threat to his authority. Duidam, *Myths of Power*, 124, 126n91. Despite his reputation to the contrary, Louis was not recklessly indulgent toward his nobles. In 1683, for example, he spent only 1.21 percent of his annual income on pensions

and gifts to courtiers. Solnon, *Cour de France,* 403. While nobles attended court in the hope of obtaining the rewards that only Louis could bestow, the king preferred to keep them in a state of hopeful anticipation.

85. Louis XIV, *Mémoires,* 31.

86. Indeed, the successful handing of a petition to the king evolved into a minor art form at court as supplicants jockeyed for position along the corridors through which the king was due to pass. Insider information was often essential for success. François Grandet, a conseiller from Angers, described his experience as a petitioner: "M. le Grand . . . informed me that I was not well placed, because as soon as the King left the Cabinet to go to Mass, the throng of courtiers following him would prevent me getting near enough to speak to him. He said that I should take up a position at the threshold of the door which connects the King's Apartment with the Salle des Gardes, and since the Salle des Gardes was both broad and long, those accompanying would disperse somewhat and I would be free to speak with the King at leisure. . . . When I told [M. de Châteauneuf] that I had handed over my petition to the King at his command, he said: 'Your audience was completely wasted: when the King changes his clothes this afternoon, before going hunting, the petition will remain in the pocket of the first coat, and it will be as good as lost.'" Quoted in Ziegler, *Court of Versailles in the Reign of Louis XIV,* 148.

87. For a thorough analysis of such transactions, see Kettering, "Brokerage at the Court of Louis XIV." Brokers received payment for their services; go-betweens did not.

88. Madame de Motteville, *Mémoires.* Quoted in Ziegler, *Court of Versailles in the Reign of Louis XIV,* 153.

89. Duindam also includes court ceremony as a factor to explain why brokers were so predominant at the court of Louis XIV. He writes, "The paralyzing weight of ritual lent special meaning to the position of intermediary. The ruler maintained his solemn aloofness, while the confidant served as broker of the king's patronage." Duindam, *Myths of Power,* 155.

90. Those who arranged the nominations to offices were able to wield a great deal of patronage that not only brought them influence at court but earned them considerable sums of money. While the king chose those who filled his principal household offices, the officeholder could (with the king's permission) select the candidates for the lesser offices under his jurisdiction. Thus the lord chamberlain named the twelve *gentilshommes de la chambre* and the *grand prévôt de l'hôtel* his lieutenants, and the *grand fauconnier* earned 50,000 *livres* each year from the sale of offices under his direction. According to Dangeau, nominating a *maître d'hôtel* was a windfall of at least 20,000 *livres* for the *grand maître.* Solnon, *Cour de France,* 353. Although the sale of the offices of the royal households had been declared illegal in 1629, the monarch might lend his consent to their sale nonetheless. Kleinman, "Social Dynamics at the French Court," 522. Each office, however, required that its occupant have a certain rank, thus limiting possible candidates.

91. Other opportunities for court brokers to turn a profit included arranging marriages (for a percentage of the dowry), negotiating tax treaties (for a gratuity or a pension), and peddling information to the government, known as acting as a *donneur d'avis* (for a specified *droit d'avis,* or fee for information). Kettering, "Brokerage at the Court of Louis XIV," 73.

92. Ibid., 76.

93. Saint Simon, *Memoirs of the Duke of Saint Simon,* 2:225.

94. Kettering, "Brokerage at the Court of Louis XIV," 73–75, and Levron, *Daily Life at Versailles,* 79.

95. Saint Simon wrote of the princesse d'Harcourt, "A gambler and a cheat. She would do business for anything from an *écu* to the largest sums of money." Quoted in Levron, *Daily Life at Versailles,* 79. She was a long-standing favorite of the king; as early as 1667 he selected her to join the group that included the queen, Louise de la Vallière, and Mme de Montespan, who accompanied him on his tour of Flanders during the War of Devolution. Wolf, *Louis XIV,* 201.

96. Or so the legendary braggart told Saint Simon, who wrote, "These are things, the recital of which takes the breath away, and terrifies at the same time." Saint Simon, *Historical Memoirs of the Duc de Saint-Simon*, 3:461–62.

97. Louis XIV, *Mémoires*, 80.

98. Wolf, *Louis XIV*, 273. For a useful chart outlining the complicated rules of seating precedence at court, see Henri Brocher, *À la cour de Louis XIV*, 29. The chart is also reprinted in Ladurie, *Saint Simon and the Court of Louis XIV*, 27.

99. Louis XIV, *Mémoires*, 80.

100. The court noblewomen implicated in the Affair of the Poisons included the comtesse du Roure, the princesse de Tingry, the comtesse de Soissons, the marquise d'Alluye, the duchesse de la Ferté, the duchesse de Bouillon, the comtesse de Gramont, the comtesse d'Armagnac, the duchesse de Vivonne, the duchesse de Foix, the duchesse d'Angoulême, the duchesse de Vitry, the vicomtesse de Polignac, and of course Mme de Montespan. "Noms des accusés nobles et gens de qualité ou qui sont en charge ou dans un état honnête au nombre de 54," APP, AA-4, fols. 288–302.

101. Visconti, *Mémoires sur la cour de Louis XIV*, 294.

102. The sorceress La Leroux, when questioned about what a ceremony for gaining someone's good graces entailed, told her interrogators that the ritual required that one "take the head of a dead man from the cemetery, and then it is necessary to burn part of it, while saying some words written down on a piece of paper." *Procès-verbal de question* of La Leroux, April 5, 1680, in Ravaisson-Mollien, *Archives de la Bastille*, 6:200.

103. Visconti, *Mémoires sur la cour de Louis XIV*, 57.

104. A ritual phrase found in the interrogation of Marie-Marguerite Montvoisin, July 12, 1680, in Ravaisson-Mollien, *Archives de la Bastille*, 6:244.

105. Interrogation of Lesage, March 6, 1680, ibid., 6:185–87.

106. See AB, MS 10357, for examples of such spells.

107. Interrogation of Lesage, March 6, 1680, and interrogations of the duc de Luxembourg, May 2 and 5, 1680, in Ravaisson-Mollien, *Archives de la Bastille*, 6:185–87 and 208. Luxembourg's rival, the minister Louvois, took advantage of the opportunity to disgrace his adversary. Luxembourg was placed in the Bastille and later tried by the Chambre de l'Arsenal. Although the judges dismissed the charges, the king ordered the duke immediately exiled from Paris. *Procès-verbal de la Chambre*, May 14, 1680, ibid., 6:210. The imprisonment and trial of the duke closely follow the pattern of accusations of political sorcery described by Peters in *Magician, the Witch, and the Law*.

108. Fourteen female and seven male courtiers were named. APP, AA-4, fols. 288–302, and Ravaisson-Mollien, *Archives de la Bastille*, vols. 4–7, passim.

109. See the Notes of La Reynie, November 5, 1680, in Ravaisson-Mollien, *Archives de la Bastille*, 6:355–56.

110. Interrogation of Lesage, November 15, 1680, ibid., 6:356–57.

111. For a more detailed discussion of the love magic purchased, see Chapters 3 and 4.

112. See the interrogation of Mariette before the judges of the Châtelet, June 30, 1668, and *Projet d'un rapport de M. de la Reynie au Roi*, undated, in Ravaisson-Mollien, *Archives de la Bastille*, 4:11 and 6:373.

113. Interrogation of Guibourg, June 26, 1680, and October 10, 1680, and *Projet d'un rapport de M. de la Reynie au Roi*, undated, ibid., 6:232, 332–36, and 369–74.

114. The king did fall ill "of the vapors" during September and October 1675, not long after he and Mme de Montespan ended the separation they had begun at the very public behest of Bishop Bossuet. Visconti, *Mémoires sur la cour de Louis XIV*, 133. For an account of the king's symptoms and the remedies prescribed by his doctor, see Stanis Perez, ed., *Journal de santé de Louis XIV, écrit par Vallot, Daquin et Fagon* (Grenoble: Jérôme Millon, 2004), 189–92. For the

original of Fagon's "Remarques sur la santé du roy," see BN, MSS fr 6998. Lisa Hilton suggests that Louis's personal physician, d'Aquin, knew that Mme de Montespan was plying the king with love potions during the 1670s but chose to close his eyes because he owed his appointment to her. Hilton, *Athénaïs*, 129.

115. Interrogation of Guibourg, October 10, 1680, in Ravaisson-Mollien, *Archives de la Bastille*, 6:336. La Reynie's notes of Guibourg's interrogation of October 10 contain an abbreviated description of the ceremony; see BN, MSS fr 7608, fols. 121–22, 239. See also 7608, fol. 249, for Marie-Marguerite Montvoisin's account of October 9, 1680.

116. The year was 1678. Visconti, *Mémoires sur la cour de Louis XIV*, 206–7.

## Conclusion

1. The edict was registered on August 31, 1682. *Edit du Roy pour la punition de différents crimes* (Paris: Jean Baptiste Coignard, 1682), BN, Collection Delamare, MS 21730, fol. 115.

2. Ibid.

3. Ibid., fols. 115–16.

4. Ibid., fol. 116.

5. Ibid., fols. 117–18. In *L'affaire des poisons*, Arlette Lebigre argues that the most important consequence of the Affair of the Poisons was the start of state regulation of the sale of toxic substances in France (143–45).

6. The edict assured the public that such people were not their own countrymen but foreigners. The former laxity in French justice had "attracted many of these imposters from foreign countries into our realm." *Edit du Roy*, BN, Collection Delamare, MS 21730, fol. 115.

7. Ibid.

8. Ibid.

9. Impiety and profaning holy objects earned stiff penalties of heavy fines and nine years' banishment.

10. *Crimes énormes* included *lèse-majesté*, treason, premeditated murder, the use of poison, simony, robbery on the *grands chemins*, abortion, and certain crimes against morals. Garnot, "Législation et la répression," 76.

11. The Chambre de l'Arsenal convicted thirty-six people of the following capital crimes: *lèse-majesté divine* (1); *lèse-majesté divine*, sacrilege, impieties, and *maléfices* (3); *lèse-majesté* (4); *lèse-majesté* and poison (1); sacrilege, profaning the holy, and impieties (3); *lèse-majesté divine*, poison, sacrilege, conjurations, and impieties (1); poison, impieties, profaning the holy, and conjurations (1); poison, abortion, impiety, and *maléfices* (2); poison, abortion, impieties, and profaning the holy (2); poison, impieties, and counterfeiting (1); abortion (3); use of poison (9); accomplice to the use of poison (1); attempted use of poison (1); distributing poison (3). APP, AA-4, fols. 303–17.

12. Quoted in Zeigler, *Court of Versailles*, 209.

13. Visconti, *Mémoires sur la cour de Louis XIV*, 300–301. While the king persisted in his newly regularized life, his court did not remain the dull seminary about which Visconti and a number of other court observers complained. John B. Wolf explains, "the court had not so greatly changed since the earlier part of the reign. The gaming table was still the center of interest for many of the people who lived in 'this strange land,' and if the stories are correct, all gallantry did not end when the king regularized his own life. What we must see is that the court of Louis XIV, like any other institution, was fluid and changing." Wolf, *Louis XIV*, 349–50.

14. *Mémoire de René Voyer, comte d'Argenson, lieutenant de police, sur les faux sorciers qui abusent de la crédulité publique*, October 9, 1702, reprinted in Robert Mandrou, ed., *Possession et sorcellerie au XVIIe siècle: Textes inédits* (Paris: Fayard, 1979), 275.

15. Ibid., 275–328.

16. Article 479:7 of the Napoleonic Code is quoted in Harvey, "Fortune-Tellers in the French Courts," 133.

17. On the French state's attempt to repress magical practices in the modern era, see ibid.

18. Louis XIV, *Mémoires*, 144–45.

# BIBLIOGRAPHY

## Abbreviations

AB     Archives de la Bastille
AN    Archives Nationales
APP   Archives de la Préfecture de Police
BA    Bibliothèque de l'Arsenal
BN    Bibliothèque Nationale

## Primary Sources

### Unpublished Sources

Archives Nationales
    U 941 and 942, "Instruction et pratique de la Chambre de la Tournelle du Parlement par Claude Amiot, greffier criminel," 1702
    C 208, "Papiers du Rosoy"
    $X^2A$ 1 033, "Procès Mariette-Lesage"
    Minutier central XXXIII 362, "Étude Chauveau"

Archives de la Préfecture de Police
    AA-4, "Notes prises au 18e s. sur l'affaire des poisons par Duval, secrétaire de la lieutenant de police"

Bibliothèque de l'Arsenal
    Archives de la Bastille, 10338–59
    For a complete listing of the documents relating to the Affair of the Poisons held in this collection, I refer the reader both to the endnotes to each chapter and to Frantz Funck-Bretano's *Archives de la Bastille: Catalogue des manuscrits*, 14 vols. (Paris: Plon, 1892).
    Manuscrits 2664, "Questions sur les empoisonneurs et autres semblables," n.d.

Bibliothèque de l'Assemblée Nationale
    MSS 1127, "Chambre Ardente 1679–82, extrait fait par M. Brunet, avocat, des Procès Criminels Instruits et Jugés Pendant Lesdites Années Contenus en Douze Cartons, qui ont été Remis entre les Mains de M. la Garde des Sceaux par les Héritiers de M. de la Reynie"

Bibliothèque Nationale de France
  Collection Clairambault
    983, fols. 1–57, "Extraits d'interrogatoires fait par la police de Paris de gens vivans
      d'industrie, dans le désordre et de mauvaises moeurs, et aussi de gens de la religion,
      de 1702 à 1714"
    984–85, "Faux sorciers et fausses sorcières (registres de Bicêtre [hommes] et de la
      Salpêtrière [femmes])"
    986, fols. 161–467, "Inventaire des papiers et interrogatoires faits par M. de la Reynie
      Lieutenant General de Police, et Commissier député par Sa Majesté, aux personnes
      detenuës dans les Chateaux de Vincennes, et de la Bastille, pour le poison, rangés
      par ordre alfabetique, fait en 1727"
    Fols. 467–68, "Informations, Recollements, et Confrontations contre les accusez, dont
      les extraits son rapportés cy-devant"
    Fols. 469–73, "Carton des Recollements et confrontations, dans lequel sont les exécu-
      toires décrirais par la Chambre au profit des officiers qui ont travaillé au fait des
      poisons, al'Exécuteur, et au questionnaire, dont les payements sont à prendre sur le
      Domaine"

  Collection Delamare
  "Affaires criminelles. Documents imprimés et mss. relatif à divers affaires criminelles,
    la plupart du temps de Louis XIV"

  Collection Dupuy
  II 634 (documents concerning the marquise de Brinvilliers)

  Collection Morel de Thoisy
  "Affaires d'hérésie, impiété, sortilège"

  Manuscrits Français
  85 (miscellaneous documents concerning the Affair of the Poisons)
  1192, "La Diablomanie de Monsieur de Luxembourg ou Histoire de la Prison de Mon-
    sieur de Luxembourg"
  7608, "Recueil des pièces originales et copies concernant les procès instruits par M. de
    la Reynie et jugés par la Chambre de l'Arsenal, 1679–91"
  7630, "Procès criminel de La Joly"
  22566–69, "Recueil de chansons, épigrammes, satires, épitaphes, sur les personnages
    et sur les événements des règnes de Louis XIV et Louis XV"

  Nouvelles Acquisitions Françaises
  21314 (correspondence of Arnoul, intendant of the galleys)


## Published Sources

Agrippa, Henricus Cornelius. *Three Books of Occult Philosophy*. Trans. J. F. London. N.p.,
  1651.
Anon. *L'esprit familier du Trianon ou l'apparition de la duchesse de Fontanges, contenant
  les secrets de ses amours, les pecularités de son empoisonnement et de sa mort*. Paris
  [Holland]: Chez la Veuve de Jean Felix, 1695.
Bensarade, Isaac de. *Metamorphoses d'Ovide*. Paris: Imprimerie Royale, 1676.

Bussy, Roger de Rabutin, Comte de. *Correspondance de Roger de Rabutin, comte de Bussy, avec sa famille et ses amis, 1666–1693.* Ed. Ludovic Lalanne. 6 vols. Paris: Charpentier, 1858–59.

Caylus, Madame de. *Les souvenirs de Madame de Caylus.* Ed. Bernard Noël. Paris: Mercure de France, 1965.

Choisy, Abbé de. *Mémoire de l'abbé de Choisy: Mémoires pour servir à l'histoire de Louis XIV. Mémoires de l'abbé de Choisy habillé en femme.* Ed. Georges Mongrédien. Paris: Mercure de France, 1979.

Corneille, Pierre. *Médeé.* In *Médeé.* Ed. André de Leyssac. Geneva: Librairie Droz, 1978.

———. *Médée.* In *Théatre II, Tragédies.* Ed. Jacques Maurens. Paris: Garnier-Flammarion, 1980.

———. *Oeuvres complètes.* Ed. Georges Couton. 3 vols. Paris: Gallimard, 1980–87.

Corneille, Thomas, and Jean Donneau de Visé. *La devineresse.* Ed. P. J. Yarrow. Exeter: University of Exeter Press, 1971.

*Discours au vrai de l'étrange cruauté d'un soldat appelé la Planche: Par luy exercée sur une jeune fille pour avoir de son lait empoisonné. . .* Lyon: Antoine Bessy, 1611.

*Encyclopédie, ou, dictionnaire raisonné des sciences, des arts et des métiers par une société de gens des lettres.* Ed. Denis Diderot and Jean Le Rond d'Alembert. 34 vols. Paris, 1751–80.

*Factum en forme de Requête pour Damoiselle Angélique et le Sieur Baron de Divette son Beau-père, accusés de l'Empoisonnement, autres crimes.* Paris: Veuve Dupont, 1681.

Ferrand, Jacques. *A Treatise on Lovesickness, or Erotic Melancholy* (1610, 1623). Ed. and trans. Donald A. Beecher and Massimo Ciavolella. Syracuse: Syracuse University Press, 1990.

Feuquières, Antoine de Pas, marquis de. *Lettres inédites des Feuquières,* ed. Étienne Gallois. 5 vols. Paris: LeLeux, 1845.

Forster, Elborg, trans. and ed. *A Woman's Life in the Court of the Sun King: Letters of Liselotte von der Pfalz, 1652–1722.* Baltimore: Johns Hopkins University Press, 1984.

Gouges, Olympe de. "Declaration of the Rights of Woman and the Female Citizen." In *The Old Regime and the French Revolution,* ed. Keith Michael Baker, 263–68. Chicago: University of Chicago Press, 1987.

Guillemeau, Jacques. *De l'heureux accouchement des femmes.* Paris, 1609.

Hardy, Alexandre. *Alcméon, ou la vengeance féminine.* In *Le théâtre d'Alexandre Hardy,* vol 5. Ed. E. Stengel. Paris: Le Soudier, and Marburg: N. G. Elwert'sche, 1884.

Isambert, François-André, ed. *Recueil général des anciennes lois françaises depuis l'an 420 jusqu'à la révolution de 1789.* 29 vols. Paris, 1821–33.

Joubert, Laurent. *Erreurs populaires.* Trans. Gregory David de Rocher. Tuscaloosa: University of Alabama Press, 1989.

Lafayette, Madame de. *The Princess of Clèves.* Trans. Terence Cave. New York: Oxford University Press, 1992.

———. *The Secret History of Henrietta, Princess of England, First Wife of Philippe, Duc d'Orléans, Together with Memoirs of the Court of France for the Years 1688–1689.* Trans. J. M. Shelmerdine. New York: Howard Fertig, 1993.

La Fontaine, *Oeuvres complètes I: Fables, contes, et nouvelles.* Ed. Jean-Pierre Collinet. Paris: Gallimard, 1991.

*Le livre des conjurations du pape Honorius, avec un recueil des plus rares secrets de l'art magique et des pratiques l'opposant aux maléfices.* N.p., 1670. Reprint, Paris: Éditions Perthuis, 1970.

Louis XIV. *Mémoires for the Instruction of the Dauphin.* Trans. and ed. Paul Sonnino. New York: Free Press, 1970.

Magne, Emile, ed. *Lettres inédites à Marie-Louise de Gonzague, reine de Pologne sur la cour de Louis XIV.* Paris, 1920.

Marat, Jean-Paul. *Oeuvres de Jean-Paul Marat.* Ed. A. Vermorel. Paris: Décembre-Alonnier, 1869.

Montaigne, Michel de. *The Complete Essays.* Trans. M. A. Screech. New York: Penguin, 1991.

Motteville, Françoise de. *Mémoires de Madame de Motteville sur Anne d'Autriche et sa cour.* Ed. M. Sainte-Beauve. Paris: Charpentier, 1869.

Ovid. *The Metamorphoses.* Trans. Horace Gregory. New York: Viking, 1958.

Perez, Stanis, ed. *Journal de santé de Louis XIV, écrit par Vallot, Daquin et Fagon.* Grenoble: Jérôme Millon, 2004.

Racine, Jean. *Phèdre.* In *Oeuvres complètes.* Ed. P. Mesnard. Paris: Hachette, 1885.

Ravaisson-Mollien, François, ed. *Les archives de la Bastille: Documents inédits.* 19 vols. Paris: A. Durand et Pedone-Lauriel, 1866–1904.

Rosset, François de. *Histoires tragiques.* Ed. Anne de Vaucher Gravili. Paris: Livre de Poche Classique, 1994.

Rotrou, Jean de. *Hercule mourant.* In *Théâtre complet 2.* Ed. B. Louvat, D. Moncond'huy, and A. Riffaud. Paris: STFM, 1999.

Saint-Maurice, Thomas-François Chabod, Marquis de. *Lettres sur la cour de Louis XIV.* Ed. Jean Lemoine. 2 vols. Paris: Calmann-Lévy, 1911–12.

Saint Simon, Duc de. *Mémoires de Saint Simon.* Ed. Arthur Boislisle. 43 vols. Paris, 1879–1928.

———. *Memoirs of the Duke of Saint Simon.* Trans. Bayle St. John. New York: Willey Book Co., 1901.

———. *Historical Memoirs of the Duc de Saint-Simon: A Shortened Version, 1691–1715.* Ed. and trans. Lucy Norton. 3 vols. London: W. W. Norton, 1967.

Sévigné, Marie de Rabutin Chantal, Marquise de. *Correspondance.* Ed. Roger Duchêne. 3 vols. Paris: Gallimard, 1972–78.

Spanheim, Ezekiel. *Relation de la cour de France en 1690.* Paris: Librairie Renouard, 1882.

Thiers, Jean-Baptiste. *Traité des superstitions: Croyances populaires et rationalité à l'âge classique.* Ed. Jean-Marie Goulemot. Paris: Sycomore, 1984.

Primi Fassiola di San Maiolo. *Mémoires sur la cour de Louis XIV.* Ed. and trans. Jean Lemoine. Paris: Calmann-Lévy, 1908.

Voltaire, François-Marie Arouet de. *Mélanges.* Ed. J. Van Den Heuvel. Paris: Gallimard, 1961.

Von der Pfalz, Elizabeth Charlotte. *Letters from Liselotte.* Ed. and trans. Maria Kroll. New York: McCall, 1971.

## Secondary Sources

Adam, Paul. *La vie paroissiale en France au XIV siècle.* Paris: Hachette, 1964.

Adamson, John, ed. *The Princely Courts of Europe: Ritual, Politics, and Culture Under the Ancien Régime, 1500–1750.* London: Weidenfeld & Nicolson, 1999.

Alexandre, Josette. "La Comète de Halley à travers les ouvrages et manuscrits de l'Observatoire de Paris." *Isis* 77 (1986): 79–84.

Andrews, Richard Mowery. *Law, Magistracy, and Crime in Old Regime Paris, 1735–1789.* 2 vols. Cambridge: Cambridge University Press, 1994.

Ankarloo, Begnt, and Stuart Clark, eds. *Witchcraft and Magic in Europe: The Eighteenth and Nineteenth Centuries.* Philadelphia: University of Pennsylvania Press, 1999.

Antoine, Michel. "La monarchie absolue." In *The Political Culture of the Old Regime.* Vol. 1, *The French Revolution and the Creation of Modern Political Culture,* ed. Keith Michael Baker, 3–24. New York: Pergamon Press, 1987.

Apostolidès, Jean-Marie. *Le roi-machine: Spectacle et politique au temps de Louis XIV.* Paris: Éditions de Minuit, 1981.

Arditi, Jorge. *A Genealogy of Manners: Transformations of Social Relations in France and England from the Fourteenth to the Eighteenth Century.* Chicago: University of Chicago Press, 1998.

Asch, Ronald G. "Introduction: Court and Household from the Fifteenth to the Seventeenth Centuries." In *Princes, Patronage, and the Nobility: The Court at the Beginning of the Modern Age, c. 1450–1650,* ed. Ronald G. Asch and A. Birke, 1–38. Oxford: Oxford University Press, 1991.

Bailey, Michael D. *Battling Demons: Witchcraft, Heresy, and Reform in the Late Middle Ages.* University Park: Pennsylvania State University Press, 2003.

Baker, Keith Michael, ed. *The Old Regime and the French Revolution.* Chicago: University of Chicago Press, 1987.

Banerjee, Pompa. *Burning Women: Widows, Witches, and Early Modern Travelers in India.* New York: Palgrave Macmillan, 2003.

Barnes, Andrew. "The Social Transformation of the French Parish Clergy, 1500–1800." In *Culture and Identity in Early Modern Europe (1500–1800): Essays in Honor of Natalie Zemon Davis,* ed. Barbara B. Diefendorf and Carla Hesse, 139–57. Ann Arbor: University of Michigan Press, 1993.

Bartrip, Peter. "A 'Pennurth of Arsenic for Rat Poison': The Arsenic Act, 1851, and the Prevention of Secret Poisoning." *Medical History* 36 (1996): 53–69.

Bastard-d'Etang, Henri Bruno. *Les Parlements de France: Essai historique sur leurs usages, leur organisation et leur autorité.* 2 vols. Paris: Didier, 1857.

Bastien, Pascal. "Usage politique des corps et rituel de l'exécution publique à Paris, XVIIe–XVIIIe siècles." *Crime, histoire et sociétés/Crime, History, and Societies* 6, no. 1 (2002): 31–56.

Baxter, Douglas Clark. "'Ah Dieu merci, me voilà française': The Acculturation of Foreign Brides at the French Court in the Seventeenth and Eighteenth Centuries (1680–1773)." *Proceedings of the Western Society for French Historical Studies* 25 (1998): 268–78.

Beik, William. *Absolutism and Society in Seventeenth-Century France.* New York: Cambridge University Press, 1985.

Bellamy, Alistair. *The Politics of Court Scandal in Early Modern England: News Culture and the Overbury Affair, 1603–1660.* Cambridge: Cambridge University Press, 2002.

Bély, Lucien. *La société des princes, XVIe–XVIIIe siècle.* Paris: Fayard, 1999.

———, ed. *Dictionnaire de l'ancien régime.* Paris: Presses Universitaires de France, 1996.

Bertelli, Sergio. *The King's Body: Sacred Rituals of Power in Medieval and Early Modern Europe.* Trans. R. Burr Litchfield. University Park: Pennsylvania State University Press, 2001.

Billacois, François. "Pour une enquête sur la criminalité dans la France d'ancien régime." *Annales* 22, no. 2 (1967): 340–49.

———. *The Duel: Its Rise and Fall in Early Modern France.* Ed. and trans. Trista Selous. New Haven: Yale University Press, 1990.

———, ed. *Crimes et criminalité en France sous l'ancien régime, 17e–18e siècles.* Paris: Armand Colin, 1971.

Blécourt, Willem de. "Witch Doctors, Soothsayers, and Priests: On Cunning Folk in European Historiography and Tradition." *Social History* 19, no. 1 (1994): 285–303.

Bloch, Marc. *The Royal Touch: Sacred Monarchy and Scrofula in France and England.* Trans. J. E. Anderson. London: Routledge & Kegan Paul, 1973.

Bluche, François. *Louis XIV.* Trans. Mark Greengrass. New York: Basil Blackwell, 1990.

Bornecque, Robert. *La France de Vauban.* Paris: Arthaud, 1984.

Bossy, John. "The Counter-Reformation and the People of Catholic Europe." *Past and Present* 47 (1970): 51–70.

———. "The Mass as a Social Institution." *Past and Present* 100 (1983): 29–61.

———. *Christianity in the West, 1400–1700.* Oxford: Oxford University Press, 1985.

———. "Moral Arithmetic: Seven Sins into Ten Commandments." In *Conscience and Casuistry in Early Modern Europe,* ed. Edmund Leites, 214–34. Cambridge: Cambridge University Press, 1985.

Boulanger, Marc. "Justice et absolutisme: La grande ordonnance criminelle d'août 1670." *Revue d'histoire moderne et contemporaine* 47, no. 1 (2000): 7–36.

Briggs, Robin. *Communities of Belief: Cultural and Social Tension in Early Modern France.* Oxford: Oxford University Press, 1989.

———. *Witches and Neighbors: The Social and Cultural Context of European Witchcraft.* New York: Penguin, 1996.

Brocher, Henri. *À la cour de Louis XIV: Le rang et l'étiquette sous l'ancien régime.* Paris: Alcan, 1934.

Brockliss, L. W. B., and Colin Jones. *The Medical World of Early Modern France.* Oxford: Oxford University Press, 1997.

Brown, Peter. "Sorcery, Demons, and the Rise of Christianity: From Late Antiquity to the Middle Ages." In *Religion and Society in the Age of Saint Augustine,* ed. Peter Brown, 119–46. London: Faber & Faber, 1972.

Bryant, Lawrence M. *The King and the City in the Parisian Royal Entry Ceremony: Politics, Ritual, and Art in the Renaissance.* Geneva: Librairie Droz, 1986.

Burke, Peter. *Popular Culture in Early Modern Europe.* New York: Harper & Row, 1978.

———. *The Fabrication of Louis XIV.* New Haven: Yale University Press, 1992.

Burney, Ian A. "A Poisoning of No Substance: The Trials of Medico-Legal Proof in Mid-Victorian England." *Journal of British Studies* 38, no. 1 (1999): 59–92.

Butler, E. M. *Ritual Magic.* Cambridge: Cambridge University Press, 1949.

Cabantous, Alain. *Blasphemy: Impious Speech in the West from the Seventeenth to the Nineteenth Century.* Trans. Eric Rauth. New York: Columbia University Press, 2002.

Cameron, Euan. "For Reasoned Faith or Embattled Creed? Religion for the People in Early Modern Europe." *Transactions of the Royal Historical Society* 8 (1998): 165–87.

Cameron, Iain A. "The Police of Eighteenth-Century France." *European Studies Review* 7 (1977): 47–75.

Carrot, Georges. *Histoire de la police française.* Paris: Tallandier, 1992.

Cavazza, Silvano. "Double Death: Resurrection and Baptism in a Seventeenth-Century Rite." Trans. Margaret A. Callucci. In *History from Crime,* ed. Edward Muir and Guido Ruggerio, 1–31. Baltimore: Johns Hopkins University Press, 1994.

Chartier, Roger. "From Texts to Manners, a Concept and Its Books: *Civilité* Between Aristocratic Distinction and Popular Appropriation." In Roger Chartier, *The Cultural*

*Uses of Print in Early Modern France,* trans. Lydia G. Cochrane, 71–109. Princeton: Princeton University Press, 1987.

Church, William F. *Richelieu and Reason of State.* Princeton: Princeton University Press, 1972.

Clark, Stuart. "French Historians and Early Modern Popular Culture." *Past and Present* 100 (1983): 62–99.

———. "The 'Gendering' of Witchcraft in French Demonology: Misogyny or Polarity?" *French History* 5, no. 4 (1991): 426–37.

———. *Thinking with Demons: The Idea of Witchcraft in Early Modern Europe.* Oxford: Oxford University Press, 1997.

Clément, Pierre. *Madame de Montespan et Louis XIV.* Paris: Perrin et Cie, 1910.

———. *La police sous Louis XIV.* Geneva: Mégariotis Reprints, 1978.

Cohen, Thomas V., and Elizabeth S. Cohen. *Words and Deeds in Renaissance Rome: Trials Before the Papal Magistrates.* Toronto: University of Toronto Press, 1993.

Cohn, Norman. *Europe's Inner Demons: An Inquiry Inspired by the Great Witch Hunts.* New York: Meridian, 1975.

Collard, Franck. "Recherche sur le crime de poison au moyen âge." *Journal des savants* (January–June 1992): 99–114.

———. *Le crime de poison au moyen âge.* Paris: Presses Universitaires de France, 2003.

Collins, James B. *The State in Early Modern France.* Cambridge: Cambridge University Press, 1995.

Constant, Jean-Marie. *La vie quotidienne de la noblesse française aux XVIe–XVIIe siècles.* Paris: Hachette, 1985.

Cosandey, Fanny. *La reine de France: Symbole et pouvoir.* Paris: Éditions Gallimard, 2000.

Courtès, Noémie. *L'écriture de l'enchantement: Magie et magiciens dans la littérature française du XVIIe siècle.* Paris: Honoré Champion, 2004.

Couton, Georges. *La chair et l'âme: Louis XIV entre ses maîtresses et Bossuet.* Grenoble: Presses Universitaires de Grenoble, 1995.

Crawford, Patricia. "Attitudes to Menstruation in Seventeenth-Century England." *Past and Present* 91 (1981): 51–69.

Curtin, Michel. "A Question of Manners: Status and Gender in Etiquette and Courtesy." *Journal of Modern History* 57 (1985): 395–423.

Davis, Ben. "A History of Forensic Medicine." *Medico-Legal Journal* 53 (1985): 9–23.

Davis, Natalie Zemon. *Society and Culture in Early Modern France.* Stanford: Stanford University Press, 1975.

———. "Boundaries and the Sense of Self in Sixteenth-Century France." In *Reconstructing Individualism: Autonomy, Individuality, and the Self in Western Thought,* ed. Thomas C. Heller, Morton Sosna, and David E. Wellbery, 53–63. Stanford: Stanford University Press, 1986.

———. *Fiction in the Archives: Pardon Tales and Their Tellers in Sixteenth-Century France.* Stanford: Stanford University Press, 1987.

Decker, Michel de. "Madame de Montespan noircie par les jaloux?" *Historama* 14 (1985): 72–77.

Delumeau, Jean. *Catholicism Between Luther and Voltaire: A New View of the Counter-Reformation.* Trans. Jeremy Moiser. Philadelphia: Burns & Oates, 1977.

Denier, Marie-Claude. "Sorciers, présages, et croyances magiques en Mayenne aux XVIIIe et XIXe siècles." *Annales de Bretagne et des Pays de L'Ouest (Anjou, Maine, Touraine)* 97 (1990): 115–32.

Desplat, Christian. "La grâce royale: Lettres de grâce enregistrées par le Parlement de Navarre au XVIIIe siècle." *Revue de Pau et du Béarn* 10 (1982): 83–99.

———. *Sorcières et diables en Béarn (fin XIVe–début XIXe siècle).* Pau: Graphique Marrimpouey, 1988.

Dewald, Jonathan. "'The Perfect Magistrate': *Parlementaires* and Crime in Sixteenth-Century Rouen." *Archive for Reformation History* 67 (1976): 284–300.

———. "Politics and Personality in Seventeenth-Century France." *French Historical Studies* 16, no. 4 (1990): 893–908.

———. "Deadly Parents: Family and Aristocratic Culture in Early Modern France." In *Culture and Identity in Early Modern Europe (1500–1800): Essays in Honor of Natalie Zemon Davis,* ed. Barbara B. Diefendorf and Carla Hesse, 223–36. Ann Arbor: University of Michigan Press, 1993.

———. *The European Nobility, 1400–1800.* Cambridge: Cambridge University Press, 1996.

Diefendorf, Barbara B., and Carla Hesse, eds. *Culture and Identity in Early Modern Europe (1500–1800): Essays in Honor of Natalie Zemon Davis.* Ann Arbor: University of Michigan Press, 1993.

Dolan, Frances E. *Dangerous Familiars: Representations of Domestic Crime in England, 1550–1700.* Ithaca: Cornell University Press, 1994.

Dooley, Brendan. *The Politics of Information in Early Modern Europe.* Florence, Ky.: Routledge, 2001.

Drew-Bear, Annette. "Cosmetics and Attitudes Towards Women in the Seventeenth Century." *Journal of Popular Culture* 9, no. 1 (1975): 31–37.

Dubois, E. T., O. W. Maskell, and P. J. Yarrow. "L'almanch de la devineresse." *Revue d'histoire du théâtre* 32, no. 3 (1980): 216–19.

Duden, Barbara. *The Woman Beneath the Skin: A Doctor's Patients in Eighteenth-Century Germany.* Trans. Thomas Dunlap. Cambridge: Harvard University Press, 1991.

Duindam, Jeroen. *Myths of Power: Norbert Elias and the Early Modern European Court.* Trans. Lorri S. Granger and Gerard T. Moran. Amsterdam: Amsterdam University Press, 1995.

———. *Vienna and Versailles: The Courts of Europe's Dynastic Rivals, 1550–1780.* Cambridge: Cambridge University Press, 2003.

Edwards, Francis, S.J. "The Strange Case of the Poisoned Pommel: Richard Walpole, S.J., and the Squire Plot, 1597–1598." *Archivum Historicum Societatis Jesu* 56, no. 111 (1987): 3–82.

Elias, Norbert. *The Court Society.* Trans. Edmund Jephcott. New York: Pantheon Books, 1983.

Essig, Marc. *How to Kill Like a Woman, How to Kill Like a Foreigner: Forensic Medicine and the Otherness of Poison Murder.* Paper presented at the annual meeting of the American Historical Association, Washington, D.C., January 7–10, 1999.

Fairchilds, Cissie. "Female Sexual Attitudes and the Rise of Illegitimacy: A Case Study." *Journal of Interdisciplinary History* 8 (spring 1978): 627–67.

———. *Domestic Enemies: Masters and Servants in Old Regime France.* Baltimore: Johns Hopkins University Press, 1984.

Farge, Arlette. *Fragile Lives: Violence, Power, and Solidarity in Eighteenth-Century Paris.* Trans. Carol Shelton. Cambridge: Harvard University Press, 1993.

———. *Subversive Words: Public Opinion in Eighteenth-Century France.* Trans. Rosemary Morris. University Park: Pennsylvania State University Press, 1994.

Farge, Arlette, and Jacques Revel. *The Vanishing Children of Paris: Rumor and Politics*

*Before the French Revolution*. Trans. Claudia Miéville. Cambridge: Harvard University Press, 1991.

Farr, James R. "The Pure and Disciplined Body: Hierarchy, Morality, and Symbolism in France During the Catholic Reformation." *Journal of Interdisciplinary History* 21, no. 3 (1991): 391–414.

———. *Authority and Sexuality in Early Modern Burgundy (1550–1730)*. New York: Oxford University Press, 1995.

———. "Death of a Judge: Performance, Honor, and Legitimacy in Seventeenth-Century France." *Journal of Modern History* 75 (March 2003): 1–22.

Farrell, Michèle Longino. *Performing Motherhood: The Sévigné Correspondence*. Hanover: University Press of New England, 1991.

Ferber, Sarah. *Demonic Possession and Exorcism in Early Modern France*. London: Routledge, 2004.

Fiume, Giovanna. "The Old Vinegar Lady, or the Judicial Modernization of the Crime of Witchcraft." Trans. Margaret A. Gallucci. In *History from Crime*, ed. Edward Muir and Guido Ruggerio, 65–87. Baltimore: Johns Hopkins University Press, 1994.

Flint, Valerie I. J. *The Rise of Magic in Early Medieval Europe*. Princeton: Princeton University Press, 1991.

Forbes, Thomas R. "The Social History of the Caul." *Yale Journal of Biology and Medicine* 23 (1953): 495–508.

Foucault, Michel. *Discipline and Punish: The Birth of the Prison*. Trans. Alan Sheridan. New York: Vintage Books, 1977.

Freedman, Jeffrey. *A Poisoned Chalice*. Princeton: Princeton University Press, 2002.

Funck-Bretano, Frantz. *Les lettres de cachet à Paris: Étude suivie d'une liste des prisonniers de la Bastille (1659–1789)*. Paris: Imprimerie Nationale, 1903.

———. *Le drame des poisons*. Paris: J. Tallandier, 1977.

Garland, David. "Punishment and Culture: The Symbolic Dimensions of Criminal Justice." *Studies in Law, Politics, and Society* 11 (1991): 191–222.

Garnot, Benoît. "La législation et la répression des crimes dans la France moderne, XVIe–XVIIIe siècles." *Revue historique* 293, no. 1 (1993): 75–90.

———. "La perception des délinquants en France du XIVe au XIXe siècle." *Revue historique* 296, no. 2 (1996): 349–63.

———. *Justice et société en France aux XVIe, XVIIe, et XVIIIe siècles*. Paris : Éditions Ophyrs, 2000.

Geertz, Clifford. *The Interpretation of Cultures*. New York: Basic Books, 1973.

———. "Centers, Kings, and Charisma: Reflections on the Symbolics of Power." In *Culture and Its Creators: Essays in Honor of Edward Shils*, ed. Joseph Ben-David and Terry Nichols Clark, 13–38. Chicago: University of Chicago Press, 1977.

Gelbart, Nina Rattner. *The King's Midwife: A History and Mystery of Madame du Coudray*. Berkeley and Los Angeles: University of California Press, 1998.

Gentilcore, David. *Healers and Healing in Early Modern Italy*. Manchester: Manchester University Press, 1998.

Genuth, Sarah Schechner. *Comets, Popular Culture, and the Birth of Modern Cosmology*. Princeton: Princeton University Press, 1997.

Giesey, Ralph. *The Royal Funeral Ceremony in France*. Geneva: Librairie Droz, 1960.

———. *Cérémonial et puissance souveraine: France, XVe–XVIIe siècles*. Paris: Armand Colin, 1987.

———. "The King Imagined." In *The Political Culture of the Old Regime*. Vol. 1, *The*

*French Revolution and the Creation of Modern Political Culture,* ed. Keith Michael Baker, 41–60. New York: Pergamon Press, 1987.

Giesey, Ralph, Lanny Hardy, and James Milhorn. "Cardinal Le Bret and Lese Majesty." *Law and History* 4 (spring 1986): 23–56.

Gijswijt-Hofstra, Marijke. "Witchcraft After the Witch-Trials." In *Witchcraft and Magic in Europe: The Eighteenth and Nineteenth Centuries,* ed. Begnt Ankarloo and Stuart Clark, 95–188. Philadelphia: University of Pennsylvania Press, 1999.

Ginzburg, Carlo. *The Night Battles: Witchcraft and Agrarian Cults in the Sixteenth and Seventeenth Centuries.* Trans. John and Anne Tedeschi. New York: Penguin, 1983.

———. *Ecstasies: Deciphering the Witches' Sabbath.* Trans. John and Anne Tedeschi. New York: Penguin, 1991.

———. *The Cheese and the Worms: The Cosmos of a Sixteenth-Century Miller.* Trans. John and Anne Tedeschi. Baltimore: Johns Hopkins University Press, 1992.

Golden, Richard M. "Satan in Europe: The Geography of Witch Hunts." In *Changing Identities in Early Modern France,* ed. Michael Wolfe, 216–47. Durham: Duke University Press, 1997.

Goubert, Pierre. *Beauvais et les beauvaisis de 1600 à 1730.* Paris: Librairie Plon, 1960.

Goulemot, Jean-Marie. "Sexual Imagination as Revealed in the *Traité des superstitions* of Abbé Jean-Baptiste Thiers." Trans. Odile Wagner and Arthur Greenspan. *Eighteenth-Century Life* 9, no. 3 (1985): 22–30.

Graham, Lisa Jane. "Crimes of Opinion: Policing the Public in Eighteenth-Century Paris." In *Visions and Revisions of Eighteenth-Century France,* ed. Christine Adams, Jack R. Censer, and Lisa Jane Graham, 79–103. University Park: Pennsylvania State University Press, 1997.

Greenshields, Malcolm. "Women, Violence, and Criminal Justice Records in Early Modern Auvergne." *Canadian Journal of History* 22 (August 1987): 175–94.

———. *An Economy of Violence in Early Modern France: Crime and Justice in the Haute Auvergne, 1587–1664.* University Park: Pennsylvania State University Press, 1994.

Grissa, Mohamed. *Pouvoirs et marginaux à Paris sous le règne de Louis XIV (1661–1715).* Tunis: Publications de l'Université de Tunis, 1980.

Guillais, Joëlle. *Crimes of Passion: Dramas of Private Life in Nineteenth-Century France.* Trans. Jane Dunnett. Cambridge, UK: Polity Press, 1990.

Hallissey, Margaret. *Venomous Woman: Fear of the Female in Literature.* Westport, Conn.: Greenwood Press, 1987.

Hamscher, Albert N. *The Parlement of Paris After the Fronde, 1653–1673.* Pittsburgh: University of Pittsburgh Press, 1976.

Hanley, Sarah. *The Lit de Justice of the Kings of France: Constitutional Ideology in Legend, Ritual, and Discourse.* Princeton: Princeton University Press, 1983.

———. "Engendering the State: Family Formation and State Building in Early Modern France." *French Historical Studies* 16 (1989): 4–27.

———. "Social Sites of Political Practice in France: Lawsuits, Civil Rights, and the Separation of Powers in Domestic and State Government, 1500–1800." *American Historical Review* 102 (1997): 27–52.

———. "The Pursuit of Legal Knowledge and the Genesis of Civil Society in Early Modern France." In *Historians and Ideologues,* ed. Anthony T. Grafton and J. H. M. Salmon, 71–86. Rochester: University of Rochester Press, 2001.

Hardwick, Julie. *The Practice of Patriarchy: Gender and the Politics of Household Authority in Early Modern France.* University Park: Pennsylvania State University Press, 1998.

Hariman, Robert. *Political Style: The Artistry of Power.* Chicago: University of Chicago Press, 1995.

Harth, Erica. *Ideology and Culture in Seventeenth-Century France.* Ithaca: Cornell University Press, 1983.

Hartman, Mary S. *Victorian Murderesses: A True History of Thirteen Respectable French and English Women Accused of Unspeakable Crimes.* New York: Schocken Books, 1977.

Harvey, David Allen. "Fortune-Tellers in the French Courts: Antidivination Prosecutions in France in the Nineteenth and Twentieth Centuries." *French Historical Studies* 28, no. 1 (2005): 131–57.

Henein, Eglal. "Les poisons dans le roman (1607–1628)." *Madame de Sévigné, Molière et la médecine de son temps: 3e Colloque de Marseille* 95 (October–December 1973): 151–58.

Herrup, Cynthia. "Law and Morality in Seventeenth-Century England." *Past and Present* 106 (1985): 102–23.

Hillairet, Jacques. *Dictionnaire historique des rues de Paris.* 2 vols. Paris: Éditions de Minuit, 1985.

Hilton, Lisa. *Athénaïs: The Life of Louis XIV's Mistress, the Real Queen of France.* Boston: Little, Brown, 2002.

Hoffman, Kathryn A. *Society of Pleasures: Interdisciplinary Readings in Pleasure and Power During the Reign of Louis XIV.* New York: St. Martin's Press, 1997.

Hsia, R. Po-Chia. *The Myth of Ritual Murder: Jews and Magic in Reformation Germany.* New Haven: Yale University Press, 1988.

Jackson, Richard A. *Vive le Roi! A History of the French Coronation from Charles V to Charles X.* Chapel Hill: University of North Carolina Press, 1984.

Jacquin, Frédéric. "Un empoisonnement à Paris: L'empoisonnement du sieur de Vaux (1742)." *Histoire, économie et société* 20, no. 1 (2001): 23–36.

Johnson, James H. *Listening in Paris: A Cultural History.* Berkeley and Los Angeles: University of California Press, 1995.

Jones, Colin. *Madame de Pompadour: Images of a Mistress.* New Haven: Yale University Press, 2002.

Kaiser, Thomas E. "Louis *le bien-aimé* and the Rhetoric of the Royal Body." In *From the Royal to the Republican Body: Incorporating the Political in Seventeenth- and Eighteenth-Century France,* ed. Sarah E. Melzer and Kathryn Norberg, 131–61. Berkeley and Los Angeles: University of California Press, 1998.

Kantorowicz, Ernst. *The King's Two Bodies: A Study in Mediaeval Political Theology.* Princeton: Princeton University Press, 1957.

Kettering, Sharon. *Patrons, Brokers, and Clients in Seventeenth-Century France.* New York: Oxford University Press, 1986.

———. "Patronage in Early Modern France." *French Historical Studies* 17, no. 4 (1992): 831–48.

———. "Brokerage at the Court of Louis XIV." *Historical Journal* 36, no. 1 (1993): 69–87.

Kieckhefer, Richard. *Magic in the Middle Ages.* Cambridge: Cambridge University Press, 1989.

———. "Erotic Magic in Medieval Europe." In *Sex in the Middle Ages: A Book of Essays,* ed. Joyce E. Salisbury, 30–55. New York: Garland Publishing, 1991.

———. "The Specific Rationality of Medieval Magic." *American Historical Review* 99, no. 3 (1994): 813–36.

———. "Avenging the Blood of Children: Anxiety over Child Victims and the Origins of the European Witch Trials." In *The Devil, Heresy, and Witchcraft in the Middle Ages*, ed. Alberto Ferrerro, 91–109. Boston: Brill, 1998.

———. *Forbidden Rites: A Necromancer's Manual of the Fifteenth Century*. University Park: Pennsylvania State University Press, 1998.

Klaassen, Frank. "English Manuscripts of Magic, 1300–1500: A Preliminary Survey." In *Conjuring Spirits: Texts and Traditions of Medieval Ritual Magic,* ed. Claire Fanger, 3–31. University Park: Pennsylvania State University Press, 1998.

Klairmont-Lingo, Alison. "The Fate of Popular Terms for Female Anatomy in the Age of Print." *French Historical Studies* 22, no. 3 (1999): 335–49.

Klaits, Joseph. *Printed Propaganda Under Louis XIV: Absolute Monarchy and Public Opinion*. Princeton: Princeton University Press, 1976.

———. *Servants of Satan: The Age of the Witch Hunts*. Bloomington: Indiana University Press, 1985.

Kleinman, Ruth. "Social Dynamics at the French Court: The Household of Anne of Austria." *French Historical Studies* 16, no. 3 (1992): 517–35.

Knecht, R. J. *Renaissance Warrior and Patron: The Reign of Francis I*. New York: Cambridge University Press, 1994.

Knelman, Judith. "Women Murderers in Victorian Britain." *History Today* 48, no. 8 (1998): 9–15.

Lacour, Eva. "Faces of Violence Revisited: A Typology of Violence in Early Modern Rural Germany." *Journal of Social History* 34, no. 3 (2001): 649–81.

Ladurie, Emmanuel Le Roy. "The Aiguillette: Castration by Magic." In *The Mind and Method of the Historian*, trans. Siân Reynolds and Ben Reynolds, 84–96. Chicago: University of Chicago Press, 1981.

———. "Versailles Observed: The Court of Louis XIV in 1709." In *The Mind and Method of the Historian*, trans. Siân Reynolds and Ben Reynolds, 149–73. Chicago: University of Chicago Press, 1981.

———. *Jasmin's Witch*. Trans. Brian Pearce. Aldershot: Scolar Press, 1987.

———. "Rangs et hiérarchie dans la vie de cour." In *The Political Culture of the Old Regime*. Vol. 1, *The French Revolution and the Creation of Modern Political Culture,* ed. Keith Michael Baker, 61–76. New York: Pergamon Press, 1987.

Ladurie, Emmanuel Le Roy, with Jean-François Fitou. *Saint Simon and the Court of Louis XIV*. Trans. Arthur Goldhammer. Chicago: University of Chicago Press, 2001.

Langbein, John H. *Prosecuting Crime in the Renaissance: England, Germany, France*. Cambridge: Harvard University Press, 1974.

———. *Torture and the Law of Proof: Europe and England in the Ancien Régime*. Chicago: University of Chicago Press, 1977.

Laqueur, Thomas. *Making Sex: Body and Gender from the Greeks to Freud*. Cambridge: Harvard University Press, 1990.

Lawrence, Paul. "Images of Poverty and Crime: Police Memoirs in England and France at the End of the Nineteenth Century." *Crime, histoire et sociétés/Crime, History, and Societies* 4, no. 1 (2000): 63–82.

Lea, Henry Charles. *Superstition and Force: Essays on the Wager of Law—The Wager of Battle, the Ordeal, Torture*. 4th ed., revised. Philadelphia: Lea Brothers and Co., 1892. Reprint, New York: B. Blom, 1971.

Lebigre, Arlette. "Les juges et la torture." *Histoire* 67 (1984): 18–25.

———. *La justice du roi*. Paris: Albin Michel, 1988.

————. *L'affaire des poisons*. Brussels: Éditions Complexe, 1989.

Lebrun, François. "Les superstitions populaires au temps de Louis XIV." *Histoire* 9 (1979): 42–50.

————. "La place du pèlerinage thérapeutique dans la piété des Bretons aux XVIIe et XVIIIe siècles." *Historiens-Géographes* 78, no. 318 (1988): 15–19.

Lemoine, Jean. *Madame de Montespan et la légende des poisons*. Paris, 1908.

————. *La des Oeillets: Une grande comédienne; une maîtresse de Louis XIV*. Paris, 1938.

Levack, Brian P. *The Witch Hunt in Early Modern Europe*. 2d ed. London: Longman, 1995.

————. "The Decline and End of Witchcraft Persecutions." In *Witchcraft and Magic in Europe: The Eighteenth and Nineteenth Centuries*, ed. Begnt Ankarloo and Stuart Clark, 1–93. Philadelphia: University of Pennsylvania Press, 1999.

Levron, Jacques. *Daily Life at Versailles in the Seventeenth and Eighteenth Centuries*. Trans. Claire Eliane Engel. New York: Macmillan, 1968.

Lidaka, Juris. "The Book of Angels, Rings, Characters, and Images of the Planets: Attributed to Osbern Bokenham." In *Conjuring Spirits: Texts and Traditions of Medieval Ritual Magic*, ed. Claire Fanger, 32–75. University Park: Pennsylvania State University Press, 1998.

Lindley, David. *The Trials of Frances Howard: Fact and Fiction and the Court of King James*. London: Routledge, 1993.

Liu, Tessie P. "Le Patrimoine Magique: Reassessing the Power of Women in Peasant Households in Nineteenth-Century France." *Gender and History* 6 (1994): 13–36.

Loriga, Sabina. "A Secret to Kill the King: Magic and Protection in Piedmont in the Eighteenth Century." Trans. Margaret A. Callucci and Corrada Biazzo Curry. In *History from Crime*, ed. Edward Muir and Guido Ruggerio, 88–109. Baltimore: Johns Hopkins University Press, 1994.

Luria, Keith P. *Territories of Grace: Cultural Change in the Seventeenth-Century Diocese of Grenoble*. Berkeley and Los Angeles: University of California Press, 1991.

————. "Rituals of Conversion: Catholics and Protestants in Seventeenth-Century Poitou." In *Culture and Identity in Early Modern Europe (1500–1800): Essays in Honor of Natalie Zemon Davis*, ed. Barbara B. Diefendorf and Carla Hesse, 65–81. Ann Arbor: University of Michigan Press, 1993.

Maes, L. Th. "Empoisonnement, procédure inquisitoriale, et peine de mort au début de XVIIIe siècle." *Revue historique de droit français et étranger* 55, no. 1 (1977): 59–72.

Major, J. Russell. *From Renaissance Monarchy to Absolute Monarchy: French Kings, Nobles, and Estates*. Baltimore: Johns Hopkins University Press, 1994.

Mandrou, Robert. *Magistrats et sorciers en France au XVIIe siècle: Une analyse de psychologie historique*. Paris: Librairie Plon, 1968.

————. *Louis XIV et son temps, 1661–1715*. Paris: Presses Universitaires de France, 1973.

————, ed. *Possession et sorcellerie au XVIIe siècle: Textes inédits*. Paris: Fayard, 1979.

Mansel, Philip. *The Court of France, 1789–1830*. Cambridge: Cambridge University Press, 1988.

Marion, Marcel. *Dictionnaire des institutions de la France, XVIIe–XVIIIe siècles*. Paris: Picard Éditeur, 1923. Reprint, Paris: Picard, 1984.

Marvick, Elizabeth Wirth. "Favorites in Early Modern Europe: A Recurring Psychopolitical Role." *Journal of Psychohistory* 10, no. 4 (1983): 463–89.

Massing, Jean-Michel. "A Sixteenth-Century Illustrated Treatise on Comets." *Journal of the Warburg and Courtauld Institutes* 40 (1977): 318–22.

Mauss, Marcel. *The Gift.* Trans. Ian Cunnison. New York: W. W. Norton, 1967.

May, Gita. *Madame Roland and the Age of Revolution.* New York: Columbia University Press, 1970.

Maza, Sarah. "Domestic Melodrama as Political Ideology: The Case of the Comte de Sanois." *American Historical Review* 94 (1987): 1249–64.

———. *Private Lives and Public Affairs: The Causes Célèbres of Prerevolutionary France.* Berkeley and Los Angeles: University of California Press, 1993.

McKenna, Antony. "Des pamphlets philosophiques clandestins." *XVIIe siècle* 49, no. 2 (1997): 243–52.

McLaren, Angus. *Reproductive Rituals: The Perception of Fertility in England from the Sixteenth to the Nineteenth Century.* London: Methuen, 1984.

Mellaerts, Wim. "Criminal Justice in Provincial England, France, and the Netherlands, c. 1880–1908: Some Comparative Perspectives." *Crime, histoire et sociétés/Crime, History, and Societies* 4, no. 2 (2000): 19–52.

Mellor, Alec. *La torture.* Paris: Horizons Littéraires, 1949.

Melzer, Sarah E., and Kathryn Norberg. "Introduction." In *From the Royal to the Republican Body: Incorporating the Political in Seventeenth- and Eighteenth-Century France,* ed. Sarah E. Melzer and Kathryn Norberg, 1–10. Berkeley and Los Angeles: University of California Press, 1998.

Merrick, Jeffrey. "The Body Politics of French Absolutism." In *From the Royal to the Republican Body: Incorporating the Political in Seventeenth- and Eighteenth-Century France,* ed. Sarah E. Melzer and Kathryn Norberg, 11–31. Berkeley and Los Angeles: University of California Press, 1998.

Mettam, Roger. *Power and Faction in Louis XIV's France.* London: Basil Blackwell, 1988.

Mollenauer, Lynn Wood. "Justice Versus Secrecy: Investigating the Affair of the Poisons, 1679–1682." *Zeitsprünge: Forschungen zur Frühen Neuzeit* 6 (2002): 179–205.

———. "The End of Magic: Superstition and So-Called Sorcery in Louis XIV's France." *Studies in Law, Politics, and Society* 37 (2005): 33–52.

Mongrédien, Georges. *Madame de Montespan et l'affaire des poisons.* Paris: Hachette, 1953.

Monod, Paul Kléber. *The Power of Kings: Monarchy and Religion in Europe, 1589–1715.* New Haven: Yale University Press, 1999.

Monter, William. *Ritual, Myth, and Magic in Early Modern Europe.* Brighton, Eng.: Harvester Press, 1983.

———. "Toads and Eucharists: The Male Witches of Normandy." *French Historical Studies* 20, no. 4 (1997): 563–95.

Muchembled, Robert. *La sorcière au village (XVe–XVIIIe siècle).* Paris: Armand Colin, 1979.

———. "Anthropologie de la violence dans la France moderne (XVe–XVIIIe siècles)." *Revue de synthèse* 108, no. 1 (1987): 31–55.

———. *Société et mentalités dans la France moderne, XVIe–XVIIIe siècle.* Paris: Armand Colin, 1990.

———. *Le temps des supplices: De l'obéissance sous les rois absolus, XVe–XVIIIe siècle.* Paris: Armand Colin, 1992.

———. *Le roi et la sorcière: L'Europe des bûchers, XVe–XVIIIe siècles.* Paris: Desclée, 1993.

Muir, Edward. *Ritual in Early Modern Europe.* Cambridge: Cambridge University Press, 1997.

Muir, Edward, and Guido Ruggerio. "Introduction." In *History from Crime,* ed. Edward

Muir and Guido Ruggerio, vii–xviii. Baltimore: Johns Hopkins University Press, 1994.

Mukerji, Chandra. "Unspoken Assumptions: Voice and Absolutism at the Court of Louis XIV." *Journal of Historical Sociology* 11, no. 3 (1998): 283–315.

Nass, Lucien. *Les empoisonnements sous Louis XIV, d'après les documents inédits de l'affaire des poisons, 1679–1682.* Paris: Carré et Naud, 1898.

Neuchel, Kristin. *Word of Honor: Interpreting Noble Culture in Sixteenth-Century France.* Ithaca: Cornell University Press, 1989.

Newton, William R. *L'espace du roi: La cour de France au château de Versailles, 1682–1789.* Paris: Fayard, 2000.

Niccoli, Ottavia. "'Menstruum Quasi Monstruum': Monstrous Births and Menstrual Taboo in the Sixteenth Century." Trans. Mary M. Galluci. In *Sex and Gender in Historical Perspective,* ed. Edward Muir and Guido Ruggerio, 1–25. Baltimore: Johns Hopkins University Press, 1990.

Niderst, Alain, ed. *Les français vus par eux-mêmes: Le siècle de Louis XIV, anthologie des mémorialistes du siècle de Louis XIV.* Paris: Robert Laffont, 1997.

Nirenberg, David. *The Gender of Poison.* Paper presented at the Gender, Health, and History Conference, Chicago, April 24–25, 1998.

Noonan, John T., Jr. "Abortion and the Catholic Church: A Summary History." *Natural Law Forum* 12 (1967): 85–131.

Norberg, Kathryn. "Incorporating Women/Gender into French History Courses, 1429–1789: Did Women of the Old Regime Have a Political History?" *French Historical Studies* 27, no. 2 (2004): 243–66.

O'Hara, Stephanie Elizabeth. "Tracing Poison: Theater and Society in Seventeenth-Century France." Ph.D. diss., Duke University, 2003.

O'Keefe, Daniel Lawrence. *Stolen Lightning: The Social Theory of Magic.* New York: Oxford University Press, 1982.

Oliver, Reggie. "The Poisons Affair." *History Today* (March 2001): 28–34.

Parker, David. "The Social Foundations of French Absolutism, 1610–1630." *Past and Present* 53 (1971): 67–89.

———. *Class and State in Ancien-Régime France: The Road to Modernity?* London: Routledge, 1996.

———. "French 'Absolutism'?" *History Review* 29 (1997): 14–20.

Perkins, Wendy. *Midwifery and Medicine in Early Modern France: Louise Bourgeois.* Exeter: University of Exeter Press, 1996.

Peters, Edward. *The Magician, the Witch, and the Law.* Philadelphia: University of Pennsylvania Press, 1978.

———. *Torture.* New York: Basil Blackwell, 1985.

Petitfils, Jean-Christian. *L'affaire des poisons: Alchimistes et sorciers sous Louis XIV.* Paris: Albin Michel, 1977.

———. *Madame de Montespan.* Paris: Fayard, 1988.

Peveri, Patrice. "Cette ville était alors comme une bois . . . : Criminalité et opinion publique à Paris dans les années qui précèdent l'affaire Cartouche (1715–1721)." *Crime, histoire et sociétés/Crime, History, and Societies* 1, no. 2 (1997): 51–73.

Plato. *The Laws.* Trans. Trevor J. Saunders. New York: Penguin, 1975.

Plongeron, Bernard. *La vie quotidienne du clergé français au XVIIIe siècle.* Paris: Hachette, 1989.

Potter, David. "'Rigueur de Justice': Crime, Murder, and the Law in Picardy, Fifteenth to Sixteenth Centuries." *French History* 11, no. 3 (1997): 265–309.

Raheja, Gloria Goodwin. *The Poison in the Gift: Ritual, Prestation, and the Dominant Caste in a North Indian Village.* Chicago: University of Chicago Press, 1988.

Ramsey, Matthew. "The Popularization of Medicine in France, 1650–1900." In *The Popularization of Medicine, 1650–1850,* ed. Roy Porter, 97–133. New York: Routledge, 1992.

Ranum, Orest. "Courtesy, Absolutism, and the Rise of the French State, 1630–1660." *Journal of Modern History* 52 (1980): 426–51.

———. *Paris in the Age of Absolutism: An Essay.* University Park: Pennsylvania State University Press, 2002.

Riddle, John M. *Contraception and Abortion from the Ancient World to the Renaissance.* Cambridge: Harvard University Press, 1992.

———. *Eve's Herbs: A History of Contraception and Abortion in the West.* Cambridge: Harvard University Press, 1997.

Riley, Philip K. "Louis XIV, Watchdog of Parisian Morality." *The Historian* 27 (1973): 19–33.

———. "Hard Times, Police, and the Making of Public Policy in the Paris of Louis XIV." *Historical Reflections/Réflexions historiques* 10 (1983): 313–34.

———. "Michel Foucault, Lust, Women, and Sin in Louis XIV's Paris." *Church History* 59 (1990): 35–50.

———. *A Lust for Virtue: Louis XIV's Attack on Sin in Seventeenth-Century France.* Westport, Conn.: Greenwood Press, 2001.

Robb, George. "Circe in Crinoline: Domestic Poisonings in Victorian England." *Journal of Family History* 22, no. 2 (1997): 176–90.

Roper, Lyndal. *Oedipus and the Devil: Witchcraft, Sexuality, and Religion in Early Modern Europe.* London: Routledge, 1994.

Rowlands, Guy. *The Dynastic State and the Army Under Louis XIV: Royal Service and Private Interest, 1661–1701.* Cambridge: Cambridge University Press, 2002.

Rubin, Miri. *Corpus Christi: The Eucharist in Late Medieval Culture.* Cambridge: Cambridge University Press, 1991.

Ruff, Julius R. *Crime, Justice, and Public Order in Old Regime France.* London: Croom Helm, 1984.

———. *Violence in Early Modern Europe, 1500–1800.* Cambridge: Cambridge University Press, 2001.

Ruggerio, Guido. *Binding Passions: Tales of Magic, Marriage, and Power at the End of the Renaissance.* Oxford: Oxford University Press, 1993.

Russell, Barry. *Calendrier des spectacles sous Louis XIV (1996–1998).* Le théâtre de la foire à Paris: Textes et documents. http://foires.net (accessed March 20, 2006).

Sabean, David Warren. *Power in the Blood: Popular Culture and Village Discourse in Early Modern Germany.* Cambridge: Cambridge University Press, 1984.

Sánchez, Magdalena S. *The Empress, the Queen, and the Nun: Women and Power at the Court of Philip III of Spain.* Baltimore: Johns Hopkins University Press, 1998.

Scarry, Elaine. *The Body in Pain: The Making and Unmaking of the World.* New York: Oxford University Press, 1985.

Schalk, Ellery. *From Valor to Pedigree: Ideas of Nobility in France in the Sixteenth and Seventeenth Centuries.* Princeton: Princeton University Press, 1986.

Septon, Monique. "Les femmes et le poison: L'empoisonnement devant les juridictions criminelles en Belgique, 1795–1914." Ph.D. diss., Marquette University, 1996.

Shapiro, Ann-Louise. *Breaking the Codes: Female Criminality in Fin-de-Siècle Paris.* Stanford: Stanford University Press, 1996.

Silverman, Lisa. *Tortured Subjects: Pain, Truth, and the Body in Early Modern France.* Chicago: University of Chicago Press, 2001.

Smith, Pamela H. *The Business of Alchemy: Science and Culture in the Holy Roman Empire.* Princeton: Princeton University Press, 1994.

Solnon, Jean-François. *La cour de France.* Paris: Fayard, 1987.

Soman, Alfred. "Criminal Jurisprudence in *Ancien Regime* France: The *Parlement* of Paris in the Sixteenth and Seventeenth Centuries." In *Crime and Criminal Justice in Europe and Canada*, ed. Louis A. Knafla, 43–75. Waterloo, Ontario: Wilfred Laurier University Press, 1981.

———. "Witch Hunting at Juniville." *Natural History* 95, no. 10 (1986): 6–15.

———. "Decriminalizing Witchcraft: Does the French Experience Furnish a European Model?" *Criminal Justice History* 10 (1989): 1–30.

———. *Sorcellerie et justice criminelle: Le Parlement de Paris (16e–18e siècles).* Brookfield, Vt.: Ashgate, 1992.

———. "Sorcellerie, justice criminelle et société dans la France moderne." *Annales: Histoire, économie et société* 12 (1993): 177–217.

———. "Anatomy of an Infanticide Trial: The Case of Marie-Jeanne Bartonnet (1742)." In *Changing Identities in Early Modern France*, ed. Michael Wolfe, 248–72. Durham: Duke University Press, 1997.

Somerset, Anne. *The Affair of the Poisons: Murder, Infanticide, and Satanism at the Court of Louis XIV.* London: Weidenfeld & Nicolson, 2003.

Sonnino, Paul. "The Dating and Authorship of Louis XIV's *Mémoires.*" *French Historical Studies* 3, no. 3 (1964): 303–37.

———, ed. *The Reign of Louis XIV: Essays in Celebration of Andrew Lossky.* Atlantic Highlands, N.J.: Humanities Press International, 1990.

Spierenburg, Pieter. *The Spectacle of Suffering: Executions and the Evolution of Repression from a Principal Metropolis to the European Experience.* Cambridge: Cambridge University Press, 1984.

———. "Homicide Trends and Cultural Meanings: Amsterdam, 1431–1816." *Journal of Social History* 27 (1994): 701–16.

Spooner, Frank C. *The International Economy and Monetary Movements in France, 1493–1725.* Cambridge: Harvard University Press, 1972.

Stedman, T. L. *Stedman's Shorter Medical Dictionary.* New York: Wilcox & Follett, 1942.

Swann, Julian. *Provincial Power and Absolute Monarchy: The Estates General of Burgundy, 1661–1790.* Cambridge: Cambridge University Press, 2003.

Szarka, Andrew S. "An Outsider's View of Louis XIV's Court: The Portuguese Ambassador's *Discorso Politico* (1695–1704)." *Proceedings of the Western Society for French Historical Studies* 25 (1998): 277–88.

Tallon, Alain. *La compagnie du Saint-Sacrement (1629–1667): Spiritualité et société.* Paris: Éditions du Cerf, 1990.

Taylor, Katherine Fischer. *In the Theater of Criminal Justice: The Palais de Justice in Second Empire Paris.* Princeton: Princeton University Press, 1993.

Thomas, Chantal. *The Wicked Queen: The Origins of the Myth of Marie-Antoinette.* Trans. Julie Rose. New York: Zone Books, 1999.

Thomas, Keith. *Religion and the Decline of Magic.* New York: Charles Scribner's Sons, 1971.

Thorndike, Lynn, ed. *A History of Magic and Experimental Science.* 8 vols. New York: Columbia University Press, 1923–58.

Tulard, Jean. "La préfecture de police et ses archives." *L'Information historique* 24, no. 5 (1962): 197–98.

Turner, Victor. *The Ritual Process: Structure and Anti-Structure.* Ithaca: Cornell University Press, 1977.

Van Kley, Dale. *The Jansenists and the Expulsion of the Jesuits from France, 1757–65.* New Haven: Yale University Press, 1975.

———. *The Damiens Affair.* New Haven: Yale University Press, 1984.

———. *The Religious Origins of the French Revolution: From Calvin to the Civil Constitution, 1560–1791.* New Haven: Yale University Press, 1996.

Veenstra, Jan R. *Magic and Divination at the Courts of Burgundy and France: Text and Context of Laurens Pignon's* Contre les devineurs *(1411).* New York: Brill, 1998.

Vovelle, Michel. "La représentation populaire de la monarchie." In *The Political Culture of the Old Regime.* Vol. 1, *The French Revolution and the Creation of Modern Political Culture,* ed. Keith Michael Baker, 77–86. New York: Pergamon Press, 1987.

Walker, D. P. *Unclean Spirits: Possession and Exorcism in France and England in the Late Sixteenth and Early Seventeenth Centuries.* Philadelphia: University of Pennsylvania Press, 1981.

Wells, Charlotte. "Leeches on the Body Politic: Xenophobia and Witchcraft in Early Modern French Political Thought." *French Historical Studies* 22, no. 3 (1999): 351–77.

Williams, Alan. *The Police of Paris, 1718–1789.* Baton Rouge: Louisiana State University Press, 1979.

Williams, Gerhild Scholz. *Defining Dominion: The Discourses of Magic and Witchcraft in Early Modern France and Germany.* Ann Arbor: University of Michigan Press, 1995.

Wolf, John B. *Louis XIV.* New York: W. W. Norton, 1968.

Wygant, Amy Kay. "Pierre Corneille's Medea-Machine." *Romantic Review* 85, no. 4 (1994): 537–53.

———. "The Meanings of *Phèdre.*" Ph.D. diss., Johns Hopkins University, 1995.

———. "Medea, Poison, and the Epistemology of Error in *Phèdre.*" *Modern Language Review* 95, no. 1 (2000): 62–71.

Yarrow, P. J. "Introduction." In Thomas Corneille and Jean Donneau de Visé, *La devineresse,* ed. P. J. Yarrow, v–xxiii. Exeter: University of Exeter Press, 1971.

Zanger, Abby E. *Scenes from the Marriage of Louis XIV: Nuptial Fictions and the Making of Absolutist Power.* Stanford: Stanford University Press, 1997.

———. "Lim(b)inal Images: 'Betwixt and Between' Louis XIV's Martial and Marital Bodies." In *From the Royal to the Republican Body: Incorporating the Political in Seventeenth- and Eighteenth-Century France,* ed. Sarah E. Melzer and Kathryn Norberg, 32–63. Berkeley and Los Angeles: University of California Press, 1998.

Ziegler, Gillette. *The Court of Versailles in the Reign of Louis XIV.* Trans. Simon Watson Taylor. London: George Allen & Unwin, 1966.

# INDEX